WELCOME HOME BROTHER.

You that of late haue lefte your habitation,
And in Barnes Stables,Hayrickes, tooke your station:
With scornes and taunts though other men doe meete y
At your returne the Foole doth kindly greete you
And though your Coyne and Credit scanted bee,
Your honest Cooze will keepe you Company

Johannis Geddard fcu

GREETING THE RUNAWAYS

THE PLAGUE IN SHAKESPEARE'S LONDON

BY

F. P. WILSON

OXFORD UNIVERSITY PRESS

OXFORD
UNIVERSITY PRESS

Great Clarendon Street, Oxford OX2 6DP

Oxford University Press is a department of the University of Oxford.
It furthers the University's objective of excellence in research, scholarship,
and education by publishing worldwide in

Oxford New York

Athens Auckland Bangkok Bogotá Buenos Aires Calcutta
Cape Town Chennai Dar es Salaam Delhi Florence Hong Kong Istanbul
Karachi Kuala Lumpur Madrid Melbourne Mexico City Mumbai
Nairobi Paris São Paulo Singapore Taipei Tokyo Toronto Warsaw

with associated companies in Berlin Ibadan

Oxford is a registered trade mark of Oxford University Press
in the UK and in certain other countries

Published in the United States
by Oxford University Press Inc., New York

© Oxford University Press 1927

The moral rights of the author have been asserted
Database right Oxford University Press (maker)

Special edition for Sandpiper Books Ltd., 1999

British Library Cataloguing in Publication Data

Data available

ISBN 0-19-820810-3

1 3 5 7 9 10 8 6 4 2

Printed in Great Britain
on-acid free paper by
Bookcraft (Bath) Ltd.,
Midsomer Norton

PREFACE TO THE FIRST EDITION

In English history the plague is associated chiefly or solely with the Great Plague of 1665 and with the visitation of 1348–9 which Mrs. Markham has taught us to call the Black Death. But the importance of these has tended to obscure several intermediate epidemics, which in turn were styled 'great' before they were surpassed in magnitude by their successors. The most serious of these subsidiary plagues—those of 1603 and 1625—were described by that lively journalist of genius, Thomas Dekker, in some pamphlets which have recently been published at the Clarendon Press. Dekker was an eyewitness of, and a participant in, the scenes of which he writes with such gusto. But if his work leaves little to be desired in racy and graphic portraiture, it leaves unsaid much that is of interest to the historian of local government and to the student of manners and customs and of the English character in the time of Shakespeare. This book, which is based on the materials supplied by contemporary books and documents, aims at narrating in detail the history of the plague in London in the early seventeenth century, and at tracing the rise of the plague-orders from their inception in 1518.

The approach was in the first place literary rather than historical. To annotate Dekker's plague pamphlets it was necessary to consult the records. Then as the materials grew in my hands I became more ambitious, and from a commentary proceeded to a book. The first draft, completed in 1914, was revised and in part re-written in 1921. The delay in publication has enabled me to make use of a few books and articles bearing on this subject which have recently been published.

For permission to reproduce the illustrations given in this book I am indebted to the Librarian and Curators of the Bodleian Library, to the Cambridge University Press, to the Committee of the Guildhall Library, London, to the London Topographical Society, to the Master and Fellows of Magdalene College, Cambridge, to the Society of Antiquaries of London, to the Librarian of Trinity College, Dublin, and to the authorities of St. Saviour's, Southwark. It is also a pleasure to acknowledge the generous help received at the libraries and record offices where I have had occasion to work.

F. P. W.

Oxford,
March, 1927.

PREFACE TO THE REPRINT
OF 1963

IN this reprint a few errors have been corrected, two illustrations (nos. 11 and 22) have been added, and two (nos. 17 and 18) have been reproduced from better copies. I have removed from p. 113 a baseless speculation about what Shakespeare was doing in 1603, being now content to say that I do not know; with the expert assistance of Dr. F. N. L. Poynter, Chief Librarian of the Wellcome Historical Medical Library, to whom I am also indebted for other kindnesses, I have brought up to date the reference to modern medical theory and practice with regard to the plague (note on pp. 2–3); and I have used some empty spaces on pp. 13 and 215 and in a few footnotes to supplement, rather than correct, what I had written before.

What is most in need of supplementation is the account of weekly printed bills of mortality on p. 192. When in 1927 I searched for weekly bills printed before 1625, I could find very few. It is the more remarkable that recently the Houghton Library, Harvard University, has been able to acquire forty-two broadside bills published in 1603 and 1604. These bills are docketed in a hand identified by Dr. R. W. Hunt as Sir Julius Cæsar's. For all but five weeks Harvard now has a complete run of weekly bills from 14 July 1603 till 12 April 1604 and from 24 May till 21 June 1604. The bill for the week 14–21 July 1603 is the earliest printed bill now known. Twenty-nine more copies of weekly bills for 1603 and early 1604 and a yearly bill have just come to light, the property of Sir Charles Ponsonby, sold at Christie's on 13 December 1962 (lot 96); but these I have not seen. With the generous permission of the Librarian of the Houghton Library, Professor W. A. Jackson, the illustrations facing pp. 106 and 114 are reproduced from the Harvard copies. For the illustrations facing pp. 62 and 160 I am indebted to the British Museum and the Huntington Library.

F. P. W.

Oxford,
December, 1962.

CONTENTS

LIST OF ILLUSTRATIONS

LIST OF ILLUSTRATIONS

ABBREVIATIONS

Cal. S. P. Dom. or *Ven.* = The Calendar of State Papers, Domestic or Venetian.

D. P. P. = The Plague Pamphlets of Thomas Dekker, edited by F. P. Wilson (1925).

G. = The Non-Dramatic Works of Thomas Dekker, edited by A. B. Grosart in five volumes (1884–6).

J. = The Journals recording the proceedings of the London Court of Common Council : preserved at the Guildhall Record Office.

Letter Books = The Letter Books of the City of London : preserved at the Guildhall Record Office.

P. C. R. = The Registers of the Privy Council : preserved at the Public Record Office.

R. = The Repertories recording the proceedings of the London Court of Aldermen : preserved at the Guildhall Record Office.

Remembrancia = The Remembrancia of the City of London : preserved at the Guildhall Record Office.

S. P. Dom., Eliz., or *Jas. I,* or *Chas. I* = The Domestic State Papers of the reign of Elizabeth or James I or Charles I : preserved at the Public Record Office.

NOTE.—The spelling and punctuation of quotations from printed books have been preserved, except where they were likely seriously to mislead the modern reader. The spelling and punctuation of quotations from manuscript sources have been modernized (except on pp. 178–9, 181, and 182–3), and contractions have been expanded. Dates are given in old style, and the year is reckoned from the first of January.

I

THE CAUSE AND THE CURE

FORTY years ago the interest taken in the plague was mostly antiquarian. The infection still lingered in obscure places in Persia, Arabia, India, Africa, and China, but it was held too remote ever to startle and dismay the world as it had done two hundred years before. This feeling of false security was shattered by the Bombay epidemic of 1896, and the impression has been deepened by subsequent plagues that the infection is by no means effete, but is full of menace for Asia, if not for Europe. One result of the return of the plague into the consciousness of the world of science has been an important advance in our knowledge of its nature and causes. In 1891 it was possible to say ' with some confidence ' that the plague was a soil-poison generated out of the products of cadaveric decay.[1] But in the Hong Kong epidemic of 1894 Kitasato discovered the plague bacillus, and further investigation has shown that the disease occurs in two chief forms, the bubonic, involving the lymphatic glands, and the rarer pneumonic, causing an acute and rapidly fatal inflammation of the lungs. The two are often found together in the same epidemic.

Pneumonic plague is directly infectious, as the bacilli are sprayed into the air by coughing ; but the latest researches seem to have proved that contagion plays no part in the propagation of bubonic plague. The infection in man is caused by the disease in the rat, and is

[1] Cf. C. Creighton, *A History of Epidemics in Britain* (vol. i, 1891), i. 173.

transmitted from rat to rat and from rat to man by the bite of rat-fleas. These fleas only prey upon man when deprived of their usual food by the death of the rat. Bubonic plague may be transmitted from place to place by imported fleas, which are carried by people on their persons or in their baggage, or in merchandise. In this way the human agent often escapes infection. In England, it is said, ' the most favourable temperature for transporting infected rat-fleas is about 50° F. when the atmosphere is damp, and the most unfavourable temperature is one above 80° F., or even a lower temperature, when the atmosphere is dry '. Under favourable conditions a flea has been known to live without food for 125 days.

The disappearance of the plague from Europe in the seventeenth and eighteenth centuries coincided in the main with the appearance of the brown sewer rat and the disappearance of the old English black or house rat. Both can take the plague, but the black rat, a tame, confiding creature which likes to breed in houses, is more dangerous to man than the shyer brown rat, which breeds usually in burrows outside houses, or in drains and sewers. A house in an Elizabethan slum, with a wooden framework filled in with clay and plaster, a refuse-heap before the door, and filthy rushes upon the floor, provided the black rat with an ideal home. This animal has disappeared from English towns, not because it has been exterminated by the brown rat but because the more cleanly modern house of brick or stone is not congenial to its habits. It still thrives in the slums of the East, with which in filth and poverty the Elizabethan slums are comparable.[1]

[1] For modern views on the causes of the plague see L. F. Hirst, *The Conquest of Plague. A Study of the Evolution of Epidemiology*

In the light of modern discoveries the theories held in the sixteenth and seventeenth centuries seem ludicrous, and the futility of the prophylactics which were valued so highly is not without its irony. But although such theories have long been discarded, it is only by their help that we can understand the attitude of the age towards the infection and interpret the attempts made to grapple with it.

These theories may be divided into two classes according as they were of learned or popular origin. The popular superstitions are ridiculed by many contemporary writers. About the year 1477 a raven bred on Charing Cross, the harbinger of a mighty plague that lasted three years.[1] In 1593 the ' vulgar menialty ' foretold an increase of the plague because a heron sat for an afternoon on the top of St. Peter's Church in Cornhill. There was also talk of an ox that tolled the bell at Woolwich, and of how from an ox he transformed himself into an old man, from an old man to an infant, and from an infant to a young man.[2] Defoe tells us that similar wonders were observed in 1665. Flaming swords, hearses, coffins, and corpses were seen in the air, as were ghosts, and angels clothed in white and wielding fiery swords.

In the opinion of more learned writers the infection was due to four causes, the first and chiefest of which was supernatural. The plague was God's instrument for the punishment of sin. It was God's angel[3] (2 *Samuel* xxiv.

(Oxford, 1953) and R. Pollitzer, *Plague* (World Health Organization, Geneva, 1954). The statement in the text that the black rat has disappeared is false. In 1961, I am informed, brown rat infestation in the City of London was only slightly predominant.

[1] *The Brut*, ed. F. W. D. Brie, pt. ii, p. 604.

[2] T. Nashe, *Works* (ed. R. B. McKerrow), ii. 172.

[3] Cf. John Donne, *Poems* (ed. Grierson), i. 346. In 1603 it was said that six or ten men died for every woman. Francis

17), the arrow of God (*Psalm* xxxviii. 2) flying through the
air, the hand of God stretched out to smite the wickedness
of men and cut them off from the earth (*Exodus* ix. 15).
Texts like ' There is wrath gone out from the Lord : the
plague is begun ' (*Numbers* xvi. 46) were seized on by
preachers and moralists, and the literature of the plague
abounds in vigorous condemnations of sin and in earnest
appeals for repentance and amendment. The need for
preserving spiritual as well as bodily health if the plague
was to be warded off is ingeniously expressed in this
parody of medical jargon :

> ' First, fast and pray, and then take a quart of Repentance
> of *Nineve*, and put in two hand-fuls of Faith in the blood of
> Christ, with as much Hope and Charity as you can get, and
> put it into the vessell of a clean Conscience : then boyle it on
> the fire of Love, so long till you see by the eye of Faith, the
> black foame of the love of this world stinke in your stomacke,
> then scumme it off cleane with the spoone of faithfull Prayers.
> When that is done, put in the powder of Patience, and take
> the cloth of Christs Innocency, and straine all together in his
> Cup : then drinke it burning hot next thy heart, and cover
> thee warme with as many clothes of Amendment of life, as God
> shall strengthen thee to beare, that thou mayst sweate out
> all the poyson of covetousnesse, pride, whoredome, idolatrie,
> usury, swearing, lying, and such like. And when thou feelest
> thy selfe altered from the forenamed vices, take the powder of
> Say-well, and put it upon thy tongue : but drinke thrice as
> much Doe-well daily.' [1]

Hering was careful to point out that this was not because women
were holier than men, but because they were ' more tractable
and easily perswaded to keepe themselves warme, to keepe house
and bed '. *A Modest Defence of the Caveat Given to the Wearers of
impoisoned Amulets* (1604), sig. A 4ᵛ.

[1] See T. Vicary, *The English Mans Treasure* (1613), p. 223,
and see *Lord have mercy upon us* (1636). Cf. Dekker's ' Julep to
sweeten the mouth of thy Stomacke ' (*D. P. P.* 190), and the

A second cause was the corruption of the air. Shakespeare couples together the first and second causes in *Timon of Athens* (IV. iii) : [1]

> a planetary plague, when Jove
> Will o'er some high-vic'd City, hang his poison
> In the sick air.

As defined by Marsilius Ficinus the plague was ' Venenosus quidam vapor in aere concretus, vitali inimicus spiritui '. It was thought to be engendered ' by a rotten and corrupt ayre by a hidden and secret propertie which it hath ',[2] and it sent out its poison into the air as the violet its odours.[3] Thomas Coghan, translating Ficinus, enumerates these signs of an approaching plague :

' where the ayer of that place varyeth from his naturall temperature, declyning to heate and moysture, when it seemeth clowdie and dustie : When the Wyndes are grosse and hoat : when the Waters and feelds smoke and smell : and the fishes are yll both in savour and taste : When manie Woormes breede of putrifaction of the earth : Toade stooles and rotten herbes abound : The fruites and beastes of the earth are unsavourie : The wines becomes muddie : Manie birds and beastes flye from that place, strange Agewes arise, raging continuall, burning, phrantike, when the small Pockes, and Mesels are rife, and wormes abound in children and olde folkes '.[4]

Thirdly, the opinion that the conjunction of the stars and the aspect of the planets had potent influence upon the

---

pills taken by Christiana's son ' three at a time fasting, in half a quarter of a Pint of the Tears of Repentance '.
[1] Cf. also *King Lear* (III. iv) :
  Now all the plagues, that in the pendulous air
  Hang fated o'er men's faults, light on thy Daughters.
[2] S. H., *A New Treatise of the Pestilence* (1603), sig. A 2.
[3] Wither, *Britain's Remembrancer* (1628), 48 b.
[4] *The Haven of Health* (1584), 263–4. See also *D. P. P.* 82, 83.

health of the nation was widespread.   Ulysses expresses
Elizabethan sentiments in the words (*Troilus and Cressida*,
I. iii) :

> when the Planets
> In evil mixture to disorder wander,
> What Plagues, and what portents, what mutiny . . .
> Divert, and crack, rend and deracinate
> The unity, and married calm of States
> Quite from their fixure !

Astrologers were not slow to observe that in 1603 there
was a conjunction of Saturn and Jupiter in Sagittarius,
and just before that an eclipse of the sun.   A comet of
great magnitude also appeared.   The plague of 1625 again
‘ was the consequence of a great *Conjunction* of *Saturn,
Jupiter*, and *Mars*, in the Celestial sign *Leo*, a sign of the
fiery triplicity, and representing the heart in the *Micro-
cosme, Ergo*, the more dangerous ’.[1]

A fourth cause was aptness of body—‘ those bodies
wherein there is *Cacochymia*, corrupt and superfluous
humours abounding, are apt and lightly infected ’.[2]
Prophylactic treatment varied according to the humour
predominating in the body.   The sanguine were let blood,
and the choleric were purged with an infusion of rhubarb
if they were rich, or with the electuary of the juice of roses
if they were poor.   Other medicines were recommended

---

[1] John Gadbury, *London's Deliverance predicted* (1665), 7.   The
influence of Saturn was especially noxious.   An extraordinary
conjunction of Saturn with other planets was thought by a
contemporary astrologer to be responsible for the plague of 1348.
Cf. *The Vision and Creed of Piers Ploughman* (ed. T. Wright, 1856),
i. xii.   And the conjunction of Saturn and Jupiter was believed
to be the cause of the plague of 1365.   Cf. D. W. Singer, *Some
Plague Tractates (Fourteenth and Fifteenth Centuries)* (1916), p. 11.
[2] Thomas Thayre (or rather Phayre), *A Treatise of the Pestilence
1603), sig. B 1.   On this book see Creighton, *op. cit.*, i. 489–90.

for the purgation of the phlegmatic and the melancholy, with the proviso that they were to be administered under the direction of a learned and diligent physician, ' and not according to the fancie of foolish chare-women, and ignorant practizers '.[1]

Many of these doctrines are not so absurd as they may appear at first sight. We no longer believe that Jupiter and Saturn have pre-eminence over us, but the theory is still upheld that the activity of the plague bacillus is affected by atmospherical conditions. Almost all the English plagues were virulent in the summer and declined at the approach of cold weather.[2] Moreover many doctrines, false in themselves, resulted in the enforcement of excellent prophylactic measures. For example, the belief that the infection was fostered by the corruption of the air induced the authorities to establish a more rigorous system of sanitation : and the opinion that bodies filled with corrupt humours were apter to take the disease led to a more careful diet and method of life. Again, it must be remembered that on points which are non-technical and non-scientific the Elizabethan physicians were essentially sound. Their attitude is well summed up by Thomas Lodge in words which would be endorsed by any physician of to-day :

' Briefly, to live in repose of spirit, in al joy, pleasure, sport

---

[1] T. Lodge, *A Treatise of the Plague* (1603), sig. D 1ᵛ.

[2] Cf. John Woodall, *The Surgeons Mate* (1639), 322 : ' heretofore the *Plague* with us hath begun in Summer, and was commonly most fierce, predominate and untractable to Medicines in the heat of Summer, and chiefly in Harvest, which is the unseasonable time that we doe usually call the Canicular or Dog dayes '. A plague which flourished in the winter was thought to be most pernicious. Cf. *J.* xxvi. 26 b and *The White Divel* (v. iii) : ' Equally mortall with a winter plague.'

and contentation amongst a mans friendes, comforteth heart and vitall spirits, and is in this time more requisite then any other things.'

The prophylactics recommended to a trustful public by contemporary doctors were of a respectable antiquity. Little store was set by originality, and the writers of the day made no parade of first-hand knowledge or research. They preferred to lean upon Hippocrates, Galen, Ficinus, Paracelsus, and ' all the learned and authentic fellows ',[1] and the formula ' as Avicen testifieth ' was of greater virtue than ' my judgement is '.   A few of the innumerable remedies are mentioned here.   It was thought good to chew angelica root or a gentian or zodoary root or the rind of a lemon or pomecitron.[2]   A pomander much favoured by doctors was 'a good Sivill Orenge stuck with cloves '.[3]   Cardinal Wolsey, says Cavendish, would hold in his hand ' a very fair orange, whereof the meat or substance within was taken out, and filled up again with the part of a sponge, wherein was vinegar, and other confections against the pestilent airs ; the which he most commonly smelt unto, passing among the press, or else when he was pestered with many suitors '.   Excellent also was wormwood steeped in vinegar and kept in a close-stopped pewter-piece. A ' fume of great experience ' for correcting the air of a room was obtained by dipping a red-hot brick into a basin of vinegar : [4] another by the burning of old shoes.[5]   A more fragrant ' fume ' is recommended in the

---

[1] *All 's Well That Ends Well*, II. iii.
[2] Lodge, *op. cit.*, sig. C 4^v.
[3] J. Woodall, *The Surgeons Mate* (1639), 339.
[4] *Present Remedies against the Plague* (1594), sig. A 4^v and B 3.
[5] See quotation from Holinshed in P. Stubbes, *The Anatomie of Abuses* (ed. Furnivall), i. 282.

SVNDRÆ
APPROOVED REMEDIES
againſt the Plague.

I.

A remedie againſt the Plague, ſent to the Lord
Maior of London from King Henry
the eight.

Ake a handfull of Sage, a handfull
of Elder leaues, a handful of redde
Bramble leaues, ſtampe them all
and ſtraine them through a fine
cloth, with a quart of Wnite wine
and then take a quantitie of Gin-
ger, and mingle them together,
& ſo take a ſpoonefull of the ſame,
and you ſhall be ſafe for foure and twentie daies: and
ſo being nine times taken, ſhall be ſufficient for all the
whole parte by the grace of God. And if it be ſo that
the party be ſtricken with the Plague before hee hath
dunke of this medicine : Then take the water of
Scabions a ſpoonefull and water of Betonie a ſpoonefull,
and a quantitie of fine Treacle, and put them altogether, and cauſe him to drinke it, and it ſhall put out all
the venome. If it fortune the Botche to appeare,
then take the leaues of Brambles, Elder leaues, Muſtard
ſeede, and ſtampe them altogether, and make a Plaiſter thereof, and lay it to the ſore, and it ſhall draw out
the venome, and the partie ſhall be whole by the
grace of God.

II.

A medicine taught vnto King Henrie the ſeuenth
by his Phiſition againſt the
Plague.

Ake halfe a handfull of Rew, likewiſe of Mandra-
gories, Feather-few, Sorrell, Burner, and a quantitie of crops and rootes of Dragons, waſh them
cleane, and ſeeth them with a ſoft fire in running water, from a Bottle to a Quarte, and then ſtraine them
together through a cleane cloth : And if it be bitter, put
thereto a quantitie of Suger-Candy, or of other Suger,
and if this medicine bee vſed before the Purples doe
ariſe: ye ſhall be whole by Gods grace.

III.

Another remedie.

Ake three ſlips of Herbe grace, and ſire ſpoonefuls
of Vineger, and beate the ſame together, then
ſtraine the iupce out thereof, and put thereunto
one ounce of fine Treacle, and one ounce of Suger, and
ſtir it together, then ſet it ouer the fire, and make thereof a Sirrop, and put it in a Boxe cloſe : then take a
Sage leafe, and euerie Morning faſting, ſpread as
much as a Beane thereof vpon the ſame leafe, and ſo
eate it. And if hee that taketh it, be infected it will diue
it from his heart: and if the partie that taketh it Euening and Morning be not infected, it will preſerue him
for twentie foure houres after.

IIII.

Another.

Mongſt other excellent and approoued Medicines for the Peſtilence, there is none more wor-
thy auaileable when the ſore doth appeare, then
to take a Cocke, Pullet, or Chicken, and let the feathers
of the taile of the higheſt pa   lucke off, till the
rump: be bare, then holde the ſaide   re of the Pullet to
the ſore, and the Pullet will gape and labour for life,
and in the ende will die: then haue another Pullet, and
do the like to the Patient, and if that die, yet ſtill apply
the Patient with Pullets ſo long as any doe die: for
when the Poyſon by the ſaide Chicken is drawen
forth, the ſaid Chickens that be offered thereunto will
liue, then the ſore preſently will ſwage, and the partie
forth-with recouereth: This Medicine is neceſſarie
to drue the venome from the heart.

V.

A Plaiſter to draw the Sore to a head, and
to breake it.

Ake two Lyllie rootes, one handfull of ſowre
Dowe, two handfuls of Mallowes, one handfull
of Linſeede, ſtampe all theſe together ſmall, and
boyle it in a quarte of the Lees of Wine till it be thicke,
then lay it an inch thicke vpon Leather, broader then
the Sore, and let the borders of the Leather be plai-
ſtred with Corleos waxe, to make it cleane: it ſhall
bring out the Botch in twelue houres, and breake it
ſhortly.

VI.

A drinke to be taken euery Morning for a preſeruatiue
againſt the Plague, and for the voyding
of infection.

Ake Sauerie the quantitie of a handful, and boyle
the ſame in a quart of good Wine vinegar, with
a ſpoonefull of Graines being beaten, and put into
the ſame: then drinke the ſame with a quantitie of Suger euery morning faſting.

VII.

Another drinke to be viually drunke of euery one
being infected.

Ake Roſemarie the quantitie of eight or nine
crops, then take of Marigolds being brown within, of Burner, and of Bourage, euery one a handfull
thereof, let them be ſod in a quarte of ſtale Ale clariſhed:
then put into it a cruſt of bread, a little whole Mace,
and a quantitie of Suger, and let him drinke the ſame at
all times during his ſickneſs: and put Pimpernel in his
broth.

VIII.

Another drinke againſt the Plague.

Ake an ounce of Sorrell water, and as much Dra-
gon water, a dragme of Treacle, and put thereto a
dragme and a halfe of Powder imperial, & giue it
to the Patient with Ale, within twenty foure houres
after hee is infected, and hee ſhal with Gods grace e-
ſcape and do well.

Imprinted at London by E. Alde for E. White, and are to be ſolde at the little North doore of
Paules Church at the ſigne of the Gun.

Remedies against the plague

General Orders against the plague issued in 1592—dried rosemary, juniper, bayleaves or frankincense burnt in a chafingdish and carried about from room to room. Edward Alleyn, when on tour in the country during plague-time, charged his wife, who was in London, to keep in the windows good store of rue and herb of grace.[1] Face in *The Alchemist* (v. i) put his trust in the burning of rose-vinegar, treacle, and tar. But the best fortification against the plague was the onion. Three or four peeled onions left on the ground for ten days would gather all the infection in the neighbourhood.[2] Sir Politick Would-be was well acquainted with their wonderful powers of absorption. His ingenious method of discovering whether a ship was 'guilty of the plague' was to blow air with bellows upon sliced onions (*Volpone*, iv. i) :

> Now, sir, your onion, which doth naturally
> Attract th' infection, and your bellowes, blowing
> The ayre upon him, will shew (instantly)
> By his chang'd colour, if there be contagion,
> Or else, remaine as faire, as at the first.

A more cumbersome method was to put two or three sheep in an infected room three or four days ' before the full or change ' and leave them there for a month. Then wash them in warm water and give the wash to swine to drink. If these die, the infection is mostly taken out of the house.[3]

---

[1] *Henslowe Papers* (ed. W. W. Greg), 35. As late as 1760 the price of rue and wormwood in Covent Garden Market rose 40 per cent. in consequence of a false rumour that the plague had broken out in St. Thomas's Hospital. Cf. Chambers's *Book of Days*, ii. 141.

[2] *Present Remedies against the Plague* (1594), sig. B 3ᵛ.

[3] James Manning, *A New Booke, intituled, I am for you all. Complexions Castle* (1604), sig. E 2.

An elaborate ritual is commended by a London physician to visitors of the infected. The chamber is to be well perfumed with ' odoriferous trochiskes ', the windows ' laid ' with herbs, the floor swept clean and sprinkled with rose-water and vinegar. A fire of sweet wood should burn in the chimney, and the casements after being shut for an hour are to be opened towards the north. ' Then let him wash his face and hands with rose-water and rose-vineger, and enter into the chamber with a waxe candle in the one hand, and a sponge with rose-vineger and wormewood, or some other Pomander, to smell to. Let him hold in his mouth a peece of Mastic, Cinamon, Zedoarie, or Citron pill, or a Clove. Let him desire his sicke friend to speake with his face turned from him.' Finally, on his departure he must wash again in rose-vinegar and water, and lay by for a time the garments worn during the visit.[1]

The use of amulets was approved by some physicians and condemned by others. Two London doctors, Peter Turner and Francis Hering, argued at some length in 1603 for and against the wearing of bags of arsenic next the skin.[2] Lodge followed Avicenna in praising the special qualities of the Eastern Hyacinth stone. Carried in the mouth or about the breast near the region of the heart, it had the excellent property of quickening the vital spirits.

There was an infinite variety of inward medicines for warding off the infection. The grocer in *The Knight of the Burning Pestle* (i. iii) did good business by selling mithrida-

---

[1] F. Hering, *Certaine Rules, Directions, Or Advertisments* (1625), sig. B 2.   See also Lodge, *op. cit.*, sig. L 1.

[2] This preservative was recommended to Walsingham in 1582. Cf. *Cal. S. P. Dom., Addenda*, 1580–1625, 78. Lodge and Kellwaye also approved of it.

tum and dragon-water to plague-stricken houses. Several
kinds of triacle were put on the market, London triacle
being cried up by some in preference to that 'filthy and unwholesome baggage composition, termed commonly Triacle
of Geane'.[1] ' Venice ' triacle was even more famous than
that of Genoa. A poor-man's triacle, greatly commended
by Galen, was garlic eaten with butter and salt at break-
fast.[2] Others put their trust in tobacco, ' a most rare Anti-
dote and Preservative, either being smelled unto, or taken
fasting in the morning : provided, that presently after the
taking thereof, you drinke a deepe draught of six shillings
Beere, and walke after it '.[3] A less pleasant remedy was
a draught of sack, salad oil, and gunpowder. This made
the patient sweat.[4] But the sovereign specific was
unicorn's horn. Half a dram mixed with the same weight
of angelica root made ' a good Opiat to expell venem and
provoke sweat '.[5] Many quacks grew rich on the sale of
this commodity. It was ' worth halfe a City ' ; [6] yet the
outlay was inconsiderable, for a piece of old shoeing-horn
easily deceived the ignorant. True, there were ways of
testing whether the horn was ' right ' or not. Topsell's
method was to ' put silke upon a burning cole, and upon
the silke the aforesaid horne, and if so be that it be true
the silke will not be a whit consumed '.[7] Another method,

[1] *London Tryacle, Being the enemie to all infectious diseases*
(1612), sig. A 4. Triacle of Geane (= Genoa) cost 4*d.* a lb. in 1545.
Cf. Sir E. Brydges, *The British Bibliographer*, ii. 507.
[2] Simon Kellwaye, *A Defensative against the Plague* (1593),
sig. C 1.
[3] *The Red-Crosse : Or Englands Lord have mercy upon us* (1625).
[4] This saved 100 lives in 1625. Cf. manuscript note on sig. B 3ᵛ
of B.M. copy (C. 31 e. 7) of *Present Remedies against the Plague*
(1594).   [5] S. Kellwaye, *op. cit.*, sig. F 3ᵛ.
[6] *The Guls Horne-booke* (1609), sig. C 2ᵛ (*G.*, ii. 221).
[7] *The Historie Of Foure-Footed Beastes* (1607), 720.

described by Webster in *The White Divel* (II. i), was to make ' a preservative Circle ' of the powder of unicorn's horn and in it to place a spider. The spider was charmed to remain within the circle. The boy Davenant, having bought a horn from a famous apothecary, made this trial ' without the expected success : the Spider would go over and thorough and thorough, unconcerned '.[1]   But few were sceptical enough to test their purchases. Doctors, however, were well acquainted with the rarity of this beast, and remembered that Alexander the Great was at great charge and expense to procure one, ' neither may it be taken alive, for that it liveth in places desart and solitary in the extreamest parts of *India* and the East '.[2]

A favourite remedy for those actually infected with the plague is given in the General Orders : ' Take a white *Onion* cut in pieces, of fresh butter iii. ounces, of *Leven* the weight of xii.d, of *Mallowes* one handful, of *Scabious* if it may bee had one handfull, of *Cloves* of garlike the weight of xx.d. boyle them on the fire in sufficient water, and make a pultesse of it, and lay it warme to the sore.' Another good remedy for drawing out the venom was to pull the feathers from the tail of a cock, pullet, pigeon, or chicken, and apply him to the sore :

' and the *Pullet* will gape and labour for life, and in the ende will die : then have another *Pullet*, and do the like to the Patient, and if that die, yet still apply the Patient with *Pullets* so long as any doe die ; for when the Poysen by the saide *Chicken* is drawen foorth, the said *Chickens* that be offered thereunto will live, then the sore presently will swage, and the partie foorth-with recovereth '.[3]

[1] MS. Aubrey 6, fo. 46 (*Brief Lives*, ed. A. Clark, i. 205).
[2] Lodge, *op. cit.*, sig. H 3ᵛ.
[3] See the broadsheet at p. 8. See also Lodge, *op. cit.*, sig. l 2ᵛ ;

When a man struck another within the precincts of the court his right hand was chopped off, not without merciful medical care, the yeoman of the poultry standing by with a cock to lay to the stump. The treatment was for

The Unicorn, from Topsell, after Gesner.

rich and poor. The extremity of Prince Henry's disease in 1612 appeared to be in his head, 'for remedie wherof they shaved him, and applied warm cocks and pigeons newly killed, but with no successe'. The test for hydrophobia was not unlike. Take an old cock, pluck the feathers from its breech, and apply it to the bite. If the dog is mad the cock swells and dies; if the cock lives, the dog is not mad. *Teste* the Royal Society in 1687.[1]

A man's faith and physique would need to be robust to withstand some of these nostrums, and we can sympathize with Margaret Paston's anxiety for her husband in 1464: 'for Goddys sake be war what medesyns ye take of any fisusyans of London; I shall never trust to hem be cause of your fadr and myn onkyl, whoys sowlys God assoyle'.[2]

J. Bamford, *A Short Dialogue*, sig. D 4; S. Kellwaye, *op. cit.*; T. Vicary, *The English Mans Treasure* (1613), p. 81. Webster (*Dutchesse of Malfy*, ii. i) writes of a dead pigeon being taken from the soles of the feet of one sick of the plague.

[1] Harrison's *Description*, ed. Furnivall, i. 276; J. Chamberlain, *Letters*, ed. McClure, i. 388; *Transactions Royal Soc.* xiv. 410.

[2] *Paston Letters* (ed. J. Gairdner, 1904), iv. 106.

II

THE PLAGUE-ORDERS

THE elaborate plague-orders of 1603 and 1625 were the logical outcome of the theories of sixteenth-century England about the cause and the cure of the plague. They were not shaped in a single year, but were the result of long and bitter experience. This chapter will attempt to explain not only what these orders were, but how far and in what way they were the accretion of a century.

At the outset it is important to distinguish between two sets of orders. The ' Orders, Thought Meete . . . to be executed throughout the Counties of this Realme, in such Townes, Villages, and other places, as are, or may be hereafter infected with the plague, for the stay of further increase of the same ' were drafted and issued by the Privy Council and applied only to the towns and villages outside London.[1] London, which was already large enough to require special consideration, had its own set of orders, similar in most respects to the General Orders, but differing in proportion as the needs of a large town differ from those of a small town and still more from those of a village. The London Orders are the more important intrinsically and historically, for they were earlier and more detailed, and set the pattern from which the General Orders were copied.

The compilation and execution of the London Orders

---

[1] The book was printed in 1592 and reissued without alteration in 1593, 1594, 1603, and 1625. The book is referred to in *Acts of the Privy Council*, 1592, 204, as being ' lately set out' on 19 September. This edition appears to be the earliest extant, but similar orders were probably printed as early as 1578. See *Acts of the Privy Council*, 1577–1578, 387–8.

were undertaken by the Lord Mayor and the aldermen
and councillors of the City, and our knowledge of them
is mainly derived from the Repertories and Journals
recording the proceedings of the Court of Aldermen and
the Court of Common Council. The Privy Council was
sometimes consulted on methods of procedure, as also—
in the seventeenth century—were the Justices of the
Peace for the districts in the immediate neighbourhood.
But those who had a special knowledge of the government
of the City—and in particular the Lord Mayor and the
aldermen—were the most competent to decide the best
practical methods of fighting the infection.

Although the plague had been endemic in England
since the Black Death, it was not until 1518 that the
Government, stirred to action no doubt by the example
already set by France and Italy,[1] drew up and enforced
a set of orders for its prevention. The primitive arrange-
ments then instituted were gradually amplified and
altered in succeeding years, and at various times the
orders were tabulated and published in collected form.
In August 1543, for example, the Privy Council commanded the Lord Mayor to devise and execute precepts
and articles, and to communicate them to each of the
aldermen.[2] The severe plagues of 1563 and 1570 led
to the issue of several additional orders,[3] and in 1574,
perhaps for the first time, the orders were printed and
fixed upon posts.[4] In 1583 an important collection of
twenty-one orders was devised by the Lord Mayor and

[1] See below, pp. 34, 55, 62, and 179.
[2] R. x. 350. The precepts may be seen in J. xv. 47 b–49 and
55–55 b. A summary is in B.M. Addit. MS. 4376.
[3] J. xviii. 123 b, 136, 139, 145 b, 152 b, and xix. 219.
[4] J. xx, pt. i, 184.

aldermen with the help of the Privy Council.[1] Twenty printed copies were delivered to each alderman, one for every deputy-alderman, constable, warden, and beadle in his ward, and the rest to be set up in parish churches, on posts, and in other public places.[2] Minor changes and additional orders were introduced into the recensions of 1592, 1603, 1606, 1608, 1609, 1625, 1630, and 1636, but in essentials the orders of 1583 agree with all subsequent collections, including the last collection published in 1665.

In considering the London plague-orders it will be convenient to follow the arrangement of the General Orders, which were grouped under three sections according as they treated (1) of the officials responsible for their execution, (2) of sanitation, and (3) of segregation.

1. OFFICIALS

In the appointment of officials the policy of the City authorities throughout was to use as much as possible the services of those already employed by the City, and to resist all proposals (emanating chiefly from the Privy Council) to make additional appointments. Their point of view was as practical as it was praiseworthy, for they argued that the fewer officials there were to pay, the more money there would be for the infected poor. In time the appointment of additional officials became necessary, but the City maintained its efforts to limit their number and their salaries.

[1] No printed copy appears to be extant. The orders may be found *in extenso* in *J*. xxi. 285–286 b.

[2] *J*. xxi. 284 b. An abstract of the orders of 1583 is in B.M. Lansdowne MS. 74, fo. 69, and is reprinted in the Malone Society's *Collections*, i. 206–10. It is dated 1593 in the *Catalogue of the Lansdowne Manuscripts*.

The Lord Mayor, Aldermen, &c.

The men who bore the brunt of the responsibility for the City's health were the Lord Mayor, the aldermen, and the deputy-aldermen. The Lord Mayor was directly responsible to the King and to the Privy Council, the aldermen to the Lord Mayor. Apart from their many other duties, aldermen were required to see that the prescribed orders were duly executed in the ward which they represented. During a severe plague meetings of the Court of Aldermen or the Court of Common Council were out of the question, but each alderman was supposed to be in his place, and to him or to his deputy were addressed the precepts issued from time to time by the Lord Mayor. The provost-marshal, whose duty it was to attend on the Lord Mayor together with his men, exercised a general supervision over inferior officials. Subordinate to the aldermen, councillors, and marshal, yet an important personage in his ward, the beadle saw that infected houses were marked, and that lantern and candlelight were hung from every man's door on a winter's night.[1] The two churchwardens and the clerk of each parish were held responsible for the proper conduct of burials, for searching out infected houses, and for seeing that they were properly shut up.[2]

Constables

The normal duties of the constable are indicated in the oath which he was required to swear when admitted to office.[3] In plague-time it was his arduous and thankless

[1] Cf. *J.* xxiii. 130 (1592) and xxvi. 141 b (1603).
[2] For the clerk's duties with regard to the bills of mortality see the Appendix.
[3] See the illustration at p. 18.

task to report to the Lord Mayor the true number of those
who died in his precinct, to shut up and mark infected
houses, and to arrest wandering beggars and idle persons.
In 1609 any constable who neglected his duty was fined
twenty shillings, of which two shillings went to the in-
former and the rest to the poor of the parish.[1] But punishment was often more severe. In the same year a constable
in the Tower Ward was sent to Newgate for allowing a
house which he knew to be infected to stand without any
bill, cross, or warder,[2] and in 1625 two churchwardens and
a constable of St. Helen's Parish were sent to the same
prison for concealing plague-deaths at the Angel Inn in
Bishopsgate Street.[3] Constables were in great danger of
taking the infection or of being mauled by plague-stricken
maniacs. But the places of casualties were quickly filled
by deputies, since acceptance of the post was compulsory,
recalcitrant citizens being brought before the Lord Mayor
and duly punished.[4] Many constables ran away in plague-
time, but flight gave only temporary relief. The names of
defaulters who fled without appointing deputies were
taken by the beadle,[5] and on their return they were made
to suffer for this betrayal of their trust.

[1] *J*. xxvii. 319.
[2] *R*. xxviii. 329 b. For another case see *Middlesex County
Records* (ed. J. C. Jeaffreson), ii. 41.
[3] *R*. xxxix. 262. Cf. also *J*. xxvi. 103 b (June 1603).
[4] *J*. xxvi. 131 b and *The Account Books of the Parish of St. Bartholomew Exchange* (ed. E. Freshfield), 23.
[5] *J*. xxxiii. 130 (1625). In 1630 William Thompson of Edgware,
gent., was bound to good behaviour and to appear at the next
Sessions ' for that he being Constable of Edgware in the last time
of the infection . . . deserted the town and left it without any
care or without a deputy to do his duty whereby much disorder
followed '. See *S. P. Dom., Chas. I*, vol. 175, Doc. 24, and
Middlesex County Records, iii. 33.

The O th of the Conſtables within the City of *London*.

YE ſhall ſwear, that pe ſhall keep the Peace of our Soveraign Lord the King well and lawfully after pour power: And pe ſh, I arreſt all them that make Conteſt, Riot, Debate, oz Affray, in Bzeaking of the ſaid Peace, and lead them to the Houſe oz Comp er of one of the Sheriffs: and if pe be withſtood by ſtrength of miſdoers, pe ſhall rear on them an out-cry, and purſue them from Street to Street, and from Ward to Ward, till they be arreſted: And pe ſhall ſearch at all times, when pe be required by the Scavengers oz Beadles, the common noiſance of pour Ward: And the Beadle and Raker pe ſhall help to rear and gather in their Salary and Quarterage, if pe be thereupon by them required. And if any thing be done within pour Ward againſt the Ozdinance of this City, ſuch defaults as pe ſhall find there done, pe ſhall them preſent to the Mapoz and Miniſters of this City: and if pe be letted by any perſon oz perſons, that pe may not duly do pour Office, pe ſhall certifie the Mapoz and Council of the City of the name oz names of him oz them that ſo let pou. Pe ſhall alſo ſwear that during the time that pe ſhall ſtand in the Office and occupy the room of a Conſtable, pe ſhall once at the leaſt every month certifie and ſhew to one of the Clerks of the Mapoz’s Court, and in the ſame Court, as well the names as ſurnames of all Free-men which pe ſhall know to be deceaſed within the month in the Pariſh wherein pe be inhabited, as alſo the names and ſurnames of all the childzen of the ſaid Freemen ſo deceaſed, being Ozphans of this City. And pou ſhall enquire of all and every the Offences done contrary to the Statutes made 1, 4, & 21 Jac. to reſtrein the inozdinate haunting and tipling in Inns and Alehouſes, and foz repzeſſing of Dzunkenneſs and other diſozders, and thereof due pzeſentments make, accozding to the ſame Statutes. And thus pe ſhall not leave to do, as God pou help, &c. God ſave the King.

The oath of the Constables

Examiners

These were the duties of the permanent officials in time of infection. But the exceptional needs of the City made necessary the appointment of special officials, whose duties began and ended with the rise and decline of the plague. The most important of these were the surveyors, or examiners as they were afterwards called. In 1583 each alderman was required to choose monthly two substantial and discreet citizens to be surveyors in each parish. Refusal to take office or negligence in the performance of duty was punished by a committal to ward.[1] By the Act of Parliament passed in 1604 ' for the charitable Relief and ordering of persons infected with the Plague ', the title of surveyor was changed to that of examiner, and this name persisted as long as the office. It will be remembered that the hero of Defoe's *Journal of the Plague Year* was appointed examiner in the Great Plague of 1665, ' which I was at first greatly afflicted at, and very much disturb'd about '. The examiner's duties were to ensure that all orders were duly observed, to discover infected houses, to appoint and supervise warders, searchers, and other plague-officials, and to render account of the due execution of his charge before the Lord Mayor, aldermen, and deputy-aldermen. He was required to keep to himself and to carry a red wand in his hand when

---

[1] *J.* xxi. 285 b. The earliest reference I have found to the appointment of surveyors is dated November 1578 (*J.* xx, pt. ii, 450 b). In the orders in *S. P. Dom.*, *Eliz.*, vol. 98, Doc. 38 (December 1578 ?), surveyors are called general overseers. In 1581 surveyors were also appointed to prevent the entry into the City of idle vagrants and masterless or suspected persons (*J.* xxi. 91 and 93 b). For an account of the commissioners of health appointed in 1609 and 1610 to supervise the examiners see Note A, p. 177.

he walked abroad. In some parishes he received subscriptions for the relief of the poor, paid out wages to searchers, warders, and dogkillers, and bought padlocks, staples, printed orders, and other necessary things.[1] In May 1609 and subsequently examiners were appointed for two months, and those who refused the office were imprisoned ' until they shall conform themselves accordingly '.[2]

Physicians and Surgeons

An account of the minor officials to whom were entrusted matters of sanitation and segregation is given later : [3] but something may be said in this place of the appointment and duties of physicians and surgeons in time of infection. Surgeons from the hospitals were appointed to heal the plague-stricken as early as 1569.[4] Some years later the Privy Council proposed the engagement of two physicians at a stipend of 13s. 4d. a day,[5] but the Lord Mayor and aldermen objected that there was no need for any pay-

[1] See the accounts of the examiners for St. Martin's-in-the-Fields in 1625 and later years, preserved at City Hall, Westminster (MSS. 4511, 4512, and 4513).

[2] J. xxvii. 365 b.

[3] See below, p. 26 (scavengers), p. 28 (rakers), p. 39 (dogkillers), p. 45 (bearers), p. 64 (searchers and viewers), p. 67 (nurses), p. 68 (warders), and p. 179 (providers).

[4] J. xix. 186.

[5] S. P. Dom., Eliz., vol. 98, Doc. 38. This document gives a list of twenty-two orders drawn up by the Privy Council with suggestions and corrections by the aldermen and common councillors. It is dated 1574 in Cal. S. P. Dom. In November and December 1578 the Court of Common Council considered articles touching the plague sent by the Privy Council (J. xx, pt. ii, 451 b, 453 b, and 455), and the document possibly gives the result of their deliberations. The reference to the mark for women-keepers— ' to be a red wand '—is an interlineation in a different handwriting and was probably added in 1583 or later (see Note C, p. 179).

The Apothecary's Shop opened.

Sold by N: Brooke at ye Angell in Cornhill.

The Doctors' Dispensatory.
or the Art of Phisick restored to practise

Apothecary's Shop and Doctor's Dispensary

ment if the infected resorted to these physicians only :
for the rich could afford to pay for themselves, and the
' stock ' (i. e. the fund for charitable purposes) would pay
for the poor. For similar reasons they refused to pay
the surgeons and the two apothecaries whose appointment
was also suggested. The same attitude was taken in 1583
when a ' certain and convenient ' number of physicians
and surgeons were appointed by the College of Physicians
for the counsel and cure of the sick. They were required
to give their whole attention to the infected and were
recompensed by their patients, if of ability, and alterna-
tively by the parish.[1] In 1609 the Privy Council proposed the election of six doctors at an annual stipend
of 400 crowns each. The City refused to pay so extravagant a wage, but engaged three ' able and discreet ' surgeons besides the three that belonged to the Pesthouse,
and allotted a district to each of the six. They joined
with the searchers in viewing bodies ' to the end there
may be a true report made of the disease ', they had to
attend all who sent for them or who were sent to them
by the examiners, could only deal with infected cases, and
were paid either by their patients or by the parish at
the rate of twelve pence for every body searched.[2]

In 1625 the attempts to secure the effective co-operation
of competent physicians were more elaborate than in
former plague-years. On 28 June a committee of aldermen
and doctors (including Sir William Paddy, physician to
King James I) met to consider the engagement of one
or two skilful physicians for the cure of the infected.
On 14 July the Lord Mayor informed the Court of

[1] *J.* xxi, 285 b.
[2] *Cal. S. P. Ven.*, 1607–1610, 273 ; *J.* xxvii. 365 b.

Aldermen that 'the Spanish Doctor' and Nicholas Heath, a surgeon, had agreed to give their services to healing the sick in the City, the one for 100 marks and the other for £50 per annum.[1] As much as £290 6s. 8d. was spent by the City in 1625 on doctors, physicians, surgeons, and apothecaries.[2] The name of the author of *Rosalynde* was mentioned at a meeting of the Court of Aldermen held on 7 July : ' Item for and touching the entertainment and employment of Doctor Lodge to be one of the Physicians for cure of those visited with the plague within this City the same is by this Court referred to the Lord Mayor to deal with him as his Lordship shall think fit.'[3] It is not known what action his Lordship thought fit to take, but it is certain that Lodge remained at his post. He died in September in the parish of St. Mary Magdalen, Old Fish Street, probably of the plague.

2. SANITATION

The City of London proper was and is little more than one square mile in area. Its houses were low-roofed and commonly of two or three stories, seldom of four. They were built of wood, those of the richer sort of brick. The streets were narrow and the stories overhung so that in many lanes and alleys the tops of the houses almost met. This propinquity encouraged gossip and the wit-combats of neighbours, but it darkened the streets and shut out the pleasant and healthy light of heaven. The circumference of the horizon was diminished to a narrow slit of sky.

[1] *R*. xxxix. 255 b and 279 b. £20 was paid the Spanish doctor in part payment of this sum on 9 March 1626 (*R*. xl. 154 b). For Nicholas Heath, see below, p. 76.

[2] See below, p. 168.   [3] *R*. xxxix. 274 b.

Copy of a Letter from James I to the Lord Mayor, 29 April 1605
Requesting him to test the efficacy of a remedy for the plague invented by
Henry de Ommeren et d'Ashenbrook, a German

Distinguished foreigners thought the houses of the City very handsome and the streets very clean, but distinguished foreigners were shepherded into the better quarters of the town. They were dazzled by the magnificent display of gold and silver in Goldsmith's Row, but they were not shown the more populous parishes in the liberties, like St. Sepulchre's ; St. Giles's, Cripplegate ; and St. Saviour's and St. Olave's, Southwark : and they were carefully screened from the eight out-parishes which included St. James's, Clerkenwell ; St. Leonard's, Shoreditch ; and St. Mary's, Whitechapel. These districts, some of which were outside the jurisdiction of the City, were far from being ' white and clean '. Instead of wide streets were to be found narrow lanes and alleys, and instead of handsome houses mean tenements where families of poor people were thickly crowded into small and dirty rooms. The suburbs were notorious for poverty and disease. They were the haunt of vice and the breeding-place of the plague.[1]

In a report presented to the Privy Council and dated 20 April 1630, the College of Physicians gave it as their opinion that the following ' Annoyances ' were most potent in fostering the contagion : increase of the buildings in and about the City ; inmates by whom the houses were so pestered that they became unwholesome ; neglect of cleansing of common sewers and town ditches, and permitting standing ponds in divers inns ; uncleanness of streets ; the laystalls so near the City, especially on the north side ; the slaughter-houses in the City ; burying of

---

[1] Cf. W. B. Rye, *England as seen by Foreigners*, 110, 166, and 283. Cf. also the letter from More to Colet in T. Stapleton, *Tres Thomae* (1588), Vita Thomae Mori, p. 21.

infected people in the churches and churchyards of the
City ; that churches were ' overlaid ' with burials ; the
carrying up of funnels to the tops of houses from privies
and from vaults of the dead ; the selling of musty corn in
the public markets ; bakers baking unwholesome corn ;
butchers killing unsound cattle ; tainted fish.[1] Add
the abuses resulting from infected goods and infectious
animals and we get a comprehensive list of annoyances
all of which may be grouped roughly under the general
heading of ' Sanitation '.

Housing

The authorities of sixteenth-century and seventeenth-
century London were bent on preserving the ancient limits
of the City. In their view, an increase in population dis-
turbed the ordinary jurisdiction, enhanced the price of
food, and unpeopled other towns. But the rapid expansion of commerce, the immigration of foreigners through
the troubles in France and the Netherlands, and the influx
from the country caused in part by enclosures and the
conversion of arable land into pasture, set them a problem
which they were powerless to solve. Innumerable statutes
and proclamations were directed against the division of
single tenements and the erection of new buildings about
the City and suburbs. In 1564, for example, the Lord
Mayor ordered that no one was to receive into his house
any persons ' but such as without fraud or covin were well
known to be of his family to dwell or abide, otherwise than
guests or strangers which do abide or hire their lodging

[1] *Hist. MSS. Comm.*, 8th Report, Appendix, 229. An abstract
of this document in *S. P. Dom., Chas. I*, vol. 25, Doc. 97, has
been wrongly dated April 1626. It adds ' mussels ' to the list
given above.

within common inns or other places for a small season '.[1]
In 1580 a royal proclamation forbade any new buildings
within three miles of the City gates, and in 1596 the Privy
Council drew the attention of the Middlesex Justices to
the ' great number of dissolute, loose, and insolent people
harboured in such and the like noisome and disorderly
houses, as namely poor cottages, and habitations of
beggars and people without trade, stables, inns, alehouses,
taverns, garden-houses converted to dwellings, ordinaries,
dicing-houses, bowling-allies, and brothel-houses'.[2] Elizabeth's successor and his advisers were equally diligent
in fighting an evil which menaced the City both with
pestilence and riot. A proclamation of 16 September 1603
complained of the crowding of dissolute and idle persons
into small and narrow rooms, and ordered all houses in-
fested with multitudes of dwellers to be razed to the
ground and not to be rebuilt. A proclamation dated
October 1607 deplored ' the filling and pestering of houses
with Inmates [3] and several dwellers (and those of the
worse sort) almost in every several room '. It forbade the
erection of new houses in London except by special
licence, the division of a dwelling-house into tenements,
and the reception of inmates.

Attempts to check the growth of London were vain and,
far from remedying the evils, led to gross overcrowding
and the erection of mean hovels in holes and corners of the
City and suburbs. In spite of a multitude of regulations
housing conditions were worse at the end of James's reign
than at the beginning. The inefficacy of the Privy Council's

[1] *J.* xviii. 204 and 215.
[2] John Stow, *Survey of London* (ed. C. L. Kingsford), ii. 367
and 368.
[3] i. e. houses with more than one family or household.

orders was lamented by many. John Chamberlain remarked in June 1602 that it had spied an inconvenient increase of housing in and about London caused by building in odd corners, in gardens and over stables, and he condemned its sporadic action in pulling down one building here and one there, ' lighting in every parish on the unluckiest, which is far from removing the mischief '.[1] Stow's comment on the proclamation of 1603 is also significant: ' but nothing was done touching that matter '.[2]

Foul Streets

The unauthorized midden which stood near John Shakespeare's house in Henley Street twelve years before the birth of his illustrious son has become to posterity the symbol of Elizabethan methods of sanitation. It is only just to remember that the offence was not committed with impunity, and that John was forced to use the authorized ' comyn mukhyll ' which stood before the house of his neighbour, William Chambers.[3] In London the fines for unauthorized ' filths and dunghills ' were collected by the sergeant of the Channel. He took an oath that he would ' spare no person for favour, neither grieve any person for hate '. A yeoman of the Channel assisted him in his task of general supervision.[4] The duty of cleaning the streets devolved mainly upon householders, but partly also upon scavengers and rakers. In Shakespeare's time two scavengers were appointed to each

---

[1] *Cal. S. P. Dom.*, 1601–1603, 209.

[2] *Annales* (1605), 1417.

[3] *Minutes and Accounts of the Corporation of Stratford-upon-Avon* (Dugdale Society, 1921), i. xxxiv and 42.

[4] See the Book of Oaths in the Guildhall Record Office compiled towards the end of Elizabeth's reign.

The Oath of the Scavengers.

YE shall swear, that ye shall diligently o=
versee that the Pavements within your
Ward be well and sufficiently repaired,
and not made too high in noysance of your
Neighbours; And that the Ways, Streets
and Lanes, be cleansed of Dung, and all
manner of Filth, for the honesty of this City:
And that all the Chimnies and Furnaces be
of Stone or Brick, sufficiently and defensibe=
ly made against peril of Fire. And if ye find
any the contrary, ye shall shew it to the Al=
derman of your Ward, so that the Alderman
may ordain for the amendment thereof. And
thus ye shall do, as God you help.

God save the King.

Printed by *Samuel Roycroft*, Printer to the Honourable
City of *LONDON.*

The oath of the Scavengers

parish and held office for a year. Like the constables they gave their services, willingly or unwillingly, for nothing. Their office was not menial : they were citizens and house-holders, men of some importance in the parish, civic digni-taries. They did not clean the streets themselves, but were responsible for the rakers who did.[1] Dr. Johnson's definition expresses the exact truth : ' SCAVENGER : . . . A petty magistrate, whose province is to keep the streets clean.' He took an oath diligently to oversee that pave-ments were kept in repair and not made too high ' in noisance of ' his neighbours, that ways, streets, and lanes were cleansed of filth for the honesty of the City, and that all the chimneys, ' Furnees ' (furnaces), and ' Reerdoes ' (fire-backs) were of stone and safe against the peril of fire.[2] But though the office might easily be a stepping-stone to higher things, few coveted it. One of the great merits of life in the Virginian settlement, claimed a sea-captain in *Eastward Hoe* (III. iii), was that the means of advancement were not preposterously mixed : ' You may be an alder-man there, and never be scavenger.' In London the office was unpaid and unpleasant, and scavengers often found themselves out of pocket at the end of their term of office.[3] It was no easy task to collect taxes for rakers' wages from householders who had no passion for cleanliness. Citizens sometimes secured exemption at the expense of a fine : among the church plate of St. Giles's, Cripplegate, are

[1] But ' scavenger ' might also mean ' raker ' in the sixteenth and seventeenth centuries. Cf. *Oxford English Dictionary* and D. Lupton, *London and the Countrey* (1632), p. 94.
[2] Cf. the Book of Oaths referred to on p. 26, n. 4. The illustra-tion is from a sheet printed between 1678 and 1709. See above, pp. viii–ix.
[3] *R.* xxvi, pt. ii, 485, and xliv, 85, 86.

a parcel gilt beaker, date-mark 1608, inscribed ' This was the fine of R. M. Vaus for beinge released from beinge scavenger ', and two silver cups inscribed ' The fyne of Peter Phillips for being released from beinge scavenger 1612 '.

The raker's duties were those of the modern scavenger. His office was ancient if not honourable. A sweeper of litter had scandalized the aldermen as early as 1299 by accusing them of turning public money to their own profit,[1] and ' a rakyer of chepe ' was among the company in *Piers Plowman* (v. 322) who drank good ale with Gluttony in a London alehouse. In 1535 and later years this officer blew his horn before every door on Mondays, Wednesdays, and Fridays to warn citizens to bring out offal into the open street.[2] He was required to clean the streets and to carry away dirt and refuse every week-day before 6 o'clock in the morning.[3]

Elaborate instructions were issued in medieval times, for example in 1357 and 1375,[4] to ensure the greater cleanliness of the streets, but the efforts of the authorities were redoubled at the threat of an approaching plague. In 1547 all wells and pumps in infected wards were drawn three times a week, and at each drawing twelve bucketfuls of water were poured into the channels which ran along the middle of each street.[5] These orders became more and more stringent. In 1583 every inhabitant owning a well

---

[1] H. T. Riley, *Memorials of London*, 41 and 299.
[2] *R.* ix. 134 b. Cf. also *J*. xxvii. 366 b (1609).
[3] *J*. xxiii. 130 (1592) and xxvi. 98 (1603).
[4] H. T. Riley, *op. cit.*, 299 and 389.
[5] *R*. xi. 387. The channels often harboured filth instead of carrying it away. Hence Mistress Quickly's anger (*2 Henry IV*, II. i) when Falstaff says : ' throw the quean in the channel '.

or pump had to flush the channel with at least twenty bucketfuls of water every morning before 6, and every evening after 8 o'clock. At the same time he had to clean and sweep those parts of the street and channel facing his house, taking particular care that the water was kept within the channel and not swept ' to the sides of the streets nor the stones wet, except only sprinkling for delaying [sic] the dust '. Mud and filth were to be swept together in heaps, not carried away by the water poured down the channels, and pavements were to be kept in good repair with no holes in which filth might collect ' to increase corruption and infection '.[1]

Simon Eyre in *The Shomakers Holiday* (ii. iii) made his servants get up betimes to clean his walks and to ' sweepe me these kennels, that the noysome stench offende not the nose of my neighbours '. But other citizens ignored the elaborate rules of their magistrates and continued to use the streets as receptacles for all kinds of rubbish. Sensitive folk complained of the dunghills which pestered narrow lanes and alleys, and a physician, Francis Hering, begged that the dung-farmers should be ' tied to their stint of time in winter, and not suffered (unlesse urgent necessitie require) to perfume the streetes all sommer long '.[2] Barber-surgeons after letting blood often cast it into the street to the great annoyance of the citizens.[3] Pudding-wives and tripe-wives were accustomed to throw into the channels paunches, guts, and entrails, and also the water in which these were boiled. The order of 1569, that their refuse was to be carried in tubs to the river Thames,[4]

[1] *J.* xxi. 285 b.
[2] *Certaine Rules, Directions, or Advertisments* (1625), sig. A 4.
[3] S. Kellwaye, *A Defensative against the Plague* (1593), 13 b.
[4] *J.* xix. 187.

reminds us that Falstaff (*The Merry Wives*, III. v) was thrown into the Thames at Windsor ' like a barrow of butcher's offal '.

The presence of slaughter-houses in the heart of the City resulted in many abuses. In the fourteenth century the putrefied blood of slaughtered beasts was allowed to run in the streets,[1] and in spite of several efforts to remove them the shambles in the parish of St. Nicholas-within-Newgate were still a menace to health in 1603. In that year Lodge recommended that the City slaughter-houses be discontinued, and ' placed in some remote and convenient place neere unto the river of the Thames, to the end that the bloud and garbige of the beasts that are killed may be washed away with the tide ', but his recommendation was not adopted, and the shambles were looked upon as a contributory cause of the plague of 1625. No wonder that Shakespeare's London was a ' city of kites and crows '. Kites and ravens were protected birds, and grew fat on the offal of the streets. Kites were so tame, it is said, that they often snatched bread and butter out of the hands of little children.[2] In changing our habits we have expelled from our cities, almost from our country, the kite, the raven, and the carrion crow.

[1] H. T. Riley, *Memorials of London*, 339 and 356. Cf. Creighton, *A History of Epidemics*, i. 216–17 and 324–5. For the prohibition of slaughter-houses within the walls of Coventry cf. *The Coventry Leet Book* (ed. M. D. Harris), 25–32. In More's Utopia (ed. J. H. Lupton, p. 158) the filthiness and ordure from the meat markets were ' clene washed awaye in the runnynge ryver, without the cytie, in places appoynted, mete for the same purpose '.

[2] Fynes Moryson, *An Itinerary* (1617) (MacLehose edition, iv. 167) ; *A Relation . . . of the Island of England* (Camden Society, 1847), p. 11. The ' Relation ' was written in 1498 by the Venetian ambassador, Andrea Trevisan. Cf. *Cal. S. P. Ven.*, 1202–1509, 269. Also, Herrick, *Poet. Wks.*, ed. Martin, 486.

To correct the noisomeness and corruption of the air in plague-time fires were sometimes burnt in the streets of the City. This ancient practice was adopted in London in July 1563, when fires were ordered to be made on Mondays, Wednesdays, and Fridays, at 7 p.m.[1] In 1603 pitch bonfires were lit twice a week between 8 and 9 o'clock at night,[2] and in July 1625 the College of Physicians recommended the burning of ' a good quantity of coarse myrrh, coarse frankincense, or stone-pitch', provided by the churchwardens of each parish.[3] Earthen pans with charcoals were set ' in the most needful places the distance of four houses one from another, and the same is conceived to be better for purging of the air than those bonfires of wood which make great flames '. In 1636 it was suggested that the Tower ordnance might sometimes be shot off ' for the correcting of the infectious aire '.[4] In the Great Plague of 1665 bonfires were tried as a last resource early in September, but as the air did not seem infected, it was felt by many that this showy and expensive project was as superfluous as it was ineffectual. In less than three days the fires were extinguished by rain.[5]

Ditches, Sewers, and Rivers

Among the nuisances especially needing reform was the foulness of the ditch which encompassed the City wall. It had been originally constructed for defensive purposes, and at one time was carefully cleaned and scoured. Men

---

[1] *J.* xviii. 123 b.   [2] *J.* xxvi. 115 b.

[3] *J.* xxxiii. 129 b. At St. Christopher's in 1625 £1 8s. 4d. was paid for earthen pans, charcoals, stone-pitch, frankincense, and incense. *Accomptes of the Churchwardens* (ed. E. Freshfield).

[4] *Certain necessary Directions* (1636), sig. C 2.

[5] N. Hodges, *Loimologia* (translated by J. Quincy, 1720), pp. 19, 20 ; *Transactions of the Bibliographical Society*, xiv. 204.

still alive in 1603 could remember the large stock of good
fish it once contained. But towards the end of the sixteenth century it was much neglected and either forced
into a narrow and filthy channel or filled up for the
planting of gardens or building of houses. Elizabethan
Londoners thought their City better fenced with men
than with stones and moats.[1] In May 1595 a petition
was presented in favour of stopping up the whole of the
Town Ditch. In 1593, so ran the petition, more had
died of the plague in its neighbourhood than in three
parishes besides. The ditch was the origin of infection
and the only noisome place in the City, and its abolition
would not only save 2,000 marks every ten years (when
it had to be scoured), but would enable the ground to be
turned into gardens. The petition was rejected. In the
same year the Common Council granted two fifteenths for
cleaning and widening the part between Bishopsgate and
Moorgate, but it quickly became choked up and unsavoury
and, wrote Stow despairingly, was ' therefore never the
better : and I will so leave it, for I cannot helpe it '.[2] The
authorities again took action in February 1603, when the
Common Council noticed that the ditches about the City
walls and the common sewer passing under the City to
the Thames, had ' for want of scouring, clean and sweet
keeping and well looking unto become of late most foul,
noisome, and dangerous for infection especially to all such
as inhabit near thereabouts or shall pass that way '.[3] A
fifteenth was voted for the reformation of these abuses,

---

[1] Camden's *Britannia* (1586), p. 229.
[2] *Survey* (ed. Kingsford), i. 20 and 164; *Cal. S. P. Dom.*,
1595–1597, 45. The ditch seems to have completely disappeared
by 1643. Cf. Stow, *op. cit.*, ii. 297.
[3] *J.* xxvi. 60.

and at the same time all vaults and latrines hanging over or issuing into any of the Town ditches or into the sewer were ordered to be pulled down. A year later a deputation of aldermen informed the Privy Council of the noisomeness of the City's ditches,[1] and in April 1606 the Common Council, threatened by another plague, considered the cleansing of the Fleet Ditch and the Town ditches and sewers.[2] Moorditch seems to have been exceptionally filthy. In 1596 or 1597 Shakespeare called the ' melancholy of Moorditch ' a most unsavoury simile. Dekker wrote in 1606 that the river Acheron ' stinks almost worse, is almost as poysonous, altogether so muddy, altogether so black ' as Moorditch, and in 1609 that the cleansing of the world would be a ' sorer labour than the clensing of *Augeaes* stable, or the scowring of Mooreditch '.[3]

The streams and rivers were almost as foul as the ditches. Many attempts were made in the thirteenth and fourteenth centuries to clean the Thames and other watercourses in and near the City. In 1357, for example, those who threw any manner of rubbish, earth, gravel, or dung into the Thames or the Fleet or into the ditches round the City walls were threatened with imprisonment.[4] But in the seventeenth century citizens were still polluting them with rubbish and ordure. The master of the Lord Mayor's

---

[1] *R.* xxvi, pt. ii, 314 b.   [2] *J.* xxvii. 35 b.

[3] *Newes from Hell* (1606), sig. E 2ᵛ (*G.* ii. 122) ; *The Guls Horne-booke* (1609), 7–8 (*G.* ii. 212). Moorfields, however, was transformed in 1605/6 from ' a most noysome and offensive place . . . loathsome both to sighte, and sent ' into ' most faire, and royall walkes '. Cf. Stow and Howes, *Annales* (1615), 945.

[4] H. T. Riley, *Memorials of London*, 299. This was a change from the instruction of 1309 (p. 67) that ordure was to be placed not in the streets but in the Thames or elsewhere out of the City.

barge received ten shillings in 1603 ' for gathering of dogs
and other noisome things out of the River of Thames and
burying them '.[1]   Able-bodied rogues and vagabonds
found in the City were often employed in cleaning the
river and the City ditches.   In 1591 they worked from
six in the morning till six at night, and received fourpence
a day for their labour and towards their meat and drink.[2]

It is clear that the system devised for the disposal of
filth and rubbish was inadequate.   It is equally clear
that many citizens ignored the regulations of their
magistrates.   A foul street or a noisome ditch was attended
to when its condition became intolerable, but it was soon
as bad as ever.   Sewers annoyed the air of Milton's as well
as of Shakespeare's London, and in the London of Pope
the Fleet Ditch still rolled ' the large tribute of dead dogs
to Thames '.[3]

Infected Goods

The attention of magistrates and physicians was early
directed to the dangers which might lurk in the goods of
infected persons.   When two servants of the Venetian
ambassador died of the plague in 1513 all their effects
were thrown into the Thames.[4]   But perhaps these drastic measures were reserved for the property of foreigners.
In 1518 the Court of Aldermen agreed that no clothes,
garments, or bedding which had been near or about any
infected person should be sold or given away, or sent out

[1] *R.* xxvi, pt. i, 191 b.
[2] *R.* xxii. 268 b (1591); *Letter Book*, D D, 298 b (1609); *P. C. R.*
xl. 422 (1631).
[3] *The Dunciad* (1728), ii. 250.
[4] Creighton, *op. cit.*, i. 289.   In Italy the destruction of infected
goods was ordered in 1399.   Cf. J. F. C. Hecker, *The Epidemics of
the Middle Ages*, 59.

of the infected house, but that they should be kept
' still, close, and unworn ' for three months. They were
not to be ' sunned, weathered, and hanged out in any
street or lane whereby infection may grow '[1] In 1543
garments were ordered to be aired in the fields, and the
dangerous practice of throwing straw and rushes into the
streets was strictly forbidden, ' but every man wisely
and warily to burn the straw and rushes, or if the same
cannot be done in his house for danger, to truss the same up
close and to carry it straight into the fields to some place
appointed, where the said straw and rushes shall be burnt '.[2]
Twenty years later the Court of Aldermen ordered the
appointment of two honest poor men to burn any straw,
garments, etc., found in the fields.[3]

Little or no change was made in these orders in subsequent years. In 1603 Lodge recommended that the
infected garments of the rich should be burnt ' according
as the custome is in Italy ', but the suggestion was not
accepted. Certain orders affecting specific trades may be
mentioned here. On 1 June 1603 the Lord Mayor complained of ' divers idle and loitering women and boys '
who ' do daily gather rags, marrow bones, old shoes, and
sundry other noisome things cast out of men's houses
into the streets and lanes within this City, liberties and
suburbs thereof, and do afterwards wash the same things
at the common sewers and other places, and hang them
up openly to dry '. This dangerous practice was prohibited, and offenders sent to Bridewell.[4] Precepts against

[1] R. iii. 185 ; J. xi. 346 b.
[2] J. xv. 48 b. In B.M. Addit. MS. 4376, fo. 51 (1543), the
straw is ordered to be carried to the fields by night.
[3] R. xv. 281 b. Cf. also B.M. Addit. MS. 4376, fo. 52 b.
[4] J. xxvi. 98 b.

the hawking of apparel or ' any other stuff ' about the
streets were issued in 1581 and 1608, and in the latter
year brokers were ordered not to make any show outside their shops, nor to hang out ' on their stalls, shop-
boards, or windows towards any street, lane, commonway
or passage any old bedding or apparel to be sold '.[1]
In 1630 it came to the notice of the Privy Council that
those who carried malt into the City were accustomed
to return home with rags ' for manuring of the soil-
ing of the ground ', and the practice was forbidden.[2] In
the same year a Clerkenwell family was shut up for three
weeks for receiving goods out of an infected house in
Southwark.[3]

Dogs

Cats, swine, rabbits, and pigeons were thought to be
very dangerous in time of infection. The chief culprit,
the rat, was rarely suspected in this country, though in
the East it was early associated with the plague. The
priests and diviners of the plague-stricken Philistines
recommended the return of the Ark of the Covenant
to Canaan with ' images of your emerods, and images of
your mice that mar the land ' (1 Samuel vi. 5) : and the
Indian Bhagavata Parana warned men to quit their houses
when a rat fell from the roof, jumped about on the floor
in a drunken fashion, and died, ' for then be sure that
plague is at hand '.[4] There were plenty of rat-catchers in

[1] J. xxi. 140 b and xxvii. 275 b.
[2] P. C. R. xl. 157.
[3] S. P. Dom., Chas. I., vol. 175, Doc. 24.
[4] Cited by W. J. Liston, British Medical Journal, 24 May 1924.
Colonel Liston suggests that the rat escaped attention in Europe
because in this cooler climate bubonic plague was often accompanied by an epidemic of pneumonic plague or of other diseases,

Elizabethan London, and their cry added to the gaiety of the streets : ' Rats or mice ! Ha' ye any rats, mice, polecats or weasels ? Or ha' ye any old sows sick of the measles ? I can kill them, and I can kill moles, and I can

A Rat-Catcher.

kill vermin that creepeth up and creepeth down and peepeth into holes.'[1] But it is a little ironical that in time of plague nearly all the attention of the authorities

such as typhus, relapsing fever, and influenza. These were not always distinguished from bubonic plague. Hence, a mortality among rats was not associated with the outbreak of bubonic plague which followed it, but was classed with the casual occurrence of disease among domestic animals.

[1] See Richard Deering's 'Fancy' of 'London Cries' in B.M. Addit. MSS. 29372–7.

was devoted to the slaughter of the rat's enemy. The dogkiller lived in clover, while the rat-catcher was ignored. The first attempt to restrict the movements of dogs and to lessen their numbers was made apparently in 1543, when they were ordered to be banished, or killed and buried out of the City at the common laystalls. Hounds, spaniels, or mastiffs necessary for the custody of houses might remain in the City if kept within doors.[1] In 1563 this order was slightly relaxed, but a dog might only take the air if held in leash.[2] Delinquents paid a fine of 3s. 4d. or lost their dog. In the following year dogs found in the streets between 10 p.m. and 4 a.m. were ordered to be killed.[3] Many animals were left without food and without company, and their dismal howling was unpleasant to the sound and intolerable to the sick. In 1583 loose dogs and dogs that howled and annoyed their neighbours were destroyed.[4] In 1606 all dogs without exception were ordered to be sent out of the City or killed, but later orders are more like that of 1563.

The streets of Elizabethan and Jacobean London were thronged with dogs. They even invaded the churches, and it was one of the many duties of a sexton to whip them out.[5] Citizens were incredibly careless in disposing

---

[1] *J*. xv. 47 b–49.

[2] *J*. xviii. 136. A mayoral proclamation issued on 2 August 1563 ordered the slaughter of cats as well as dogs. Cf. *Hist. MSS. Comm.*, 6th Report, 455 a, and 8th Report, 227 a.

[3] Bibliotheca Lindesiana, *A Bibliography of Royal Proclamations*, No. 592. In September 1578 the hours were 9 p.m. and 6 a.m. Cf. *J*. xx, pt. ii, 430.

[4] *J*. xxi. 285 b.

[5] Cf. *The Returne from Parnassus* (ed. Macray), 64. The parish of St. Mary Woolnoth bought a penny whip in 1564 'to beat dogs out of the church'. Cf. *Transcripts of the Registers* (ed. J. M. S. Brooke and A. W. C. Hallen), xxiv. See the dog-whipper

of carcasses. In 1578 it was found necessary to forbid them to throw out of doors ' any dead dogs, cats, whelps, or kitlings, or suffer them there to lie in such careless order as at this present they do '.[1] Even those who had the grace not to throw them into the streets left them unburied in the fields. In 1625 carcasses of horses, dogs, and cats lay rotting in Moorfields, Finsbury Fields, and elsewhere about the City.[2]

From 1563 special officers were appointed in plague-time to ' murder ' and bury dogs found loose in the streets.[3] In 1583 the Common Hunt, an attendant upon the Lord Mayor and aldermen and keeper of the City's kennel of hounds, was allowed fourpence for every dog he killed provided that he buried it at least four feet deep in the fields. Negligence or favouritism was punished by dismissal and imprisonment. In later years his fee fell to twopence a dog and even three-halfpence.[4] In May 1604 ' two little black hounds or beagles of his Majesty's, each of them having a cross shorn upon the right shoulder ' were reported missing.[5] Perhaps they were murdered by the Common Hunt or by one of his fellows, blissfully ignorant of the royalty of their master. Many parishes supported a dogkiller of their own. St. Margaret's, Westminster, paid only a penny a dog, yet 656 were killed there in 1592, and 502 in 1603. At St. Martin's-in-the-Fields in

at work in the painting of a sermon at Paul's Cross, now in the possession of the Society of Antiquaries. An engraving after this picture is reproduced in *Shakespeare's England*, i. 64.

[1] *J.* xx, pt. ii, 430.
[2] F. Hering, *Certaine Rules* (1625), sig. A 4.
[3] *J.* xviii. 136 and *Hist. MSS. Comm.*, 6th Report, Appendix, 445.
[4] *J.* xxi. 285 b ; cf. also *R.* xxi. 51 and xxii. 201.
[5] *J.* xxvi. 211 b.

1625, 190 dogs were slaughtered in less than a month.[1] They ' were knockt downe like Oxen, and fell thicker then Acornes '.[2] The statement mentioned by Defoe that 40,000 dogs were killed during the plague of 1665 does not sound so grossly extravagant.

Burials

The burial regulations prohibit the gathering of crowds at funerals, fix the hours of interment, reform improper methods of burial, and make some attempt to limit the fees of profiteering sextons and bearers.

In 1569 no corpses except those of persons of honour were allowed to be buried in the time of divine service, but at some convenient hour before or after; and an infected corpse, ' whether it be rich or poor ', was to be taken straight from the house to the grave without going to the church ' for any solemnity to be used for the dead '.[3] The orders of 1583 forbade children to approach a corpse, coffin, or grave, and assemblies of people to collect at the house from which the corpse was carried. In August 1603 the number of persons who might follow 'any dead corpse' to the grave was limited to six, excluding the minister, clerk, and bearers.[4] From 1609 a bell was rung by one of the bearers until the corpse was set down at the

---

[1] M. E. C. Walcott, *The Memorials of Westminster* (1851), 154–5, and *The History of the Parish Church of Saint Margaret, in Westminster* (1847), 62. Cf. also the accounts of examiners at City Hall, Westminster (MS. 4512).

[2] *D. P. P.* 33. In *The Scornful Lady*, iv. 1 (*c.* 1609), Beaumont or Fletcher suggested that during the next plague ' those harmless creatures ' the dogs should be spared, and women, ' these hot continual plagues ', should be knocked on the head in their stead.

[3] *J.* xix. 165 b and 187.

[4] *J.* xxvi. 124 b.

burial-place.[1]   Infringement of these rules was severely
punished.   The sexton of St. Giles's, Cripplegate, who in
1606 had allowed an infected corpse to remain in the
church for a whole night without burial, was set in the
stocks for four hours with a paper on his head declaring
his offence.[2]   Next year a churchwarden, two parish clerks,
and the sexton of St. Sepulchre's were sent to Newgate
for permitting an infected corpse to be accompanied to
the grave by more mourners than were allowed.[3]   But
in spite of punishment many citizens ignored the stringent
regulations of their magistrates and the godly exhorta-
tions of their ministers.   At the height of the infection
of 1603 crowds followed to the grave the bodies of those
who had died of the plague, and the streets were strewn
with flowers at the burial of a maid, and with rosemary
at the burial of a bachelor.[4]   People of the poorer sort, even
women with young children, flocked to burials, and out
of sheer bravado stood over open plague-pits to show the
world that they did not fear the infection.[5]

The easiest method of checking these abuses was to hold
the burials at night when the streets were empty, and
this method the authorities were forced in the end to
adopt.   According to Stow [6] an order issued in 1548
prohibited all burials between the hours of six in the
evening and six in the morning.   In accordance with this
order the parish clerk of Allhallows Parish, Dowgate
Ward, was sent to Newgate in 1578 for attempting to

[1] *J*. xxviii. 25 b.   The illustration on p. 149 shows a bearer with
a red wand in one hand and a bell in the other.
[2] *R*. xxvii. 319.   [3] *R*. xxviii. 82.
[4] See below, pp. 94–5.
[5] James Bamford, *A Short Dialogue* (1603), 32.
[6] *Annales* (1605), 1004.

bury the body of a plague-stricken maidservant in the night and before it had been viewed by the searchers.[1] Soon afterwards the Privy Council proposed that infected corpses should be buried between 12 and 3 a.m., but the City rejected the proposal fearing that it might lead to abuses of secret burial and to concealment of the plague.[2] In the General Orders of 1592, however, the Council ordered burials of infected bodies to be made after sunset, yet by daylight, and in May 1603 the City followed suit with the command that 'none dying of the plague be buried in the day-time before ten of the clock at night '.[3]   But, as we have seen, the order was not always obeyed.   Burials of infected corpses were made in 1608 either before sunrise or after sunset ' with the privity of the churchwardens or constable '.[4]   In after years the hours were even later, in 1630 at about 11 p.m. or 4 a.m. in summer, and in winter about 10 p.m. and before 6 a.m.[5]   The orders of 1665 are like those of 1608.

In the sixteenth century the parish churchyards in

[1] R. xix. 398.
[2] S. P. Dom., Eliz., vol. 98, Doc. 38 (December 1578 ?).
[3] J. xxvi. 98.   Creighton (i. 482) quotes The Wonderfull yeare (D. P. P. 28) : ' others fearfully sweating with Coffins, to steale forth dead bodies, least the fatall hand-writing of death should seale up their doores ', and adds that this is an evasion of the order of 1548 prohibiting night-burials.   It is rather an evasion of the order prohibiting concealment of plague-deaths, for night-burials had been legalized before Dekker began to write his pamphlet. For a graphic account of a burial by night see The Meeting of Gallants (D. P. P. 129–31).   On the other hand, it should be remembered that people who had not died of the plague, and especially people of standing, were buried by day and with many of the usual ceremonies.
[4] J. xxvii. 275 b.
[5] S. P. Dom., Chas. I, vol. 175, Doc. 3.   Cf. also P. C. R. xl. 135.

London, partly through increase of population and partly through encroachment,[1] became insufficient to contain the number of dead. In 1582, for example, no less than twenty-three parishes were using St. Paul's churchyard, and it had become so crowded that scarcely any graves could be made without corpses being exposed.[2] In the height of a plague there was the keenest competition for burial inside the churches, and the privilege was accorded only to people of family and following. John Donne spoke of this competition in a powerful sermon preached at the end of the plague of 1625 :

' Ambitious men never made more shift for places in Court, then dead men for graves in Churches, and as in our later times, we have seen two and two almost in every Place and Office, so almost every Grave is oppressed with twins ; and as at Christ's resurrection some of the dead arose out of their graves, that were buried again ; so in this lamentable calamity, the dead were buried, and thrown up again before they were resolved to dust, and make room for more.' [3]

Coffins were rare and expensive. Most corpses, especially in poor and overcrowded parishes, were covered simply with a winding-sheet, and flung without burial rites into pest-pits, the discovery of which is one of the grimmest experiences that fall to the lot of excavators in modern London. Dekker testified that in 1603 the dead were tumbled ' into their everlasting lodgings (ten in one heape, and twenty in another). . . . The gallant and the begger lay together ; the scholler and the carter in one

---

[1] See Creighton, *op. cit.*, i. 333, on encroachments.
[2] *Remembrancia* (ed. W. H. and H. C. Overall), 332. The number was reduced in this year to thirteen.
[3] *XXVI. Sermons* (*Never Before Publish'd*) (1661), sig. Qqq 2ᵛ.

bed.'[1] At Westminster in 1603 only 37s. 6d. was paid for the graves of 451 poor people—an average of one penny a burial.[2] In 1625 forty or fifty were piled up in each pit, and at one place 'the very Common-shore breakes into these ghastly and gloomy Ware-houses, washing the bodies all over with foule water'.[3] George Wither gives a gruesome account of a visit to a plague-pit :

> Lord ! what a sight was there ? and what strong smells
> Ascended from among *Death's* loathsome Cells ? . . .
> Yonn lay a heape of skulls ; another there ;
> Here, halfe unburied did a Corpse appeare . . .
> A locke of womans hayre ; a dead mans face
> Uncover'd ; and a gastly sight it was.

Wither's description is merely gruesome. Defoe begins by describing the pits as ' very, very, very dreadful, and such as no tongue can express ' : then with that economy of style and feeling which obtains its effect seemingly without effort, he bequeaths to our literature a picture which for pathos and intensity has seldom been equalled.

Men were not blind to the evil effects which might result from these methods of burial. They realized what rotten stenches and contagious damps would strike up into London's nostrils if another pestilence compelled her to break open the old plague-pits.[4] Cremation or the transport of infected corpses to places more remote from the City would have solved the problem, but the one expedient ran counter to religious scruples and the other was impracticable. Hence the authorities limited their

---

[1] *The Seven deadly Sinnes* (1606), sig. G 1ᵛ (*G*. ii. 76). Cf. *D. P. P.* 29 and 72.
[2] M. E. C. Walcott, *The Memorials of Westminster* (1851), 155.
[3] *D. P. P.* 159.
[4] *The Seven deadly Sinnes* (1606), sig. G 2 (*G*. ii. 76–7).

efforts to regulating the depth of graves. In 1543 the
parish of St. John, Walbrook, was reproved for burying
bodies one upon the other so that the uppermost did
not lie a foot and a half in the earth, ' very dangerously
for infection of all the king's liege people thereabout and
passing thereby '.[1] In later years graves had to be at
least three feet deep, and usually six feet.[2] Needless
to say, these orders were broken again and again. In
August 1603 bodies were laid so shallowly that they were
scarcely covered to the depth of one foot,[3] and in August
1625 the Privy Council had again to insist that

' the Graves be digged so deep as that those bodies which lie
next to the superficies of the earth may be interred and covered
three foot deep, at the least, the contrary whereof being
generally observed to be now practised, cannot choose but
be a great occasion of increase of the Infection, by corrupting
of the Air in greater measure. It having been found by often
experience, that even amongst bodies slain in Battle that the
not burying of them deep enough hath putrefied and corrupted
the Air in such sort as that Plagues have thereupon ensued.' [4]

The bearers whose irksome and dangerous duty it was
to carry the corpses to the graves used a cart or a barrow [5]
for the performance of their office. They were of course
required to keep to themselves and to carry a red wand
when they went abroad, but considering the risks they
ran they were extraordinarily immune from the infection.[6]

---

[1] *R.* x. 350 b. Cf. *J.* xviii. 152 b (1563).
[2] *J.* xx, pt. ii, 441 b ; xxi. 128 and 285 b ; xxiii. 130 b.
[3] *J.* xxvi. 122 b.
[4] *P. C. R.* xxxiii. 98.
[5] Cf. D. Lysons, *The Environs of London*, i. 417.
[6] Cf. Wither, *Britain's Remembrancer* (1628), 49, and *D. P. P.*
84, 85. See also below, p. 67. The observation is as old as
Procopius and has been confirmed in many later epidemics of
plague. Cf. W. J. Liston, *British Medical Journal*, 24 May 1924.

They gave notice of their approach by ringing a bell and by crying ' Cast out your dead ' or ' Have you any dead bodies to bury ? '[1] It is this grim cry which Dekker's ' excellent egregious Tinker ' parodies in the words, ' Have ye any more Londoners to bury, hey downe a downe dery, have ye any more Londoners to bury '.[2]

The bearers owed their unpopularity not only to the nature of their office but to the callous and brutal manner in which they performed it. Dekker called them ' nasty and slovenly ',[3] and Wither spoke of ' those Sharks, the shameless Bearers,' as almost ' a rout too bad, to picke out hangmen, from '. This ill odour clung to them in the plague of 1665. They were ' the hard-nedest Creatures in Town ' says Defoe, and Rugge speaks of them as a base-living, foul-mouthed crew who ' did affright the people most sadly by their swearing and cursing '.[4] They were given a weekly wage by the parish in which they were employed. At St. Martin's-in-the-Fields in 1593 there were two bearers, the one receiving sixpence, the other a shilling a week. This seems very small pay in proportion to the danger of their calling, but if they also received sixpence for every corpse buried, as they did at St. Margaret's, Westminster, in 1603, they would earn good money in plague-time.[5] St. Martin's

---

[1] Cf. Nashe, *Works* (ed. McKerrow), ii. 286, and John Davies, *Humours Heav'n on Earth* (1605), 223. In 1665 the cry was ' Bring out your dead '.

[2] See *The Wonderfull yeare* (D. P. P. 59).

[3] D. P. P. 144.

[4] B.M. Addit. MS. 10117, fo. 147. Cited by W. G. Bell, *The Great Plague in London in 1665*, 184, 185.

[5] *St. Martin-in-the-Fields The Accounts of the Churchwardens* (ed. J. V. Kitto), 582. M. E. C. Walcott, *The Memorials of Westminster* (1851), 155.

provided them with a special residence in 1625.[1] At Stepney in the same year several men acted as bearers without due authority and exacted ' cruelly of men for the bearing of the dead to the ground such sums of money as are no ways sufferable '. To reform this abuse the vestry fixed the following scale of charges : from Ratcliffe, Limehouse, Mile End, or Bethnal Green —for those who could not pay for themselves, 4d. apiece; for those who could pay, 6d. ; and for those who made use of the church cloth, 8d. From Poplar, Blackwall, Wentworth Street, Petticoat Lane, Spitalfields, Cock Lane, or Collier Row, the charges were 6d., 8d., and 12d. apiece.[2]

A Corpes Bearer

Clergymen, readers, clerks, and sextons were accused of banding together with the bearers ' to racke the dead '. Heavy charges were made for the tolling of bells which were not rung and for funeral sermons which were not delivered.[3] Dekker wrote in 1603 of the ravenous and

---

[1] Accounts of examiners preserved at City Hall, Westminster (MS. 4512).

[2] *Memorials of Stepney Parish* (ed. G. W. Hill and W. H. Frere), 107–8. The charges for the use of the ' best ' and the ' worst ' cloth in 1602 were 2s. 6d. and 2s. Cf. *ibid.* 42.

[3] Wither, *op. cit.*, 134 b–135. See Note B, p. 177, for the tolling of bells in plague-time.

unconscionable sextons of St. Giles's, St. Sepulchre's, and St. Olave's,[1] and in 1579 T. F. in *Newes from the North* deplored the ungodliness of

' the parish Clark of a Town that was sore visited with the Plague, who said unto his wife upon a day, Wife (quoth he) if there come two corpses to-day : we will have a shoulder of Mutton and a quart of Sack to supper, and if there come but one : we will have a shoulder of Mutton and but a pinte of Sack.   Content husband (quoth she).'

Unsound and Unwholesome Food

Of the causes of the plague enumerated in 1630 by the College of Physicians [2] the last five come under this heading : musty and unwholesome corn, unsound cattle, tainted fish, and mussels.   The authorities had early perceived the harm done to the City's health by unsound food, and many sellers of putrid cattle, fish, or poultry were punished in medieval times.   Modern magistrates should know the case of the taverner who sold bad wine in 1364, and as punishment was made to drink a deep draught of it, and was drenched with the remainder.[3] The authorities redoubled their vigilance in plague-time. During the infection of 1609, for example, they pointed out the dangers of stinking fish, unwholesome flesh, and musty corn,[4] and prohibitions against the sale of unsound food find a place in subsequent collections of orders, including those of 1636 and 1665.

The belief so generally held that ' aptness of body ' was a chief cause of the contagion led to much attention being paid to diet, and in plague-time the sale of ' unwholesome '

---

[1] *D. P. P.* 34.   For the misdemeanour of the sexton of St. Giles in 1606, see above, p. 41.   [2] See above, p. 23.

[3] H. T. Riley, *Memorials of London*, 318.   [4] *J.* xxvii. 366 b.

food, that is to say, of food which was thought to nourish the infection, was forbidden. In 1535 no one was allowed after the August of that year to bring oysters into the City on pain of imprisonment for forty days.[1] The sale of fruit in the streets was prohibited in 1569 : it might only be sold in houses, shops, warehouses, or in the common market-places. Fruit at the time was very plentiful and a pestilence was feared.[2] In 1581 the Common Council maintained that the eating of pork was dangerous for the infection, and no butcher in the Borough of Southwark was allowed to sell it from 3 October till the following All Saints' Day.[3] This order was still in force during the plague of 1607, when a barber-surgeon of St. Mary's, Whitechapel, had to answer ' for killing of pork, being dangerous meat for the infection '.[4] Among the foods accused of fostering the plague of 1665 were red cherries, cucumbers, melons, radishes, a dish of eels, a codling tart and cream, French beans, and a gooseberry fool.[5]

3. SEGREGATION

Assemblies

An elaborate organization was required to enforce the ' sequestration ' of individual citizens, but fear and

---

[1] *J.* xiii. 462.

[2] *J.* xix. 186. This order was renewed in September 1578 when the danger of selling pears, plums, damsons, and other like fruits to menservants and children was pointed out. Cf. *J.* xx, pt. ii, 429. In 1625 John Clift petitioned the Privy Council for power to confiscate all fruit brought into the City from infected places. Cf. *Cal. S. P. Dom.*, 1625–1626, 94. A proclamation dated 22 April 1630 forbade fruiterers and greengrocers to store fruit in their houses : it was to be kept in warehouses in Thames Street.

[3] *J.* xxi. 140 b.

[4] *Middlesex County Records* (ed. J. C. Jeaffreson), ii. 31.

[5] *The Shutting Up Infected Houses* (1665).

common sense were often sufficient to cause the abandon-
ment of meetings. From the Black Death onwards feasts
and assemblies were postponed until the abatement of the
plague. Schoolmasters were forbidden to ' make any
shows of scholars or children ', fencers ' to make any open
assemblies for playing of prizes '.[1] Bear-baitings, theatres,
dancing and bowling (especially on Sundays),[2] the going
about with drums and proclamations,[3] buckler-play and
ballad-singing,[4] were sternly put down by the authorities
in plague-time, and servants and apprentices were not
permitted to enjoy ' the outrageous play at the football '
in the streets of London[5] or Sunday indulgence in ' tippling,
gaming, tobacco-taking or needless unlawful assemblies of
waster-playing '.[6]

The authorities for the most part held that it was impossible to take the infection during the act of worship,
but their regulations do not tally with their convictions.
In 1563 and in other plague-years special fasts were ordained and sermons of repentance preached. Infected
people, however, were forbidden to attend church.[7] During

[1] *J.* xx, pt. ii, 432 (1578).
[2] *S. P. Dom., Eliz.,* vol. 98, Doc. 38 (1578 ?).
[3] *J.* xxiii. 131 (1592).   [4] *J.* xxvii, 275 b (1608).
[5] *J.* xxiii. 225 b (1593) and xxvi. 143 (1603). In 1609 a citizen
was fined 3s. for allowing his servants to play football in Cheapside
(Guildhall Library MS. 87, fo. 246 b).
[6] *P. C. R.* xxxix. 831 (1630). A ' waster ' is a cudgel. Cf. Stow,
Survey (ed. Kingsford), i. 95 : ' The youthes of this Citie also have
used on holy dayes . . . to exercise their Wasters and Bucklers.'
[7] *The Diary of Henry Machyn* (Camden Society, 1848), 310.
Before 1538 they were allowed to go to the four churches belonging
to the Grey, Black, White, and Augustine Friars, ' where there is
large room ', but were not encouraged to worship at the parish
churches. Cf. *Memoranda, References, and Documents Relating
to the Royal Hospitals of the City of London* (1836), Appendix,
pp. 1–4. See also (for Coventry) *Letters and Papers, Foreign and
Domestic, Henry VIII,* vol. xiii, pt. ii, Nos. 394 and 674.

the plague of 1543 churchwardens appointed some honest person to keep all common beggars out of churches on holidays and to cause them to ' remain for the devotion of the people, without the church doors (if they lust) ',[1] and in 1563 some ' competent part of the glass windows ' was ordered to be removed ' so that the clear and wholesome air may the more freely and abundantly enter into the said Churches for the comfort, relief and saufgard during the time of this contagious and infective sickness of the plague '.[2]   In 1569 and later all persons whose family or house had been infected, whether themselves infected or not, were told to ' tarry and serve God at home at their own houses '.[3]

Theatres

The Elizabethan theatres suffered heavily from the many epidemics of the sixteenth and seventeenth centuries. The enmity which existed between the players and the City magistrates is well known, for it led to the erection of the theatres beyond the jurisdiction of the City.   The authorities were hostile not only or chiefly for moral reasons, but partly because the playhouses were a centre of disorder and the resort of all the riff-raff of the City, partly because they distracted servants and apprentices from their work, partly also because of the danger to public health caused by crowds of vagabonds and masterless men, especially in times of sickness.   ' To play in plague-time ', wrote the City to the Privy Council, ' is to increase the plague by infection : to play out of plague-time is to draw the plague by offendings of God upon occasion of such plays.' [4]   It is clear that the City Fathers

---

[1] J. xv. 49.   [2] J. xviii. 140 b.   [3] J. xix. 187.
[4] Malone Society, Collections, i. 173 (c. 1584).

thought actors a very superfluous sort of men. They
were supported in their views by many of the clergy.
T. White in a sermon preached at Paul's Cross in 1577
pronounced this unconvincing syllogism : ' the cause of
plagues is sinne, if you looke to it well : and the cause of
sinne are playes : therefore the cause of plagues are playes ' [1]

The first occasion upon which the plague was used as
a pretext for the prohibition of plays was, as far as has
been discovered, on 12 February 1564. The plague in
the City was not then extinct, and a mayoral proclamation
forbade any person to ' set forth or openly or privately play
or to permit or suffer to be set forth or played within his or
their mansion, house, yard, yard-inn, orchard or other whatsoever place or places within the said City or the Liberties
thereof any manner of interlude or stage-play at any time
hereafter without the especial licence of the said Lord
Mayor '.[2] Ten days later Bishop Grindal complained to
Cecil that players set up bills especially on holidays, ' whereunto the youth resorteth excessively, and there taketh
infection'. He recommended that the acting of plays within
three miles of the City should be forbidden for a whole year,
' and if it were for ever it were not amiss '.[3] Henceforth
the theatres were closed whenever the plague threatened
to become serious. Thus on 3 May 1583 the Court of
Aldermen pointed out to Walsingham the danger of

' the assembly of people to plays, bearbaiting, fencers and
profane spectacles at the *Theatre* and *Curtain* and other like
places to which do resort great multitudes of the basest sort

----

[1] *Sermon* (1578), 47.

[2] *J*. xviii. 184. This proclamation is wrongly dated ' 30 September 1563 ' in B.M. Addit. MS. 4376, fo. 52.

[3] Malone Society, *Collections*, i. 148–9. The document is dated
' 22. febr. 1563 ', i. e. 1563/4.

of people and many infected with sores running on them being
out of our jurisdiction and some whom we cannot discern by
any diligence and which be otherwise perilous for contagion,
beside the withdrawing from God's service, the peril of ruins
of so weak buildings, and the avancement of incontinency and
most ungodly confederacies, the terrible occasion of God's
wrath and heavy striking with plagues '.[1]

On 3 February 1594, again, the Privy Council prohibited
any resort to common plays within the compass of five
miles from London until there was better assurance of
health.[2] This prohibition of acting in plague-time finds
expression in many of the patents granted to the companies : for example in that given to James Burbage in
1574 to show comedies, tragedies, interludes, and stage-
plays, provided that ' the same be not published or shown
in the time of common prayer or in the time of great and
common plague in our said City of London '.[3]

Most of the documents are of this indefinite kind, but
some set up an automatic restraint according as the
deaths returned in the bills of mortality exceeded a certain
number. In 1584 or 1585 the Queen's Players favoured
the suggestion that theatres should only be closed when
the deaths from the plague in London rose to 50 a week.
To this the City objected that many were infected with
the plague without dying from it, and that the number
of plague-deaths was often concealed through the fraud
or ignorance of the searchers. The average number of
deaths from all causes, it pointed out, was between 40 and
50, and usually under 40. It proposed to the Privy Council, therefore, that in future no plays should be acted unless
the number of deaths from all causes had been under

---

[1] *Remembrancia*, i. 274 b.   [2] *J.* xxiii. 232.
[3] Malone Society, *Collections*, i. 263.

50 a week for at least twenty days.[1] The suggestion was
not adopted, for there is abundant evidence to show that
the Council continued its old practice of prohibiting or
permitting the performance of plays by proclamation or
by direct letters to magistrates as occasion required.[2]

An attempt at automatic restraint in 1604 seems to
have met with more success. The warrant from the
Privy Council to the King's, Queen's, and Prince's players,
dated 9 April 1604, permitted them to act in their respec-
tive theatres ' except there shall happen weekly to die
of the Plague above the number of thirty within the City
of London and the Liberties thereof. At which time we
think it fit they shall cease and forbear any further publicly
to play until the Sickness be again decreased to the said
number.'[3] By 1608 or soon after the number had been
changed to 40,[4] and this number persisted without change
until the closing of the theatres in 1642. It is probable
that the rise from 30 to 40 was due to the inclusion of
the out-parishes in the bills of mortality.[5]

[1] B.M. Lansdowne MS. 20, fo. 23, arts. 10–13. Reprinted in the
Malone Society's *Collections*, i. 169–79, with an important note
on the date of the documents by Sir Edmund Chambers.
[2] Cf. for example *Acts of the Privy Council*, 1592–1593, p. 31 ;
1596–1597, p. 38. See also *A Bibliography of Royal Proclamations*,
passim.
[3] W. W. Greg, *Henslowe Papers*, 61. See also the Malone
Society's *Collections*, i. 265. Various writers have called attention
to the following passage in Middleton's *Your five Gallants* (entered
in the Stationers' Register on 22 March 1608) : ' tis ee'n as
uncertaine as playing now up now downe, for if the Bill rise to
above thirty, heer's no place for players ' (sig. F 2ᵛ in first edition).
[4] Cf. Lording Barry, *Ram Alley: or Merrie-Trickes* (entered
in the Stationers' Register on 9 November 1610) : ' I dwindle . . .
as a new Player does, At a plague bill certefied forty ' (sig. F 4 in
1611 edition). The passage is quoted in J. T. Murray's *English
Dramatic Companies*, ii. 175.
[5] See the Appendix, p. 195.

We must not suppose, as Fleay and some others have done, that these regulations were strictly observed. The number 30 or 40 represented a rough-and-ready figure above or below which play-acting was to be forbidden or tolerated, but in no single year perhaps was this method of automatic restraint carried out to the letter. In May 1636, for example, the Privy Council ordered the suppression of plays on 10 May, two days before the publication of the bill returning 41 plague-deaths.[1] Yet in the week ending 5 May only 4 deaths from the plague had been recorded. It is impossible therefore to tell from the bills of mortality alone for how many weeks in the year the theatres were closed. As is shown by the evidence given below,[2] the Privy Council, supported by the City rulers, were so anxious to ward off the infection that they usually closed the theatres long before the plague-deaths rose to 30 or 40, and sometimes refused to take the risk of permitting them to reopen until some weeks after the mortality had fallen below that number.

The Shutting Up of Infected Houses

Of all the preventive measures enforced against the plague those which relate to the shutting up of infected houses are by far the most important. Before the beginning of the sixteenth century there seem to have been no organized attempts to isolate the infected.[3] The

[1] Malone Society, *Collections*, i. 391. The warrant from the Lord Chamberlain reached the Master of the Revels, Sir Henry Herbert, on 12 May. Cf. Malone, *Variorum Shakespeare* (1821), iii. 239. Herbert notes that the bill published on 12 May returned 4 plague-deaths in the City and 54 (really 56) deaths in all. The plague-deaths in the liberties and out-parishes were 37.

[2] Pp. 110–12, 125–6, 170–1, and 173–4.

[3] Contrast the energy displayed in Italy where preventive measures originated in 1374, before the ill effects of the Black

sick were free to wander abroad as they pleased, and the only protection sought by most men was the time-honoured one of flight. Scores of medical treatises were written on the plague in the Middle Ages, but they do not deal with public measures, only with individual prophylaxis and treatment.[1] There were no doubt sporadic efforts made by more progressive bodies to keep the infection from their midst. In 1348, for example, the people of Gloucester tried to keep out the plague by cutting off all intercourse with Bristol.[2] In 1476 the vicar and churchwardens of St. Stephen's, Coleman Street, laid a fine of 3s. 4d. upon those parishioners who, believing that they did a work of mercy and pity, gave shelter to men, women, and children from infected houses.[3] But these were the isolated efforts of small communities, and it was not until January 1518 that a system of segregation was drawn up and enforced by the central organization of the State.

By a royal proclamation issued in this month [4] infected houses were ordered to be marked with a special mark for forty days, and no inhabitant was allowed to walk abroad without carrying in his hand a white rod four feet in length.[5] In April Wolsey was informed that Sir Thomas

Death had ceased. Cf. J. F. C. Hecker, *The Epidemics of the Middle Ages* (1859), 58–61, and W. J. Simpson, *A Treatise on Plague* (1905), 336–40.

[1] D. W. Singer, *Some Plague Tractates* (*Fourteenth and Fifteenth Centuries*) (1916), 22. [2] Creighton, *op. cit.*, i. 116.

[3] E. Freshfield, *A Discourse on Some Unpublished Records of the City of London* (1887), 8.

[4] The original proclamation does not appear to be extant, but it is mentioned in *R.* iii. 184 b and 191. Its contents are given in *J.* xi. 319.

[5] See Note C, p. 179. The period of quarantine in London varied from year to year, but from 1592 it was usually twenty-

More had ordered the inhabitants of infected houses in Oxford to ' keep in, put out wisps, and bear white rods according as your Grace devised for Londoners, the which order they be right well contented to observe '.[1] Londoners did not suffer these restrictions so gladly as the people of Oxford, and many ' murmured ' and spoke seditious words about the King's proclamation. But malcontents were punished and silenced.[2]

The City authorities adhered to the practice of shutting up infected houses until the last plague of 1665. But their regulations became more and more rigorous. In the first half of the sixteenth century all infected persons were supposed to keep in their houses, but those who were obliged to go out to earn their living were allowed to do so if they carried in their hands a white rod. In 1563 men with plague-sores were forbidden to go into the City with or without a rod on pain of losing £5 ; but others could walk about as they pleased. The leniency of these orders led to great abuses, and the City came to recognize that half-hearted measures were of no avail. Accordingly in February 1564 every citizen whose house had been infected, his wife, his children, and his household, were required to remain continuously in the same house with shut doors and windows for forty days. So that they might not have to walk abroad, the deputy-alderman appointed one ' honest, sad and discreet ' person to provide

eight days or a month after death or notification of sickness. In the General Orders from 1592 to 1625 the period was six weeks after the sickness had ceased.

[1] *State Papers, Henry VIII*, § 16, Doc. 875. The letter is endorsed ' To my lord Cardinallis grace ' : ' your Grace ' is therefore Wolsey, not Henry VIII as Creighton (i. 312) states.

[2] *R.* iii. 189 b, 191, and 192.

food, fuel, and other necessaries, the cost to be defrayed by the householder or, if he were too poor, by ' the charitable alms and devotion ' of the rich of the parish. The punishment for breach of this rule was imprisonment or disfranchisement and loss of the liberty and freedom of the City for ever.[1]   In the seventies only men with plague-sores were forbidden to go out,[2] but in 1583 a more rigorous method was again adopted. The doors and windows of the ' hall, shop, or other nether part ' of an infected house were shut up for twenty-eight days. A householder was free, however, to remove himself or any of his household to a house in the country or in the City, provided that the person removing abstained from returning to the City or from going abroad out of a house in the City for twenty-eight days.[3]   This expedient was no doubt welcome to the wealthy, who were thus able to separate the sick of their household from the sound. The lot of the poor who could not afford to keep up two establishments was far less happy, for they were cooped up without fresh air and without exercise in the same house with the infected.

The system of keeping in the infected and all those associated with the infected was very expensive, for most citizens were unable to pay for maintenance when cut off from their business. To ensure the subscription of an adequate sum of money for the use of the infected, and at the same time to give weight and authority to the regulations of magistrates and plague-officials, James's first Parliament passed in 1604 ' An Act for the charitable

[1] *J*. xviii. 139, 184, and 189 b. See Note D, p. 179, for purveyors of necessaries.
[2] *J*. xx. pt. i, 263 b (1574), and xx, pt. ii, 429 b (1578).
[3] *J*. xxi. 285.

relief and ordering of persons infected with the Plague '.[1]
This—the only Act of Parliament dealing with the plague

Chap.xxxj. # Anno primo

cured, That then such person and persons shalbe taken, deemed, and adiudged as a felon, and to suffer paines of Death, as in case of felonie. But if such person shall not haue any such Soare found about him, Then for his sayd Offence, to be punished as a uagabond in all respects should, or ought to be, by the Statute made in the Nine and thirtieth yeere of the Reigne of our late Soueraigne Lady Queene Elizabeth, for the punishment of Rogues and uagabonds, And further to be bound to his or their good behauiour for one whole yeere.

Prouided, That no attainder of Felonie by vertue of this Act, shall extend to any attainder or Corruption of Blood, or forfeiture of any Goods, Chattels, Lands, Tenements, or Hereditaments.

And be it further enacted by the authoritie aforesaid, That it shalbe lawfull for Iustices of Peace, Mayors, Bailiffes, and other head Officers aforesaid, to appoint within the seuerall limittes, Searchers, watchmen, Examiners, Keepers, and Buryers for the persons and places respectiuely Infected as aforesayd, and to minister vnto them Oathes for the performance of their offices of Searchers, Examiners, watchmen, Keepers and Buryers, and giue them other Directions, as vnto them for the present necessitie shall seeme good in their discretions. And this Acte to continue no longer then vntill the ende of the first Session of the next Parliament.

Prouided alwayes, and be it enacted by authoritie of this present Parliament, That no Mayor, Bayliffes, head Officers, or any Iustices of Peace, shall by force or pretext of any thing in this Act conteined, Doe or execute any thing before mentioned, with in either the uniuersities of Cambridge or Oxford, or within any Cathedrall Church, or the Liberties or Precincts thereof, in this Realme of England, or within the Colledges of Eaton or winchester, But that the uice-chancellor of either of the uniuersities for the time being, within either of the same respectiuely, and the Bishop and Deans of euery such Cathedrall Church, or one of them, within such Cathedrall Church, and the Prouost or warden of either of the said Colledges within the same, shall haue all such power and authoritie, and shall doe and execute all and euery such Act and Acts, thing and things in this Act before mentioned, within their seuerall Precincts and Iurisdictions abouesayd, as wholly, absolutely, and fully to all intents and purposes, as any Mayor, Bayliffes, Head Officers, or Iustices of Peace within their seuerall Precincts and Iurisdictions may elsewhere by force of this Act doe and execute,

¶ A a

A page from 1 Jac. I, c. 31 (printed by Robert Barker, 1604).

—gave the magistrates of any city, borough, or town the
authority to assess inhabitants ' at such reasonable taxes

[1] Cf. *Statutes of the Realm*, 1 Jac. I, c. 31. The Act was continued in 21 Jac. I, c. 28.

and payments as they shall think fit for the reasonable relief of such persons infected '. Any one refusing to pay might be sent to jail without bail or mainprize, and if a place were unable to relieve its infected poor, permission was given to tax and assess the inhabitants of the county within a radius of five miles. The Act made it lawful to appoint searchers, examiners, watchmen, nurses, and buriers, and to bind them by oaths to the performance of their duties. It confirmed the order of 1583 that all inhabitants of an infected house, whether themselves infected or not, were to keep at home. The punishment for disobedience was made more severe. Those who went abroad with a sore on them were to be judged as felons and to suffer the pains of death : if without sore they were to be judged as vagabonds, and whipped and set in the stocks.[1]

Little change was made in these orders in the following sixty years, though they were perforce relaxed in times of heavy mortality. One example of many will serve to illustrate the punishment inflicted upon transgressors. Henry Ross of St. Bartholomew's the Great, whose house had been shut up in May 1603, did ' most lewdly presume to go to the King's Majesty's Court at Greenwich and there thrust himself in Company amongst his Majesty's household servants and others '. He was put into the dungeon at Newgate, and next day was stripped naked from the waist upwards, tied to a cart's tail with a paper on his head declaring his offence, and then whipped from Newgate through Cheapside to the bars without Aldgate back to Temple Bar and so to Newgate.[2]

---

[1] This ' base durance ' usually lasted for two hours. Cf. R. xxvii. 337 b (1607).

[2] R. xxvi, pt. i, 151 b. See also Stow's *Annales* (1605), 1416.

The Marking of Infected Houses

Infected houses were first marked with a special sign in 1518—the year that they were first shut up. This sign warned passers-by to give the house on which it was placed as wide a berth as the street permitted. The red cross and the inscription ' Lord Have Mercy Upon Us ' are familiar to us from many references in our literature. Nashe used the inscription as a refrain to the great poem suggested by the plague of 1592-3, in which he sings of the insecurity of life and the transience of human joy and beauty :

> Beauty is but a flowre,
> Which wrinckles will devoure,
> Brightnesse falls from the ayre,
> Queenes have died yong, and faire,
> Dust hath closde *Helens* eye.
> I am sick, I must dye,
>   Lord have mercy on us.

Shakespeare refers to the inscription in *Love's Labour's Lost* (v. ii), and it has been argued that this comedy was written in 1592 on the ground that the inscription was first used in that year.[1] But as will appear below, these words were being set on plague-stricken houses many years before Shakespeare paid his first visit to London.

In January 1518 the Privy Council commanded that in any future plague the chief inhabitant of an infected house, man or woman,

' should immediately provide a pole of X feet in length and set forth the same on the street side with a convenient bundle of straw hanging [2] in the end or top of the same pole, so that

---

[1] *Modern Language Review*, xiii. 389-91.
[2] Cf. Sir Thomas More's injunction to the people of Oxford in April 1518 to ' put out wisps ' (see above, p. 57).

the said pole hang clearly without the house into the street
VII foot to the intent that all persons passing thereby may
have certain knowledge that the said house is infected with the
said plague, which setting out of the said pole should continue
XL days after the last sickness or visitation of God '.[1]

This device was not invented by the Privy Council :
like many plague-measures it was borrowed from the
Continent. The people of Lille in 1480 were ordered to place
before infected houses ' une botte d'estrain d'une aulne
de long, de demie aulne de tour pour que les reconnaissant
on puisse s'en écarter ' ; and at Paris in 1510 it was
commanded ' de mettre à l'une des fenêtres ou autre lieu
plus apparent, une botte de paille, et de l'y laisser encore
pendant deux mois après que la maladie sera cessée '.[2]
But the mark proved too elaborate for London, and in
September 1521 proclamation was made that ' every person
that God hath visited with the common sickness shall have
a sign of tau otherwise called Saint Anthony's Cross set
up openly upon his door, and to continue XL days, and
that in alleys the said sign to be set up at the alley door '.[3]
St. Anthony's Cross, a headless cross shaped like the
Greek letter τ, resembles the staff with a bar at the top
carried by St. Anthony the Great. It was painted on
paper, and delivered by the beadle of each ward to each
parish clerk or sexton, who in turn was required to fasten

[1] *J.* xi. 319. The time which elapsed between the setting up
and the removal of the mark varied with the period of segregation
(see note on p. 56).

[2] É. Caplet, *La Peste à Lille au XVIIᵉ Siècle* (1898), 36 ; N. de
La Mare, *Traité de la Police*, tome I (1705), p. 617.

[3] *R.* iv. 89. Cf. also *R.* v. 219. So in Paris by 1531 ' une botte
de paille ' had been superseded by ' une croix de boys '. Cf. *Les
ordonnances . . . de ceste ville de Paris. Pour eviter le dangier de
peste* (1531), ed. A. Chereau, p. 116. A drawing of St. Anthony's
Cross appears in the margin of *R.* ix. 190 b.

Lord have Mercy upon Vs.

The VVorld, A Sea,
A Pest-house.

The one full of Stormes, and dangers, the
other full of Soares and Diseases.

The observance from These, (though especially accomo-
dated to the times of this heavy Contagion,) fitted
for all times.

For all Men, and all Times are sicke, of the Cause
of this *Sicknesse.*

Imprinted at *London* for *Henry Gosson.* 1636.

'Lord have Mercy upon Vs', the title-page of a rare pamphlet by
Thomas Brewer, published in 1636

it on the outermost post of every infected house.[1] The cross was 'in sign and token of God's visitation'.[2] In 1563 blue headless crosses 'painted in a white paper' were used, the clerk of the parish having to see every morning that they had not been removed or defaced.[3] It would appear from the diary of Henry Machyn, citizen and merchant-tailor, that a writing was affixed beneath the cross.[4] This writing is not mentioned in the precepts issued by the Lord Mayor in 1563, but there can be little doubt that Machyn was referring to the inscription 'Lord Have Mercy Upon Us'. Bills displaying these words in large letters were ordered to be set upon the door of each infected house in 1568,[5] and for many years the inscription superseded the cross as a symbol of the visitation of the plague. In 1636, the date of the illustration, the inscription may have been a square, not a circle, but doubtless the border was still in red.

About the year 1578 the Privy Council suggested a device as elaborate as that in use in 1518—'a lopped clubbed staff plated with iron and painted, hanging at a chain above the door as a sign, with a hanging lock, the key whereof to be in the custody of surveyors'. But the City rejected this expensive apparatus, and preferred a 'large sheet of paper printed with a great red circle of the circuit of a foot and breadth of two inches and the words Lord have mercy upon us, printed in the midst'.[6]

[1] R. viii. 64 b (October 1529).   [2] J. xiii. 184 b.
[3] R. xv. 259 b and 260 b ; J. xviii. 136 b.
[4] B.M. MS. Vitellius F. v, fo. 162, 26 June 1563 (*The Diary of Henry Machyn*, Camden Soc., 1848, 310). See also *Notes and Queries*, 8th Series, i. 31.
[5] S. P. Dom., Eliz., vol. 48, Doc. 70. In 1570 the bill was printed (J. xix. 219).   [6] S. P. Dom., Eliz., vol. 98, Doc. 38. In the margin is a rough sketch of the inscription.

This method of marking infected houses was still in use in September 1592,[1] but by July 1593 the City had reverted to the cross, now no longer headless, and red instead of blue—a more conspicuous colour. In the same month the Privy Council ordered crosses to be nailed on the doors as painted crosses were so easily wiped away.[2] In December and in the following March both crosses and bills of ' Lord Have Mercy Upon Us ' were set up,[3] but by 1603 the bill had once more superseded the cross. Bills were even more easily defaced than painted crosses, and on 26 May 1603 the Lord Mayor, by command of King James, ordered the aldermen not only to have ' papers ' fastened over the doors of infected houses but also ' a red cross laid in oil colours to be made and painted over every such door of fourteen inches in length and the like in breadth upon the wall or boards in the most open place '.[4] The cross was usually set in the middle of the door, and the ' paper ' immediately above it or on the lintel. This use of both inscription and cross to mark infected houses persisted until 1665, and became the most distinctive and memorable of the customs which took their origin from the plague.[5]

Searchers and Viewers

The services of specially appointed officials were needed for the proper execution of this scheme of segregation. In

[1] *J.* xxiii. 130. The cost of the bills was defrayed by each parish. Forty bills cost eighteenpence in 1593. Cf. *St. Martin-in-the-Fields The Accounts of the Churchwardens* (ed. J. V. Kitto), 453. [2] *Acts of the Privy Council*, 1592–1593, 374.

[3] *J.* xxiii. 220, 238 b, and 254 b.

[4] *J.* xxvi. 98. In 1608 the length of the cross was one foot.

[5] See Note E, p. 180, for an account of the officers responsible for the erection of crosses, of their salaries, and of punishment given to defacers of crosses.

1578 two 'honest and discreet matrons' were appointed
to search and view the body of every person dying in
their parish. They took an oath to make true report to
the clerk of all who died of the plague, so that the clerk
might communicate it to the wardens of the parish clerks.[1]
They were required to keep apart from all healthy people,
and in some parishes were provided with a special residence.[2] Their usual fee was fourpence or sixpence a body.

In addition to these searchers two 'sober ancient women'
were appointed in each parish from 1583 to be viewers of
the sick or those suspected of infection. They were sworn
to report any infected house to the constable, who in turn reported to the alderman or deputy-alderman. Any woman
guilty of corruption or false reporting was threatened with
the pillory or corporal punishment. The searchers of dead
bodies were chiefly useful in ensuring greater accuracy in
the bills of mortality.[3] The viewers of the infected, on

---

[1] *J.* xx, pt. ii, 407. It is interesting that the first use of the word
'searcher' in this sense cited by *O. E. D.* is from *Romeo and Juliet*
(there dated 1592), v. ii. 8. Friar John, suspected of being in an
infected house, was shut up by the searchers and so prevented from
carrying to Romeo at Mantua the all-important letter from Friar
Laurence. No messenger could be found to return the letter to
Friar Laurence, so fearful were the citizens of Verona of the
infection.

[2] J. McMaster, *Short History of St. Martin-in-the-Fields,* 197.
In 1630 the number of searchers in each parish was raised to four,
two for infected bodies and two for bodies conceived to have died
of other diseases (*J.* xxxv. 203 b). The new arrangement must
have been expensive and impracticable, and we hear no more of it.
In 1593 the Vestry Minutes of St. Martin's-in-the-Fields speak
of two men searchers for men (who also acted as bearers) and two
women searchers for women (*St. Martin-in-the-Fields The Accounts
of the Churchwardens,* ed. J. V. Kitto, 582). I have seen no other
reference to men searchers.

[3] *J.* xxi. 285 b. See the Appendix, pp. 206–7, for an estimate
of the honesty and utility of the searchers.

the other hand, were appointed owing to the difficulty of obtaining accurate and speedy information about infected houses. An efficient viewer would be a consumer of parish-gossip and a vigilant spy upon shifty neighbours.

Viewers and searchers may have been ancient, but they were not usually honest, discreet, and sober. Respectable women would hardly accept so unpleasant an office, and it must have been given to any old hags who were willing to risk its dangers. George Wither called them blear-eyed. Their blindness was the result of bribery as well as of stupidity. ' The mist of a Cup of *Ale*, and the bribe of a two-groat fee, instead of one ' [1] would work wonders in the transmutation of a disease. The searchers continued to be notorious for dishonesty and incompetence until their office was swept away by the Registration Act of 1836. The following exposure of their manners and habits was published in 1835. It applies, *mutatis mutandis*, to the searchers of Shakespeare's London :

' The appointment of searcher is generally made by the churchwardens, and usually falls upon old women, and some-times on those who are notorious for their habits of drinking. The fee which these official characters demand is one shilling, but in some cases two public authorities of this description proceed to the inspection, when the family of the defunct is defrauded out of an additional shilling. They not unfrequently require more than the ordinary fee ; and owing to the circum-stances under which they pay their visit, their demands are generally complied with. In some cases they even proceed so far as to claim as a perquisite the articles of dress in which the deceased died. Such are the means at present employed in collecting medical and political statistics in the metropolis of England.' [2]

[1] John Graunt, *Natural and Political Observations* (1662), p. 24.
[2] *The Penny Cyclopaedia* (1835), iv. 408.

Nurses

Nurse-keepers, or ' Women-sleepers ' as Dekker called them,[1] were as dishonest and indiscreet as viewers and searchers. They were first appointed in 1578—two in every parish—to wait on the inhabitants of infected houses and to nurse the sick.[2] They were for the most part single or childless. Their chances of infection would seem to have been very great, yet it was remarked by Bamford in 1603 and by Wither in 1625 that few of them died. They had less opportunity than viewers and searchers of gaining money by the acceptance of bribes, but they made their office profitable in even more nefarious ways. Dekker in the last year of his life wrote bitterly about their inordinate appetite and excessive charges, calling them ' shee wolves ' and ' Night-crowes '. He accused them of pilfering : ' They are called keepers, because whatsoever they get but hold of, they keepe it with griping pawes never to let it goe. . . . Rats are not such gnawers of linnen, nor Moathes of woollen, as these are of both. If a rich Bacheler sicken, it is an *East Indian* voyage, when shee hoyses up sayle from her owne house into his : and when he dyes, then shee and her lading comes home : *Breda* is then taken, and shee alone has the spoyle.' Some nurses, he alleged, were not only thieves but murderers. They made up false medicines, and when death was near pulled away their patient's pillow to hasten him on his journey. But Dekker is careful to distinguish between those keepers who were ' motherly, skilfull, care-full, vigilant, and compassionate women ', and those who were ' the spoyle, ruine and confusion of many a poore

---

[1] *D. P. P.* 190.   [2] *J.* xx, pt. ii, 407.

servants life ; many a Childe hath beene made Father-
lesse by them, many a mother childlesse : May they repent
and amend '.[1]

Warders or Watchers

The watcher or warder of infected houses is not to be
confused with the ' watch ' which paraded the streets of
London every night. The watch existed in whatever
condition the health of the City might be, though it was
often doubled in time of infection.[2] But the office of
warder of infected houses was not created till late in the
sixteenth century. It does not appear in the London
Orders of 1583 and 1592, but in the General Orders of
1592 directions were given for the appointment of two
or three warders to watch by turns outside the houses of
infected people who did not duly observe the necessary
regulations, and to arrest any persons coming out of these
houses contrary to the orders. In London on 4 March
1594 the aldermen appointed two ' honest and discreet '
warders to watch each infected house from 5 a.m. till
9 p.m. and ensure that no one went in or out.[3] Ten years
later the hours were from 6 a.m. till 9 p.m. and the
warders were provided with bills and halberds at the

[1] *English Villanies* (1632), chap. xv. For an indictment, even
blacker than Dekker's, of their thieving and murderous conduct
in 1665, see N. Hodges, *Loimologia* (translated by J. Quincy,
1720), p. 8.

[2] As for instance in September 1569, when a double watch was
ordered to be held nightly from 6 p.m. till 4 a.m. (*J.* xix. 188).
In 1603 a special warder was appointed to watch from 5 a.m.
till 9 p.m. to apprehend all wandering rogues (i. e. to ' comprehend
all vagrom men ') and to ' avoid ' all infected strangers (*J.* xxvi.
103 b). In the same year a competent number of warders was
appointed to attend daily at each gate to prevent the entrance
of infected people into the City (*ibid.* 119).

[3] *J.* xxiii. 238 b.

charges of the parish.[1] From May 1609-a house was watched by night as well as by day, the warders changing duty at 10 p.m. and 6 a.m. They acted as purveyors of necessaries and, before departing on their errands, locked up the house and pocketed the key.[2] In many parishes warders received a wage of sixpence a day, though the parish of St. Martin's-in-the-Fields was generous enough to give them a shilling a day in 1625.[3]

Some watchmen neglected their duties. Two men at Westminster, for example, were put in the stocks in 1625, the one for allowing segregated people to leave their houses and the other for wiping off a red cross. In the same year a Holborn watchman was sentenced to three weeks' hard labour at the House of Correction for breaking off padlocks from infected houses and suffering infected goods to be removed.[4] Others failed in their duty through no fault of their own. A fever-maddened wretch cared little for the menace of a bill or halberd, and most watchmen no doubt let him go and thanked God they were rid of a knave. Fletcher is giving us a slice of life in that scene in his version of *The Taming of the Shrew* in which the infuriated Petruchio, falsely shut up by a ruse of his second wife, frightens away the watchmen with a fowling-piece :

1 *Watch.* Let 's quit him,
It may be it is trick : he 's dangerous.
2 *Watch.* The devill take the hinmost, I cry.
Exit watch running.[5]

[1] *J.* xxvi. 171 b.
[2] *J.* xxvii. 365 b. See also Note D, p. 179.
[3] See accounts of examiners at City Hall, Westminster (MS. 4512).
[4] *S. P. Dom., Chas. I*, vol. 175, Docs. 3 and 24.
[5] *The Woman's Prize : or, The Tamer Tamed*, 1647 folio, p. 113.

Contemporary Opinion

Englishmen have never submitted gladly to the restriction of their liberty, and it is not surprising that the plague-orders were hated by men, women, and children cut off from their business and their friends. Many 'reproachful and unseemly' speeches were made to magistrates and their underlings, and the hardships which segregation inevitably entailed were bitterly resented.[1] One rebel went so far as to assert that segregation actually increased the infection, and pointed out that the plague of 1625 began to dwindle only when the sick were so many that they could not be watched or kept in by the sound.[2]

The most troublesome opponents of law and order were those whose objections were religious or conscientious. By the General Orders of 1592 clergymen publishing the doctrine 'that it is a vaine thing to forbeare to resort to the infected, or that it is not charitable to forbid the same, pretending that no person shall die but at their time prefixed' were forbidden to preach : laymen guilty of airing these views were sent to prison. The modern view that the plague is not contagious was held by the 'rude multitude' and by many of the better sort, but the orthodox James Bamford, Vicar of St. Olave's, Southwark, took a firm stand against this 'bloudy errour'. He thought that the segregated ought to regard their sufferings as an excellent opportunity for the exercise of faith by patience.[3]

[1] Cf. *S. P. Dom., Chas. I*, vol. 175, Doc. 3. Some hardships were by no means inevitable, as, for example, the failure to provide the segregated with food. Cf. *D. P. P.*, p. 71, l. 27–p. 72, l. 3.

[2] *The Shutting Up Infected Houses* (1665). Wither (*Britain's Remembrancer*, 1628, p. 49) seems to hint at the same thing.

[3] *A Short Dialogue* (1603), sig. A 2ᵛ. See also Lancelot Andrewes's sermon on the pestilence preached at Chiswick on 21 August 1603. *Ninety-Six Sermons* (Oxford, 1843), v. 225.

Several heretical books were published in defiance of the authorities. In 1603 appeared *A Casting Up of accounts of certain Errors* by one W. T., who preached the doctrine that the plague was but the arrow of God flying through the air. It was not infectious, and therefore those sick of it ought to be visited. Henoch Clapham, a London clergyman at one time minister to the English Congregation in Amsterdam, maintained in *An Epistle Discoursing upon the present Pestilence* (1603) that the plague was a punishment for sin, and that those who died of it died through want of faith. He was understood to mean that the plague was not infectious and that all who died of it were damned, as dying without faith. From prison he issued a defence complaining of unjust treatment, and protesting that he assigned the outbreak of the plague to both natural and supernatural causes. His faith was that the plague which resulted from the taint of natural corruption was infectious, but that the plague which resulted from the stroke of an angel was not infectious.[1] To-day men of science call the ' natural ' plague bubonic and the ' supernatural ' pneumonic, and agree that the bubonic plague is not directly contagious whereas the pneumonic is highly so.

Evasion of Orders

Many ways and means were found to evade the network of regulations slowly and laboriously constructed by the London magistrates. Sixteenth-century and seventeenth-century legislators devised schemes which worked out

---

[1] *Henoch Clapham His Demaundes and Answeres touching the Pestilence : Methodically handled, as his time and meanes could permit* (1604).

admirably on paper but frequently failed when put into practice. Their society was insufficiently organized to carry out with success an elaborate set of unpopular orders. Accordingly, as will appear in the account of the plagues of 1603 and 1625, when the pestilence became virulent the populace got out of control, and the authorities were forced to sit with folded hands until the plague had spent itself.

The most serious charge, apart from that of desertion, which can be laid at the door of the London magistrates is that they often deferred action in the earliest stages of the infection in the hope that it would die out. In September 1536, for example, an order to set up crosses was countermanded for a week ' trusting to God that the sickness shall cease ', and in later epidemics some time elapsed before the first outbreak of the infection and the enforcement of segregation.[1] The blame for this delay did not rest wholly upon the magistrates. They had provided as good machinery as their knowledge and resources enabled them to provide. But they were working with human nature and not with machinery which obeys regulations and fixed laws. They might charge constables and viewers to search for infected houses, but these officials, as we have seen, were often stupid or dishonest. They might order the master of every house to notify the examiner within two hours of the plague's appearance, but a householder often found it possible to conceal the infection or to remove himself or the infected person from his house. Few citizens were as public-spirited as

[1] *R.* ix. 191. Lodge recommended that an outbreak of the plague should not immediately be made known to the public, but he did not advocate the postponement of segregative measures.

Pepys's physician, Dr. Burnett, who in 1665 ' caused himself to be shut up of his own accord : which was very handsome '.[1] Sometimes a corpse was laid five or six doors away, and the driver of the dead-cart bribed to remove it. Or a sexton was persuaded to bribe another sexton to give it burial many parishes off. Or a porter was hired to carry it in a sack to a workman in the out-parishes, who dared not refuse it shelter for fear of losing employment. Servants and apprentices were often sent away as soon as they were stricken with the plague, and left to perish in the fields or in garden-houses ' where they either died before next morning, or else were caried thither dead in their coffins as tho they had lyen sicke there before and there had died '.[2] A house-to-house visitation would have failed to put a stop to these abuses. Even after the infection had been traced and the house shut up, there were many ways of deceiving and eluding the watchman and escaping into the country. In fact from every restriction of their liberty wily citizens found a loophole of escape, and the literature of the plague is full of anecdotes, some merry and some sad, narrating the ingenuity or cruelty of these malefactors.

As illuminating an example as any in Dekker or Defoe of the contrariness of human nature, and especially perhaps of English nature, is to be found in the parish books of St. Margaret's, Lothbury. The first house infected in 1625 was shut up in April. It was some years since the parish had seen a plague-stricken house, and so

---

[1] *Diary* (ed. H. B. Wheatley), iv. 435 (11 June).

[2] *D. P. P.* 130–2, 151 ; *The Seven deadly Sinnes* (1606), sig. G 2, and *Lanthorne and Candle-light* (1608), sig. K 4ᵛ (*G*. ii. 77 and iii. 300, 301). Cf. also P. Stubbes, *The Anatomie of Abuses* (1583), sig. E 5ᵛ (ed. Furnivall, New Shakspere Society, i. 60).

many flocked to view it that the vestry was forced to remove the household to the pesthouse : ' for many did venture and hazard themselves, both strangers and others, to see them, to the great danger of their neighbours, notwithstanding there was a warder '.[1] The show was as novel and as fascinating as a strange fish or a dead Indian, and much cheaper.

The Pesthouse

One method of segregation remains to be mentioned which commended itself to the more enlightened writers of the time. The hardships and dangers of the sound who were compulsorily shut up with the sick aroused the sympathy of all merciful men. The one way of escape lay in the erection of pesthouses where the sick might be properly isolated, housed, and fed.

The proposal to build temporary cabins and shelters for the infected was made in the middle of the sixteenth century,[2] but does not seem to have been acted upon until 1625. In that year the Privy Council ordered the Lord Mayor to cause to be erected ' small Tents and Cabins to be made of a few boards, and such materials as may be soonest put together, and to be set a competent distance from each other, in all such several places and fields without the City, as shall be most convenient to erect them in '. Infected persons were to be removed to these cabins and their houses shut up as before. On recovery they might

---

[1] *Archaeologia*, xlv. 71. See also below, p. 183. Horace Walpole had heard of this or a similar case (*Letters*, ed. Mrs. Paget Toynbee, i. 51).

[2] In Venice a lazaretto was established for the treatment and isolation of plague-patients as early as 1403. Cf. W. J. Simpson, *A Treatise on Plague*, 337. In Scotland there was a plague-hospital on the island of Inchkeith before 1475. Cf. Creighton, *op. cit.*, i. 235 and 360–1.

return home at the end of a month, but the cabins and their clothes were to be burnt.[1] This method was also recommended in 1630,[2] but at no time was it extensively observed.

Another proposal, adopted in 1569, 1571, and 1582,[3] advocated the use of empty houses instead of temporary huts. In 1583 the City recorder, William Fleetwood, recommended the appointment of a ' Harbinger of the Plague ' who should have the power to take over any houses newly built contrary to the proclamation of 1580. Here the infected might be ' lodged and cherished till they be whole '.[4] About the same time it was suggested to the Privy Council that a convenient number of ' public houses ' should be provided in fit places within or without the City to which the sound in an infected house might be removed.[5] These houses were to be of two sorts—some for the rich who were able to pay their own charges, and others for the poor. Each house was to contain several wards, so that the sound might be kept apart from the sick and might follow their usual occupations while in quarantine, ' as in Christ's Hospital is already used '. Physicians, surgeons, and nurses were to be appointed for the healthy and the sick, the rich and the poor. This new method was devised because the usual method of shutting up the sound and the infected in one house increased rather than decreased the infection,

' for when many be pestered together in a house infected,

[1] *P. C. R.* xxxiii. 98 b. See also *Cal. S. P. Dom.*, 1625–1626, 90.

[2] *P. C. R.* xxxix. 750, 762, and 775.

[3] *R.* xvii. 2 b, 105 b, and xx. 414.

[4] B.M. Lansdowne MS. 38, fos. 23 and verso. The document is cited in Stow's *Survey* (ed. Strype, 1720), v. 439.

[5] B.M. Lansdowne MS. 74, fo. 75, reprinted in the Malone Society's *Collections*, i. 202–6. In the *Catalogue of the Lansdowne Manuscripts* it is assigned to the year 1593.

commonly for want of room and shift of beds and bedding, the
sound and infected remaining together, there do very few of
them escape the infection, but the most die, and the rest have
the disease, and very hardly escape with their lives.'

It is unlikely that this scheme was put into practice,
but empty houses were still being used for plague-cases
in 1625, when the plague-doctor, Nicholas Heath, took
a house in or near Coleman Street for the curing of the
sick, and frightened several neighbours of note from their
homes.[1]

Although Sir Thomas More had recommended in *Utopia*
(1515/16) the erection of large hospitals in which ' they
which were taken and holden with contagious diseases,
suche as be wonte by infection to crepe from one to an
other, myght be laid a part farre from the company of
the residue ',[2] yet it was not until 1594 that this wise
suggestion was adopted by the citizens of London.   On
21 April 1583 the City Fathers were scolded like naughty
children.   The Queen, so ran the Privy Council's letter,
' perceiving that her princely care of the safety of her
subjects so often recommended unto you taketh so small
place with you, as therewithal the safety of her own
person residing with her court always near unto the City
is nothing at all regarded, whereat her Majesty doth the
less marvel when she considereth how slenderly you
respect the preservation of your own lives, preferring your
desire of trade and gain before duty and nature ', now
expresses her displeasure that no house or hospital has
been built without the City, in some remote place, to
which infected people may be removed—' wherein many
cities of less antiquity, fame, wealth, circuit and reputa-

---

[1] *R.* xl. 65 b.   [2] Ed. J. H. Lupton, p. 159.

tion are to be preferred before that of London as being in all countries provided of such a place, specially whereby the lives of the inhabitants are in all times of infection chiefly preserved '.[1] The same month the City, spurred on by this rebuke, decided to build a hospital for the plague-stricken, and appointed a committee for the consideration of a convenient site ' near the little lane between Moorgate and Cripplegate without the walls of the City '.[2] The committee chose nine acres of land on the north of London, close to the footpath leading to Canonbury (then pronounced ' Canbury '), three acres being the property of St. Bartholomew's Hospital.[3] Order was made at the time for the speedy erection of the hospital and for the provision of necessaries, but the infection declined, and the scheme was dropped.

In the epidemic of 1592–93 Thomas Nashe complained of the absence of plague-hospitals in London. In other countries, he wrote, they had one for those who had been in infected houses and were not yet tainted : another for those that were tainted but whose sores had not yet broken : and a third for those whose sores had broken. In London, he complained, no provision was made ' but mixing hand over heade the sicke with the whole '.[4] The chief reason for the delay in the erection of a hospital was, no doubt, that of expense. In 1592 the City received a windfall which enabled it to meet this expense with ease and convenience. The expedition of this year in search of Spanish and Portuguese treasure-ships is a famous incident in the

[1] *Remembrancia*, i. 250 b.
[2] *Letter Book*, Z, 291.
[3] See Note F, p. 181. Canonbury is north-east of Islington and adjoining it.
[4] *Works* (ed. R. B. McKerrow), ii. 160–1.

career of Sir Walter Raleigh. Raleigh himself had been recalled by the Queen as the fleet was sailing and sent to the Tower ; but the adventure had been organized and planned by him, and his ship *The Roebuck*, under the command of Sir John Borough, captured the largest and richest of the ' Indian carracks ', the *Madre de Dios*. This vessel alone was valued at £150,000, and all the adventurers except Raleigh reaped a rich harvest. The London merchants had invested some £6,000 in the expedition and received a gross profit of 100 per cent.[1]

On 10 May 1593, when the pestilence was still raging, the Court of Aldermen ordered a motion to be made to the next Common Council ' that the surplusage of all such money as shall be raised of the sale of the Carrack goods allotted to this City over and above twelve thousand pounds may be employed towards the building of a house for receiving of infected persons '.[2] In December certain members of the Council were appointed to choose a site.[3] In May 1594 the cost of building and maintaining a hospital was estimated at £6,000, and precepts were issued to the masters and wardens of those companies which had adventured in Raleigh's expedition, urging them to give a third part of their gains to a work ' so famous and notable and so beneficial for the good of this City '.[4] This would amount only to £2,000, and the inhabitants of every ward were asked to give liberally. In December £100 was paid to ' the bricklayer and carpenter that built the pesthouse ', but

[1] For an account of the expedition see *Hakluyt* (ed. 1599), vol. ii, pt. ii, 194. For an estimate of the financial side of the venture see W. R. Scott, *Joint Stock Companies*, i. 98 and iii. 504–6.   [2] *R.* xxiii. 60.
[3] *J.* xxiii. 224 b.   [4] *J.* xxiii. 266.

it was not yet finished in April 1595, when a committee was appointed to see to its completion.[1] Two years later it was ordered to be repaired, and a gate and brick wall were built to enclose the grounds.[2] Yet in 1603 Lodge still spoke of it as unfinished : ' Towards the finishing whereof, all they that have the zeale of our Lorde in their heartes, and that have the means to distribute their goodes to the poore, ought to be diligent and charitable.' A proclamation issued in 1615 claimed it as one of the edifices tending ' to publique use and ornament ' erected in the reign of James, but this claim may have been made on the ground that extensive alterations and additions had been made to the old fabric.

The pesthouse of 1594 was built upon three acres of land belonging to St. Bartholomew's Hospital,[3] doubtless upon the same three acres mentioned in 1583 as abutting on the east on the footpath leading from London to Canonbury. From the notice given to the tenants on 19 January 1594 by the governors of St. Bartholomew's Hospital it appears that this piece of ground was near the old Butts in the parish of St. Giles-without-Cripplegate.[4] The

[1] R. xxiii. 331 ; J. xxiii. 400. The word ' pesthouse ' was perhaps first used in 1594. The earliest example given by the New English Dictionary is dated 1611.

[2] R. xxiv. 74, 143 b, 268 b, and 399. Sixty yards of the west end of the Pesthouse Close were reserved for a burial-ground for St. Giles's, Cripplegate, in 1609. Cf. R. xxix. 2, 32, and xxxi, pt. ii, 322 b. The old St. Giles's burial-ground is now the garden behind St. Luke's Lunatic Asylum. Cf. Mrs. Basil Holmes, The London Burial Grounds (1896), 123.

[3] R. xxiii. 470.

[4] Norman Moore, The History of St. Bartholomew's Hospital, ii. 292. Cf. also the Letters Patent, containing the Grant and Establishment of the Hospitals by Henry VIII in 1547, reprinted on pp. 22–49 of the Appendix to Memoranda, References, and

London Pesthouse stood on this site until 1736, when its ruins were removed, and the three acres and twelve perches of land let on a lease of 990 years to the French Protestant Hospital.[1] The old footway to Islington and Canonbury was formerly called Pesthouse Row. The name has been changed to Bath Street, but the street remains pestiferous. The site of the pesthouse is a little to the north of the existing buildings of the French Protestant Hospital, a few hundred yards up Bath Street on the left-hand side as you walk from Old Street.[2]

The accommodation at the pesthouse must have been very limited. The burials there in the nine weeks from 21 July to 22 September 1603 were 18, 19, 12, 21, 12, 6, 5, 10, and 10. Defoe says that in 1665 it could at most accommodate two or three hundred people. But its limited space was eked out by the erection of sheds in the Pesthouse Close. In 1604, for example, the church-wardens of St. Michael's, Cornhill, built a shed of deal board adjoining the pesthouse at a cost of £5 for the use of the infected of their parish.[3] Other buildings, such as

Documents relating to the Royal Hospitals of the City of London, 1836. On p. 31 reference is made to three separate pieces of land in the parish of St. Giles-without-Cripplegate, one piece containing by estimation six acres and lying by the Butts.

[1] *J.* lviii. 15 b and 23 b.

[2] The parish of St. Giles, Cripplegate, was formerly divided into two parts: (1) the Freedom part lying within the City of London; (2) the Lordship part lying within the county of Middlesex. In 1732 the latter division became the parish of St. Luke, in the county of Middlesex. Pesthouse Row was therefore formerly in the parish of St. Giles, Cripplegate.

[3] *The Accounts of the Churchwardens* (ed. A. J. Waterlow), 193 and 255. On 24 June 1665, when the plague was rapidly increasing, the Court of Aldermen ordered sheds to be built round the pest-house ground within the wall (*R.* lxx. 136).

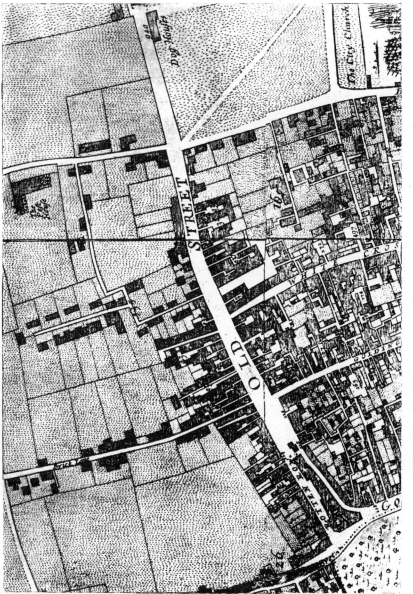

THE SITE OF THE PESTHOUSE.   From a Map published in 1682

Bridewell,[1] various lazar-houses,[2] the City hospitals,[3] and the cages,[4] sometimes admitted plague-cases, but in spite of these makeshifts the accommodation for the infected remained miserably inadequate.[5] Dekker, who had infinite compassion for the poor and defenceless, wrote bitterly of London's cruelty in not providing ' more and more convenient Cabins ' for the forsaken wretches who

[1] The deaths in Bridewell from all causes in the six weeks from 11 August to 22 September 1603 were respectively 7, 8, 5, 17, 7, and 19. In 1625, £400 was spent by the City on the poor people in Bridewell. See below, p. 168.

[2] Sir Norman Moore informed me that outhouses and lazar-houses (at first six and later but two) existed in connexion with St. Bartholomew's Hospital, some of these being also supplied from St. Thomas's. Chronic cases of all kinds were sent there, but they were not intended for plague-cases. On 9 July 1603 the masters of these lazar-houses presented a petition (not preserved) in which they complained that patients with the plague were sent to them. See also Norman Moore, *The History of St. Bartholomew's Hospital*, ii. 296.

[3] Nineteen died of the plague at St. Thomas's in 1582 and 14 at St. Bartholomew's.

[4] The parish registers for 1603 and 1625 show that many prisoners in the cages died of the plague. In 1603 they were used almost as pesthouses. See below, p. 94.

[5] The pesthouse in St. Giles's, Cripplegate, was kept solely for the needs of the citizens of London and its liberties. Cf. *Middlesex County Records* (ed. J. C. Jeaffreson), ii. 93, and R. xliv. 233 b. In 1636 there was a pesthouse in Lambeth Marsh. Cf. *Cal. S. P. Dom.*, 1636–1637, p. 316, and 1639, p. 43. The pesthouse built in 1642 in Tothill Fields was intended for the needs of Westminster and was not controlled by the City. An engraving of this pest-house, dated 1796, is reproduced at p. 82. A pesthouse at Stepney is mentioned in 1651. Cf. *Memorials of Stepney Parish* (ed. G. W. Hill and W. H. Frere), 197. Pest-house Lane and Pest-house Common are marked on Gascoigne's map of the parish of Stepney (1703). For the pesthouses built for St. Giles's-in-the-Fields at Marylebone and for St. Martin's-in-the-Fields in Soho Fields in 1665, see W. G. Bell, *The Great Plague in London in 1665*, 38, 39, 316. Dublin could boast of a pesthouse in 1604 (J. T. Gilbert, *Cal. Dublin Records*, iii. 536) and Manchester in 1606 (*S. P. Dom., Add., Jas. I*, vol. 38, Doc. 23).

lay groaning in fields and ditches. ' Thou setst up posts to whip them when they are alive : Set up an Hospitall to comfort them being sick, or purchase ground for them to dwell in when they be well, and that is, when they be dead.' [1] In 1630 the King's physicians recommended the erection of three or four hospitals on the north of the river, one in Southwark, and a large brick building near Chelsea or Paddington.[2] In March of the same year the Privy Council ordered all infected houses to be emptied and shut up and the occupants to be sent to the pesthouse, a course which it regarded as better and more effectual than the customary one. But neither the recommendations of the physicians nor the Council's orders were carried out.[3] In 1665 the City still possessed only this one pesthouse, which proved absurdly inadequate for the needs of so large a City in so great a pestilence.

Nothing is known about the plan of the building. Lodge has an interesting chapter—' Of the building of an Hospitall for the Plague '. He recommends that it should be greater in length than in breadth, and that the upper and lower stories alike should contain twenty-eight or thirty chambers. He suggests the provision of two beds in each chamber to enable the sick man to change from one to the other. Apartments separate from those of the sick should be allotted to the physician, the surgeon, the minister, and the apothecary.

The barber-surgeon in July 1606 was Thomas Abbot.[4] In 1609 there were three surgeons.[5] One was William

---

[1] *The Seven deadly Sinnes* (1606), sig. G 2ᵛ (*G.* ii. 78).
[2] *S. P. Dom., Chas. I*, vol. 187, Doc. 60.
[3] *P. C. R.* xxxix, 700 ; *R.* xliv. 228. In 1630, 1,317 died of the plague in London, but only 49 of these at the pesthouse
[4] *R.* xxvii. 235 b.   [5] *J.* xxvii. 365 b.

A VIEW OF THE PESTHOUSE IN TOTHILL FIELDS, AUGUST 1796. By Dayes and Pye

King, who two years later petitioned the Court of Aldermen—

' showing his great care and diligence in curing of such persons as have been sent thither and that by reason of his attendance and employment there his friends and former acquaintance do utterly refuse to use him in his profession, and therefore desireth some reasonable allowance and yearly pension from this City for his better maintenance and the more to encourage him to continue his former care and endeavours in helping such persons as come to the Pesthouse '.

The Court granted King an annual payment of £3, which in March 1612 was increased to £5.[1] In July 1625 Thomas Smith, a surgeon, was appointed to reside at the pesthouse at a salary of £30 per annum. The Court of Aldermen granted him and the keeper, William Upton, five pounds apiece in 1630 in reward of their care and pains.[2]

The pesthouse nurses were no kinder to their patients than the other nurse-keepers of that day. Webster has immortalized their infamy in *The White Divel*. After the strangling of Brachiano, Gasparo inquires, ' What, is it done ? ' and Lodovico replies :

The snuffe is out. No woman keeper i'th world,
Though shee had practis'd seven yere at the Pest-house,
Could have don't quaintlyer. My Lordes, hee 's dead.

A wagon or coach was specially set apart to carry the sick or the dead to the pesthouse.[3] When the plague was dormant, the building was used as an ordinary dwelling-place.[4]

[1] *R.* xxx. 170 b and 306.
[2] *R.* xxxix. 279 b ; xl. 154 b ; and xliv. 256.
[3] Cf. J. Godskall, *The Arke of Noah* (1603), sig. H 3^v, and *R.* xliv. 228 (1630). Cf. also *D. P. P.* 32 and 130.
[4] *R.* xxvi, pt. i, 135 (1603). Cf. also *Middlesex County Records : Calendar of the Sessions Books* (ed. W. J. Hardy), 230 (1701).

Most of the patients were houseless, moneyless, or friendless people, who regarded the pesthouse with hatred and horror. Its management, like that of the prisons, was farmed out to keepers who were often extortionate in their charges and harsh in their treatment.[1] Bamford praises those citizens who sent their servants there, especially if they lacked convenient room and means at home, and condemns ' those that raised a slander upon that house, holding them as despisers of governement, and wicked ill speakers of them that are in authoritie '.[2] But Lodge, while he does not condemn the pesthouse administration, is full of compassion for the fright and fear of sick folks

' ravished out of the hands of their parents and friends, and committed to the trust of strangers, who very often are but slenderly and coldly inclined to their good, wanting both service and succour '.

[1] For the prices charged at the pesthouse see Note G, p. 181. In January 1611 a petition against abuses done in the pesthouse was presented to the Court of Aldermen by Stephen Bobye (R. xxx. 45 b), but it does not appear what the abuses were or whether they were remedied.

[2] A Short Dialogue (1603), 27.

III

THE PLAGUE OF 1603

ELIZABETHAN London was seldom quite free from the plague. The four years from 1597 to 1600 were commonly supposed to have been ' clear ', yet 48 plague-deaths were recorded in 1597, 18 in 1598, 16 in 1599, and 4 in 1600. These deaths may be attributed not only to the insanitary condition of the City but to its extensive trade and intercourse with the Levant and with the countries of Europe. For some years before 1603 the infection was very prevalent on the Continent. It was at Lisbon in 1599, in Spain in 1601, and, more dangerous still, in the Low Countries in 1602. The death-rate at Ostend in January 1603 was estimated at 200 a week.[1] Some citizens fled from Amsterdam in the summer of 1602 to seek shelter in England, but the Privy Council ordered Lord Cobham to prevent their landing and to compel any who had already entered the towns to withdraw into the fields for forty days ' the better to air themselves '. Acting on these instructions Cobham ' stayed ' at Graves-end several ships from Amsterdam and Encusan. He informed Cecil in October that two houses at Wapping which had taken in goods from Danzig were infected, not a person in either house escaping. Domestic trade also had its dangers. At Yarmouth in September 1602, 80 persons died of the plague in one week. On the 17th of this month the Lord Mayor forbade any intercourse with

---

[1] *Cal. S. P. Ven.*, 1592–1603, 527.

Yarmouth or Amsterdam, and trade with Yarmouth was not resumed until the 3rd November.[1]

There was a general belief that the plague of 1603 was brought into this country from the Low Countries : ' the plague of pest. being great in Holland, Sealand, and other the low countries, and many souldiers returning thence into England, the infection was also spied in divers parts of this realme '.[2] The attempts to narrow the origin of the outbreak in London to a single house are less convincing. One writer asserts very confidently that the plagues of 1603, 1609, 1625, 1630, and 1636 ' began the first time, by a surfeit in *White Chappel*, the second time, by Sea-men, about the same place, the third by reason of rotten Mutton at *Stepney*, the fourth with a pack of Carpets from *Turkey*, the fifth with a Dogge that came over from *Amsterdam* '.[3] But there is good contemporary evidence that the infection attacked the suburbs before invading the City itself. Death, writes Dekker, ' hath pitcht his tents . . . in the sinfully-polluted Suburbes : . . . the skirts of *London* were pittifully pared off, by litle and litle '.[4] On 3 March an Englishman wrote to a Venetian that the plague had begun in the City and suburbs, especially in Southwark,[5] and the Lord Mayor informed the Privy Council on 18 April that the infection was very dangerous in the neighbourhood of Kentish Street in

[1] *Hist. MSS. Comm., Salisbury MSS.*, pt. xii, 247 and 438 ; *J.* xxvi. 26 b and 41 b.

[2] Stow, *Annales* (1605), p. 1425. Edmund Howes in his continuation of the *Annales* (1631), p. 857, adds that ' many ships of War lying long at Sea became also infected '.

[3] R. Kephale, *Medela Pestilentiae* (1665), p. 2. See also p. 131 below for the notion that the plague of 1625 began in the same house in Whitechapel as that of 1603.

[4] *D. P. P.* 31, 32.   [5] *Cal. S. P Dom.*, 1601–1603, 301.

St. George's parish in Southwark.[1] We know also that
the plague was at Stepney by 25 March.[2] Unfortunately
the weekly bills of mortality for this period are not extant.
The yearly bill gives the total of weekly deaths in the
whole City, but throws no light upon the weekly deaths
in each parish.

The mortality for the first three months of the year
was as follows :

Week ending.		Buried in all.	Of the plague.
December	23	83	3
January	6	78	0
,,	13	83	1
,,	20	80	0
,,	27	82	4
February	3	104	1
,,	10	76	0
,,	17	96	3
,,	24	85	0
March	3	82	3
,,	10	101	2
,,	17	108	3
,,	24	60	2
,,	31	78	6
April	7	66	4
,,	14	79	4
,,	21	98	8
,,	28	109	10
May	5	90	11
,,	12	112	18
,,	19	122	22
,,	26	122	32 [3]

The infection attracted little or no attention before
the end of April. Scaramelli, the Venetian ambassador,
who was unusually well-informed, says nothing of the

[1] *Remembrancia*, ii. 74. See also below, p. 89.
[2] See Note H, p. 184.
[3] See a facsimile of the yearly bill for 1603 at p. 114. The
number of parishes infected in each of the four weeks in May was
6, 9, 13, and 15. Cf. *Cal. S. P. Ven.*, 1603–1607, 33, 42, 45, and 48.

plague before 12 May, and then only to mention that
it began two weeks before.   Men's thoughts were busied
with more important matters, for the death of the
great Queen on 24 March in the seventieth year of her
age and the forty-fifth of her reign eclipsed all other
news for many weeks.   Apprehensions about the future
were quickly allayed by the peaceful accession to the
throne of James VI of Scotland, and the scenes of re-
joicing which accompanied his progress from Scotland
to London attest the sincerity of the country's welcome.
James received the news of Elizabeth's death on 26 March,
was proclaimed King of England, Scotland, France, and
Ireland on the 31st at the Market Cross of Edinburgh,
and five days later began his Progress from Edinburgh
to London.   On 7 May he was met in the fields outside
London by such 'multitudes of people in high ways,
fields, meadows, closes, and on trees . . . that they covered
the beauty of the fields ; and so greedy were they to
behold the countenance of the King that, with much
unruliness, they injured one another '.[1]

James's accession caused a great influx of visitors from
the country, bent on securing preferment or on witnessing
the coronation.   This influx and the nation's enhanced
security brought about an extraordinary revival of trade.
' Trades that lay dead and rotten, and were in all mens
opinion utterly dambd, started out of their trance.'[2]
Tailors, smiths, players, tobacconists, vintners, and others
promised themselves a rich harvest ; but the infection
cheated them of their gains.   This bustling activity in-

---

[1] T. M., *The True Narration of the Entertainment of His Royal
Majesty* (1603), reprinted in *Stuart Tracts, 1603–1693* (ed. C. H.
Firth).   [2] *D. P. P. 23.*

creased the mortality, the amounts of the weekly bills rose
slowly but surely, and by May the news of an approaching plague had spread from a small band of officials to
the general populace.

The presence of the plague at Southwark had come to
the notice of the Court of Aldermen by 5 April. The
bridgemasters were then ordered to give to the churchwardens of St. George's, Southwark, and of any infected
parish in the Borough the sum of ten pounds, to be paid
at the rate of twenty shillings a week, for distribution
among the infected poor. Strict orders were given to
provide adequate watches in every ward, and rogues and
vagabonds were hunted down and sent to Bridewell, where
they could no longer menace the City's health and peace.[1]

Such brief and inadequate abstracts as we possess of the
proceedings of the Privy Council at this period reveal
clearly their anxiety to stamp out the infection. In April
they rebuked the magistrates of London, Middlesex, and
Surrey for failing to execute the accustomed orders. The
reply of the Lord Mayor, Robert Lee, gives some interesting information about the early stages of the epidemic :

' since the 24 of December last past divers Parishes to the
number of six within the City and the Liberties thereof have
been infected with the sickness but in such sort as there was
not at any time above one house infected in a parish and one
at the most in a house excepting only such of St. George's
parish in Southwark as dwell about Kentish Street in the
County of Surrey '.

The Lord Mayor denied that plague-deaths were concealed
or plague-orders not executed.[2] Entries in the Journals
for May attest his diligence in attending to matters of

[1] *R.* xxvi, pt. i, 124 b ; *J.* xxvi. 78 b, 82, and 82 b.
[2] *Remembrancia*, ii. 74.

sanitation and segregation, yet admirable as were his intentions it is clear that they were by no means fulfilled.

On 11 May the King made his solemn entry into the Tower of London, but without passing through the City. He stayed there for three days before moving to Greenwich. Scaramelli, who was received in audience at Greenwich on 17 May, declared that never before had he witnessed so great a crowd in time of peace. There were upwards of ten or twelve thousand people about, and all the efforts of the guards hardly enabled him to reach the first, let alone the inner, chamber owing to the throng of nobility.[1] The deaths from the plague in London and the liberties for the week ending 26 May were 32, ten more than for the preceding week. The King and his Council had good reason to be alarmed at the multitudes which besieged the Court, and on 29 May all who were not in attendance at Court nor had special need to remain were ordered to leave London not later than the end of the term (6 June) and not to return until the coronation.

The plague had now a firm grip and made melancholy progress through the streets of the City :

Week ending.	Total deaths.	Of the plague.
June 2	114	30
,, 9	131	43
,, 16	144	59
,, 23	182	72
,, 30	267	158
July 7	445	263
,, 14	612	424
,, 21	1,186 [2]	917
,, 28	1,728	1,396

The infection was aided by the crowds, by the hot

[1] *Cal. S. P. Ven.*, 1603–1607, 39.
[2] The eight out-parishes (including deaths at the pesthouse) were added to the bills in this week. See the Appendix, p. 195.

weather, and by the slackness of the Justices of the Peace
in the out-parishes and outlying districts. An angry letter
from the Privy Council on 2 July accused the magistrates
of Surrey of reckless misgovernment. They had taken no
steps to confine the infected, and men afflicted with sores
walked about in company to the great danger of those that
had business in public places. Moreover no maintenance
was given to the segregated, and no orderly and due bill of
mortality was made of those who died in the suburbs and
out of the liberties of the City.[1] Two days later an eyewitness wrote from Clement's Inn that the plague was so
dispersed ' as that few places are free and such ill orders
that it cannot be known where it is, and where it is known
it is not shunned by the neighbours, as myself can witness
seeing them go in and out where it was said some lay dead
and some were dying '.[2] Printed copies of the plague
orders were sent to all parish churches on 13 July. They
were read on Sundays immediately after divine service
and then displayed on some post or board.[3]

The poor in the more seriously infected parishes were
suffering great distress. In June ten guineas were voted
for the poor of St. Botolph's-without-Aldgate, the money
to be paid in weekly doles of thirty shillings, and ten
pounds (in addition to the sum voted on 5 April) were
given to the poorest infected parishes in the Borough of
Southwark. On 12 July the London Companies were forbidden to hold any public feasts in their Halls, and it was
suggested that a third of the money thus saved should be
given towards the relief of the infected poor.[4] Five days

[1] B.M. Addit. MS. 29597, fo. 13 and verso.
[2] B.M. Stowe MS. 150, fo. 190.   [3] *J.* xxvi. 115 b.
[4] *R.* xxvi, pt. i, 158 b, 163, and 179. The Lord Mayor's feast

later two or more persons were appointed in each parish to collect charitable alms and benevolence from every inhabitant ' of ability '.[1]

All public meetings, feasts, and assemblies were now being postponed. Trinity Term was adjourned by proclamation on 23 June, and after 4 July no more juries were summoned in the Lord Mayor's or Sheriffs' Court.[2] Ceremonies not absolutely necessary to the coronation were deferred on 6 July. These edicts were temporarily successful in dispersing the crowds. ' Paul's grows very thin,' wrote that prince of intelligencers, John Chamberlain, on 10 July, ' for every man shrinks away, and I am half ashamed to see myself left alone.'[3] But the town soon filled again, for many were willing to brave the terrors of the plague for so rare a sight as a coronation.

On the last day of June the King had been joined at Windsor by the Queen and Prince and an enormous retinue.[4] Whitehall was reached by way of Hampton on 23 July, and on Monday, 25 July (St. James's Day), in unusually bad weather, the King embarked on the Thames, accompanied by his Council and by the Court, and landed at Westminster, where he was crowned.[5] Access to Westminster was barred to Londoners by road and by river. Sumptuous pageants had been prepared and arches erected in honour of the King's expected

---

was also abandoned. For a good song on this ' sad mischance ' see *Wit and Drollery* (1661), 45. The song is reprinted in Charles Mackay's *A Collection of Songs and Ballads Relative to the London Prentices and Trades* (Percy Society, 1841), 29.

[1] *J.* xxvi. 117.   [2] *R.* xxvi, pt. i, 168.
[3] *The Court and Times of James the First*, i. 9.
[4] *Cal. S. P. Ven.*, 1603–1607, 63 and 66.
[5] John Nichols, *Progresses of James I*, i. 195 ; *Cal. S. P. Ven.*, 1603–1607, 75.

Variæ per urbem jubilatione s

REJOICINGS AT THE CORONATION OF JAMES I, 25 JULY 1603

From a German print (right-hand panel)

progress from the Tower through the streets of the City. ' Our pageants are pretty forward,' wrote Chamberlain on 10 July, ' but most of them are such small-timbered gentlemen that they cannot last long, and I doubt, if the plague cease not the sooner, they will rot and sink where they stand.'[1] By 25 July the journey through the City was out of the question, and James's ' Triumphant Passage ' was postponed until the winter.[2] After the coronation their Majesties returned to Hampton Court.

The plague-deaths showed an increase of more than 1,000 a week during the fortnight ending 4 August, the infection rapidly reaching its climax.

Week ending.		Total deaths.	Of the plague.
August	4	2,256	1,922
,,	11	2,077	1,745
,,	18	3,054	2,713
,,	25	2,853	2,539
September	1	3,385	3,035
,,	8	3,078	2,724
,,	15	3,129	2,818
,,	22	2,456	2,195
,,	29	1,961	1,732

The proclamation of 29 July ordering every man to return to his home was obeyed with alacrity, and all who were able fled post-haste into the country.[3] The increase in the returns for the week ending 4 August was caused partly by the effects of the coronation, and the drop of 179 in the death-rate of the following week was doubtless

[1] *The Court and Times of James the First*, i. 9.
[2] It was hoped that James would enter the City upon the occasion of his solemn opening of Parliament (fixed for October) ; but the infection was still virulent then, and the entry was not made until 15 March 1604.
[3] According to Scaramelli (*Cal. S. P. Ven.*, 1603–1607, 87) upwards of 200,000 persons fled. But even if we allow for some thousands of visitors, this is surely an exaggeration, for the whole resident population of London at the time was not much greater.

because there were fewer victims to feed the fires of the infection. But the condition of those who stayed in the City was now pitiable. With one out of every six people sick or dying of the plague it had become impossible to enforce the regulations, and people ran about headlong to plague-stricken houses and attended burials in multitudes.[1] In a letter to Cecil written from Hampstead on the last day of August, Sir William Waad, a clerk of the Privy Council, gives a vivid picture of the extraordinary panic and disorder of the time : [2]

' My very good Lord, I assure your Lordship the disorders are so many and great and the Justices in Middlesex near London removed into the Country and the Aldermen and better sort out of the City, so as if some strict course be not taken, the contagion will spread more and more.

Notwithstanding the Orders set down, there come Londoners from infected places into cottages in all the villages about London, and bring bedding and stuff with them and presume no man or officer will lay hands on them, because it is known the sickness is in their houses : so as the difficulty is, what course should be taken with these men, which I think must be to bind them to appear from sessions to sessions, until they may there be fined, or to bind some (which are of the better sort) to appear hereafter in the Starchamber, and to send some of the meaner persons to the Pesthouse : but no constable will take charge of them.

The Cages (both in the Liberties and Suburbs) are full of sick folks, and when they die, the straw thrown about the streets, fresh straw put in, and new sick persons : I have often seen three in one Cage together, and people continually about them.

Those that are carried to be buried (if they be of any sort) accompanied as in other times, and the streets strawed with flowers when maids of any sort are buried, which gathereth

---

[1] *J.* xxvi. 125 b.   [2] *S. P. Dom., Jas. I*, vol. iii, Doc. 41.

people together, and for bachelors they wear rosemary, as if it were at marriages.

Complaint hath been made unto me of five alehouses together all infected and not one shut up.

And in all places at the entering into the Suburbs, straw, old bedding, mats and rags thrown so thick in the highway, as a man can neither come in, nor go forth of the City, without passing the pikes, which Mr. Solicitor can witness.

Another very lamentable thing very common : Divers come out of the town and die under hedges in the fields, and in divers places further off, whereof we have experience weekly here at Hampstead, and come in men's yards and outhouses if they be open, and die there, and in some barns not far from London as to a Pesthouse.

In the City it is a common thing, so soon as any falleth ill at ease in any house in a great street, presently the party is sent out of the house either to his friends abroad (and he miscarrieth often by the way) or to some poor house, and so neither the houses where the infection was first taken nor the shops are shut up.

On the holidays they come forth of the City, in such numbers to all the villages about London, as if they meant to abandon the City, which must needs spread the Infection, and it were better to limit them the fields about the City.

The absence of the Aldermen from the City, and the Justices in the shire (inferior officers being not regarded) hath bred liberty, and scope, in their lamentable cases and disorders.

These things are easier to be complained of than remedied, and yet if there be not some reformation, there will be little hope of the Contagion to cease.'

Contemporary writers support the truth of Waad's statements. All restraint was thrown to the winds. Men, women, and children afflicted with running sores recklessly thrust themselves into company,[1] some striving through envy to infect others by strewing the streets with gloves,

[1] J. Bamford, *A Short Dialogue*, 43.

garters, ruffs, cuffs, handkerchiefs, and the like things.[1]
This disorder was deplored by the Lord Mayor on 17
September in a proclamation which affords a notable
example of the fear of death piercing through the verbiage
of an official document. It complains that

‘ the people infected and whose houses are infected (against
all honesty, human Civility and good conscience seeking as
it were rather the desolation of the City and of this kingdom
by dispersing of the infection than otherwise) do daily intrude
themselves into all Companies both private and public as well
at sermons as elsewhere, and do flock and follow the dead to
the grave in multitudes one still infecting another to the
displeasure of Almighty God and great grief of his Majesty ’.[2]

In all this misery the life of the prisoner was perhaps
the most miserable. His plight was wretched at the best
of times, but in plague-time, menaced on all sides by the
infection and often in the company of the infected, his
only hope of relief was a speedy death. A pathetic letter
written from Newgate on 25 July by a Roman Catholic
gentleman informs us that the bell of St. Sepulchre’s
never ceased tolling by day or night. The common jail
was infected, many being sick and others buried. The
ward in which the writer lay was without walls or
chambers, and therefore was the more dangerous for all
‘ if any infection by one should come amongst us ’.[3] It
was no doubt owing to the fear of the plague that thirty
prisoners in the King’s Bench Prison in Southwark broke
out on the evening of 22 September. Most of them were
captured and committed to stricter ward.[4] In September
the Tower was infected, three dying of the plague in three

[1] John Davies of Hereford, *Humours Heav'n on Earth* (1605),
240.   [2] *J.* xxvi. 127.
[3] *Hist. MSS. Comm.*, 12th Report, Appendix, pt. iv, 392.
[4] Stow, *Annales* (1605), 1417.

days. The Lieutenant sent away his wife and children
' because he will not venture all his fortune in one bark,
but meaneth to ride it out himself '.[1]

Heartrending scenes were witnessed in the City. People
were alive and merry one hour and dead the next. Many
died suddenly in the streets or perished miserably in some
brake or ditch. ' A poor boy that died under St. John's
wall ', ' a poor wench died in the Cage ', ' a poor child
found at Mistress Bake's door '—such entries are common
in the burial-records of this year. In the parish of
St. Peter's, Cornhill, a girl twenty-one years of age
sickened on the day of her marriage, and in the same
parish a man died at the door of the house in which he
was born.[2]

> Whole housholds, and whole streets are stricken,
> The sick do die, the sound do sicken,
> And *Lord have mercy upon us*, crying
> Ere Mercy can come forth, th'are dying.
> No musick now is heard but bells,
> And all their tunes are sick mens knells ;
> And every stroake the bell does toll,
> Up to heaven it windes a soule.[3]

A sad commentary on Dekker's lines is given in the Parish
Register of Kensington. John, the son of Richard Sperwigg, was buried on 1 October 1603, his sister Mary on the
26th, his brother Richard four days later, his mother Alice

[1] *S. P. Dom., Jas. I*, vol. iii, Doc. 72 (Waad to Cecil). Sir Walter
Raleigh was in the Tower at the time. He had been sent there on
17 July on suspicion of complicity in a plot to place Arabella
Stuart on the throne. It was not till 12 November that he was
removed, and then to be taken to his trial at Winchester.

[2] *The Registers of St. Peter's Cornhill* (Harl. Soc. publications),
155 and 156. Dekker's anecdote in *The Wonderfull yeare* (*D. P. P.*
44–6 and note on 44, ll. 14 ff.) may relate to this girl.

[3] *D. P. P.* 94.

on 2 November (' the most thick and stinking misty day
that ever was '), his brother Thomas on the 7th, and lastly
Richard Sperwigg himself on the 23rd.

Ross's account of the state of Scotland (*Macbeth*, IV. iii)
exactly describes the lamentable condition of London in
this terrible summer :

> It cannot
> Be call'd our Mother, but our Grave ; where nothing
> But who knows nothing, is once seen to smile :
> Where sighs, and groans, and shrieks that rent the air
> Are made, not mark'd : where violent sorrow seems
> A Modern extasy : the Dead mans knell
> Is there scarce ask'd for who, and good men's lives
> Expire before the Flowers in their Caps,
> Dying, or ere they sicken.

The town was deserted and grass grew in Cheapside.
Those who were forced to go out of doors walked near the
channel in the middle of the street, chewing orange peel or
angelica root or smoking tobacco, and keeping to windward of all who seemed infected.[1] A ' fearefull pittifull
Coach ' scudded through London in August ' all hung
with Rue from the top to the toe of the Boote, to keepe
the leather and the nayles from infection ; the very
Nosthrills of the Coach-horses were stopt with hearb-
grace '.[2] The timid shunned the sound as well as the
sick, and feared to touch ' even the Platters and Candle-
stickes, which come out of straunge houses, as though
death did surely sticke therein '. Hence came it that the
infected were often suffered to die without any to see to

---

[1] So sixty-two years later the sight of infected houses put
Samuel Pepys ' into an ill conception of myself and my smell, so
that I was forced to buy some roll-tobacco to smell to and chaw,
which took away the apprehension ', *Diary* (ed. H. B. Wheatley),
iv. 428 (7 June).   [2] *D. P. P.* 117.

their wants, and women with child were forsaken in the hour of their need.[1] From many houses might be heard the groaning of sick persons or the wailing of mourners, while above all was heard the continual tolling of the bells. Fever-maddened wretches ran from house to house infecting others,

> Who, though they menac'd were with Sword, and Shot,
> Yet forward ran, and feare nor God nor man ! . . .
> So flies the Bill-man, and the Muskettire
> From the approaching desperate plaguy wight.[2]

Some hurled themselves out of windows or drowned themselves in the Thames.[3] Many blasphemed openly against God and sought to drown their fear of the terrible and invisible foe in drink and riotous living.

If the plague drove some to the taverns it drove others to the churches. Wednesday, 10 August, was ordered to be kept as a holiday and a fast throughout the kingdom, and on that day and every following Wednesday during the plague special prayers were offered, sermons of repentance preached, and collections made for the relief of the poor.[4] On fast-days ' all Persons (children, olde, weake, and sicke folks, and necessarie Harvest labourers, or the like excepted) are required to eate . . . but one competent and moderate Meale, and that towards night after Evening prayer : observing sobrietie of diet without superfluitie of ryotous fare, respecting necessitie and not voluptuousnesse '.[5] Observance of the fast and

---

[1] T. C., *A Godly and Learned Sermon, upon the 91. Psalme* (1603), sig. A 5ᵛ.

[2] J. Davies, *Humours Heav'n on Earth* (1605), 241.

[3] Beatrice refers to the frenzy of the plague-stricken. Benedick ' is sooner caught than the pestilence, and the taker runs presently mad ' (I. i).   [4] Stow, *Annales* (1605), 1418.

[5] *A Fourm of Prayer* (1603), sig. D 3ᵛ.

attendance at the service were obligatory, offenders being
haled before the Lord Mayor by the constable or beadle.[1]
The parishioners of St. Olave's were particularly diligent
in their devotions : James Bamford, the vicar, praised
them for their attendance at

' the Sacrament of Baptisme, from which in most places people
runne away most contemptuously ; Ye frequent Friday
Lecture as diligently (ever since the Plague was kindled) as
in winter nights : . . . and ye fill Gods house upon the daies of
humiliation, and holy rest, notwithstanding there have died in
our parish from the 7. of May to this day [13 October] 2640.
Wheras before the Plague our Church was partly filled by
strangers, both on Sondayes and Fridayes '.[2]

Bamford was one of the few clergymen who braved the
dangers and shared the horrors of this plague. His
conduct was the more courageous in that his parish
suffered more heavily than any other. It consisted
mainly of narrow lanes and alleys, where families of poor
people were thronged together as thickly, it was said, as
men pack woolsacks one upon another, so that one could
scarce breathe beside his fellow's face.[3] Henoch Clapham
also continued his ministry through the summer, preach-
ing in public, and in private comforting his flock night
and day as occasion demanded, at a time when the City
was almost empty of due ecclesiastical cure.[4] The name
of Dom. Joanne Marvino, commonly called Roberts, de-
serves commemoration. He was almost the only Roman
Catholic priest at liberty in London, and was indefatigable
in visiting and consoling the sick, thus ' saving the lives
of various persons and the souls of many more '.[5] In 1611

[1] *J.* xxvi. 127 b.   [2] *A Short Dialogue*, sig. A 4.
[3] F. Hering, *A Modest Defence* (1604), sig. B 1.
[4] *Henoch Clapham His Demaundes and Answeres* (1604), sig. A 2.
[5] *Cal. S. P. Milan*, 1385–1618, 649.

CERTAINE

Prayers collected out of a forme
of godly Meditations,

Set forth by his Maiesties Authoritie:

And most necessary to be vsed at this time
in the present Visitation of Gods heauy
hand for our manifold
sinnes.

❧ Together with the order of a Fast
to be kept euery Wednesday during
the said Visitation.

¶ Imprinted at London by Robert
Barker, Printer to the Kings
most Excellent Maiestie.

ANNO 1603.

Title-page of a book of prayers used in the plague of 1603.

E

the City in which he had worked rewarded his zeal and self-sacrifice with martyrdom at the scaffold.

Aldermen and justices ran away from ' the token'd pestilence, Where death is sure '.[1] They all fled, jeered Dekker, ' crying out onely, Put your trust in God my Bullies, and not in us '.[2] Their absence aggravated the disorder which prevailed at the height of the infection, for the populace paid little heed to the deputies who filled their places and still less to beadles and constables.

It was, however, the defection of physicians and surgeons which was felt most keenly, and the runaways of the medical profession are severely whipped by the lash of Dekker's satire. Dr. Simon Forman, astrologer, remained at his post, and in doggerel verse boasted of his invaluable services : [3]

> Then came the plague in sixty [sic] three
> Whence all these Doctors fled :
> I stayed, to save the Lives of many
> That otherwise had been dead.

He and his household were sick, but all escaped except one who died of an imposthume. A better physician than Forman also scorned to run from the danger. At his house in Warwick Lane on 19 August, Thomas Lodge, Doctor in Physic, wrote the preface to his *Treatise of the Plague*. This book has attracted less attention than Lodge's more purely literary work. It was not written like *Rosalynde* ' to bewitch the eares and minds of the reader ' with the airs and graces of euphuism, but, in a plain and homely style more suited to its subject and

[1] *Antony and Cleopatra*, III. x.
[2] *D. P. P.* 71. See also p. 94 above.
[3] Bodleian MS. Ash. 802, fo. 133. Forman was only 10 years old in 1563 : by ' sixty three ' he means ' 1603 '.

more intelligible to its readers, it reveals through its
sincerity and honest compassion the charming personality
of its author. When Lodge sent his book to the press nearly
three thousand people were dying weekly of the plague.

If many of the regular practitioners deserted the City
in the hour of its greatest need, plenty of impostors and
empirics sprang up to fill their places. The genuine physician had high ideals, and felt that his mystery required
at least the rudiments of omniscience: ' the *Greeke* tongue,
exactly, àll the learning, and skill of *Philosophie, Historie*
of all sorts (especially naturall), knowledge of all vege-
tatives and Minerals and whatsoever dwels within the
foure elements. Also Skill in *Astronomy, Astrologie*. And so
much of the *Judicialls* upon all manner of Calculations as
may be well warranted with much other kind of learning,
art and skill.' [1]   But the quacks, arguing that even with
the best physicians fortune prevailed more than skill,
dispensed with study and knowledge, and traded upon
the ignorance and terror of the populace. Being beggars,
these tinkers of all infirmities had at their command
potable gold, the natural balsamum, the philosopher's
stone, dissolved pearl, and all the riches of art and
nature.[2]   Their advertisements were on every post,
promising such miracles ' as if they held the raine of
desteny in their own hands, and were able to make old
Aeson young againe '.   One of their number was Lodge's
neighbour—' who because at the first he underwrit not
his billes, everyone that red them came flocking to me,
conjuring me by great profers and perswasions to store

[1] Thomas Powell, *Tom of all Trades* (1631), 29.
[2] John Cotta, *A Short Discoverie of the Unobserved Dangers of
several sorts of ignorant and unconsiderate Practisers of Physicke
in England* (1612), 34.

them with my promised preservatives, and relieve their sicke with my Cordiall waters '.[1] Their ranks were mostly recruited, wrote another physician, from runagate Jews, thrasonical and unlettered chemists, shifting and outcast pettifoggers, dull-pated and base mechanics, stage-players, pedlars, prittle-prattling barbers, toothless and tattling old wives, chattering charwomen, scape-Tyburns, ' and such like baggage, and earthdung'. ' These jolly [i. e. bold, arrogant] Quacksalvers . . . know not whether Anatomy be a Man or Woman, an Horse, or a Cow.' [2]

Contemporary writers were agreed that of all persons, ministers, magistrates, and doctors ought to remain in the City. The well-to-do were also censured for their selfish cowardice. At the best of times many people were dependent for their livelihood upon the charity of others ; but in time of plague, when trade was at a standstill, households dissolved, and servants dismissed, the number of the destitute and starving was multiplied many times. Some rich runaways, it is true, left money to be distributed amongst the poor, but others fled without giving a thought to the misery and want of those whom they were abandoning. The two persons appointed in each parish on 17 July to collect alms for the poor had met with little success, and on 14 August more collectors were appointed to charge those who had already contributed to enlarge their charity and to send messages to those absent in the country to give a portion ' of that which God hath put them in trust

---

[1] These ' cordial waters ' were often taken from Tower Hill, the water of which was much praised and sought after. See Dekker's *Newes from Hell* (1606), sig. F 3ᵛ (*G.* ii. 132), and Nashe's *Works* (ed. R. B. McKerrow), iii. 162.

[2] F. Hering, *The Anatomyes of the True Physition* (1602), 4 and 29.

A direction concerning the Plague
or Pestilence, for Pooore and Rich.

THe Plague which is called of the Greekes *Epidemia*, and in Latine *Lues pestis* or *pestilentia*, and I a stranger and a German who many times haue beene imployed in this sicknes, as at *Callas, Ostend, Amsterdam* and many other Townes more, may with great credit beare me witnesse of it, so I can say & write of this fearefull disease more then any other can. The cause is euident, that it is a punishment from God, whereof many examples may be set downe, which I leaue for breuity sake, for it is a matter which belongs to Diuines; the other cause is, that the vpper parts haue infected the Astris with a Distemperature where through the Plague hath his dominion into our bodies, whereof we leaue this besides to our learned Philosophers. Now to come to my intent which is out of loue, more then for gaine, for to take such a dangerous matter vpon me in mine old age (The which God be thanked haue no great need of, but beeing first mooued to it, by diuers of this City, for to do something in this time of sicknesse, I haue sayd nothing all this while (but finding the sicknes increasing more and more, do determine to shew my best skill for it, thus through my experience, where I haue in former times (putting my trust in God & with his helping hand) saued many a mans life. First, pray to God to forgiue your sinnes, and after vse the naturall meanes which God hath ordained to euery sicknes, and as well for this sicknes, as for any other, I haue a preseruatiue which euery body shall find by me. Also a certaine precious Pill, to keepe in your mouth, when you goe abroad or perceiue any danger.

1. First seuerall Antidotes for the preseruation of mans body from the Plague with certaine directions.

2. Secondly a certaine *Elixer*, or a water for them that are infected, besides certaine orders and directions for the perfuming of their houses, chambers & roomes, for to alter the ayre, to preserue their houses, besides for those houses that are already Infected to cleanse them, with certaine directions, washing them with waters wherein certaine hearbs are boyled, and after stroying the house with hearbs, fitting for this sicknes, and perfume. Now after many and seuerall medicines both in Physicke and Chirurgery, which are necessary in this sicknes, as Cordials, Iulips, cooling waters Conserues, Oyles, Oyntments, smelling or smoaking balls, as Pomanders, Quilts, with other Chirurgicall medicines for Carbonckles, Antraxs, or other swelling as Byles, and Impostumes. The Professor hath Poultesles, Ballomes, Oyles, Plaisters & all things else belonging to this disease, besides it is necessary for euery one to be solible in his body, or to take some conuenient purge by directions from the Physitions. Likewise Fountenell or Issues, are very commendable, the which I haue made in Germanie and other places, in vehement Plagues, as a preseruatiue against Infection. Such people are not apt to be Infected that haue any running sores, as Vlsers, nor those which are troubled with other maladies which run. There are certaine rules to be obserued, as to forbeare to go in stinking places, & not too goe abroad till the Sun be vp, principally in moist and foggy weather; in the euening auoyd the streets, & goe not to late abroad, which is principally hurtfull for Children, and yong people, ouer fill not your bodies with meat which is hard of disgesture, for it breeds ill humors. All these medicines euery body may haue in his owne house for a reasonable price, with certaine directions in print. This I take out of ancient writers, which haue bin many times approoued, this I do through & with counsell of diuers learned Physitions, some of the Kings Maiesties, & others of my friends, although there will be some Caluminating night-Oules, perhaps, will speake against my intent. Let them show a better or else let this alone.

Viuat Rex.

The Professor hereof dwelleth in Great Woodstreete at the Signe of the Meere Mayde neere the corner of Mayden Lane.

A quack's advertisement

with for relief of the great necessity of their poor brethren here at home and requiring them that now they will lend but the Lord by pitying the poor, and exhorting them by such other good means and with such persuasions as they shall think meet to move them to compassion '. On 6 September the Court of Common Council ordered the London Companies to lend £500 for the relief of the poor and needy. The list of the amounts to be paid by each company is headed by the Merchant Taylors Company with £46 16s.[1] The inhabitants of Westminster, the Strand, and St. Martin's-in-the-Fields did not come under the jurisdiction of the City, and consequently did not share in this charity. On 10 September they informed the Privy Council that all their rich had fled and that they were in great distress through lack of food and money. Two days later the Council entreated the burgesses of Westminster to disburse £100, the money to be repaid as speedily as possible.[2] The churchwardens' accounts for the parish of St. Martin-in-the-Fields show that the benevolences in 1603 were £70, as against £14 in 1601. But in spite of this increase a deficit of over £25 was due to the overseers at the end of the year.[3]

With the approach of the colder and shorter days the plague lost much of its virulence :

Week ending.		Total deaths.	Of the plague.
October	6	1,831	1,641
,,	13	1,312	1,146
,,	20	766	642
,,	27	625	508

[1] *J*. xxvi. 123, 126, and 126 b. See also *Letter Book*, BB, 205.
[2] *S. P. Dom., Jas. I*, vol. iii, Doc. 63, and B.M. Addit. MS. 11402, fo. 90 b.
[3] *St. Martin-in-the-Fields The Accounts of the Churchwardens* (ed. G. V. Kitto), 577.

Week ending.		Total deaths.	Of the plague.
November	3	737	594
,,	10	585	442
,,	17	384	251
,,	24	198	105
December	1	223	102
,,	8	163	55
,,	15	200	96
,,	22	168	74

While the plague was so rife in and about London [1] it was still found necessary to discourage public assemblies. All fairs within fifty miles of London were prohibited on 8 August. As the hope that the plague would cease in the autumn was not realized, the Michaelmas Term was adjourned on 18 October to Winchester. Strict precautions were taken to ward off the infection, and no person who had had the plague in his house since 20 July was allowed to attend. In a crowded town lawyers and clients were made to pay through the nose for food and lodging.[2]

The Court during the summer was continually haunted with the fear of sickness. Followed in its migrations by a disorderly company which it could not shake off, it infected all the places to which it came.[3] On 16 August the Court was at Oatlands, where the plague suddenly attacked a groom of the Wardrobe in the Princes' service. It moved at once to Richmond, and by the end of the month had reached Woodstock, where the King sank into a lethargy of pleasures, hunting most of the time and remitting all

[1] See the illustration for deaths in the City, liberties, and out-parishes for the week ending 20 October, and see Note H for the mortality in the outlying districts for the latter half of the year.

[2] John Milner, *History of Winchester*, i. 390. See also Note J, p. 184.

[3] So in 1578 when Elizabeth and her Court took the infection to Norwich. Cf. W. J. C. Moens, *The Walloons and their Church at Norwich* (Huguenot Soc. publications), pt. i, 44.

THE TRVE COPIE OF ALL THE BVRIALS AND CHRISTNINGS

aſwell within the City of LONDON as the Liberties thereof, as in other Pariſhes in the ſkirts of the City, and out of the Freedome, according to the report made to the Kings moſt excellent Maieſtie, by the Company of Pariſh Clearkes of the ſaid Citie, From the 13.of October, 1603. to the 20. of the ſame. Whereunto is added the true Relation of the whole nummber of all that haue dyed of this Viſitation from the 17.of December, 1602.to the 26.of this preſent moneth of October 1603. with the whole number of all that haue dyed in Weſtminſter, the Sauoy, in Stepney, Newington, and ſundry other places, ſince the ſickneſſe began there.

		Buried in all	Of the Plague		Buried in all	Of the Plague
London within the Walles.	Albones in Woodſtreet	3	2	Margrets Pattons	2	0
	Alhallowes Lumberſtreet	3		Margrets Moyſes	2	0
	Alhallowes the great	12	11	Margrets Lothbery	3	2
	Alhallowes the leſſe	5	3	Martins in the Vintry	8	7
	Alhallowes Bredſtreet	3	0	Martins Orgars	4	4
	Alhallowes ſtayninge	7	4	Martins Iremonger Lane	4	4
	Alhallowes the Wall	6	4	Martins at Luſtgate	5	0
	Alhallowes Hony-lane	0	0	Martins Outwich	2	0
	Alhallowes Barking	12		Mary le Boee	2	0
	Alphage at Cripplegate	3	1	Mary Bothawe	0	
	Andrewes by the Wardrope	4		Mary at the hill	4	4
	Andrewes Eaſtcheape	7	6	Mary Abchurch	6	
	Andrewes underſhaft	4	4	Mary Woolchurch	6	6
	Annes at Alderſgate	4	4	Mary Colchurch	2	2
	Annes Blacke Fryers	6	6	Mary Woolnoth	6	6
	Auntlins Pariſh	0	0	Mary Aldermary	4	4
	Auſtins Pariſh	2	2	Mary Aldermanbery	4	4
	Barthelemew at the Exch.	4	4	Mary Stayninge	4	
	Bennets at Pauls-Wharf	4	4	Mary Mount one	3	2
	Bennets Grace-Church	4		Mary Summerſet	4	
	Bennets Finck	2	2	Mathew Friday ſtreet	3	1
	Buttols Billinsgate	3	3	Maudlins Milke ſtreet	3	
	Chriſt Church Pariſh	11		Maudlins by Olaſſiſtreet	6	
	Chriſtophers Pariſh	0	0	Mighels Baſſie ſhawe	4	4
	Clements by Eaſtcheape	1		Mighels Corne hill	2	
	Dennis Backe-Church	3		Mighels in Woodſtreet	5	5
	Dunſtones in the Eaſt	4		Mighels in the Ryall	6	5
	Edmundes in Lumbard-ſt.	9	8	Mighels in the Querne	4	
	Ethelborow within Biſhops.	2	2	Mighels Queene-bithe	6	4
	S. Faithes	2		Mighels Crooke lane	5	
	S. Foſters in Foſter-lane	3	3	Mildreds Poultry	7	
	Gabriel Fan-Church	5	5	Mildreds Bredſtreet	4	
	George Botolph lane	1		Nicholas Acons	5	4
	Gregories by Paules	12	10	Nicholas Cole-abbay	4	
	Hellens within Biſhops.	4		Nicholas Olaues	5	4
	Iames by Garlike hithe	4		Olaues in the Iury	4	
	Iohn Euangeliſt	0	0	Olaues in Hartſtreet	6	
	Iohn Zacharies	0	0	Olaues in Siluer ſtreet	5	4
	Iohns in the Walbrooke	6	5	Pancras by Soperlane	1	
	Katherines Cree-Church	15	11	Peters in Cornehill	6	6
	Katherine Colemans	5		Peters in Cheape	0	
	Lawrence in the Iury	10	9	Peters the poore in broadſt.	1	
	Laurence Pountney	1		Peters at Pauls wharf	0	
	Leonards Foſter-lane	4	4	Stephens in Colemanſtreet	14	10
	Leonards Eaſtcheape	0		Stephens in the Walbrook	5	
	Magnus pariſh by the Bridge	3	2	Swithins at London ſtone	3	1
	Margrets New fiſhſtreete	2		Thomas Apoſtles	1	
				Trinity pariſh	8	5

The number buried within the Walles of London is 351. Whereof of the Plague 251

		Buried in all	Of the Plague		Buried in all	Of the Plague
London without the Wals, and within the Liberties.	Andrewes in Holborne	39	36	Dunſtones in the Weſt	13	9
	Barthelmew the leſſe Smith.	8		Georges in Southwarke	19	7
	Barthelmew the great Smith.	2		Giles without Cripplegate	37	22
	Brides pariſh	23		Olaues in Southwarke	21	17
	Buttols Algate	23	21	Sauiours in Southwarke	39	36
	Bridewell Precinct	4		Sepulchers pariſh	40	32
	Buttols Biſhopſg.	7		Thomas in Southwarke	4	2
	Buttols without Alderſg.	21	19	Trinity the Minories	3	2

The number buried without the wals, and within the liberties is 296. Whereof of the Plague 255

		Buried in all	Of the Plague		Buried in all	Of the Plague
Out Pariſhes adioyning to the City.	Clements without Templeb.	25	19	Martins in the Fields	20	17
	Giles in the fields	21	19	Mary Whitechappell	20	17
	Iames at Clarkenwell	9	7	Magdalens in Barmondſey ſtreete	5	
	Katherines by the Tower	4	3		5	4
	Leonards in Shurditch	14	9	At the Peſt-houſe	1	1

Buried without 119 Whereof, Of the Plague 96

Chriſtnings — 67 — Pariſhes cleere of the Plague — 19 — Pariſhes infected — 93
Buried in all, within the places aforeſaid — 766.
Whereof, of the Plague — 642.

From the firſt great plague in our memory after the loſſe of Newhauen, from the firſt of Ianuary, 1562.to December, 1563.there died of the plague twenty thouſand one hundred thirtie ſixe.

And in the laſt viſitation, from the 22.of December, 1592. to the 21.of the ſame moneth in the yeare 1593.died in all, 25886. of the plague in and about London, 11503. And in the yeare before 2000.

And now in this preſent viſitation which it pleaſeth God to ſtrike vs both, there hath bin from the 17.of December 1602. to the 14. of Iuly, 1603. The whole number in London and the Liberties, 4571. whereof, of the Plague, 3310. Where of are ſet downe as they haue followed weekely.

	Buried in all	Of the plague			
From the 14 of Iuly, to the 21. of the ſame	867	In the out pariſhes	303	Whereof, of the plague	846
Buried in all this weeke	1186.	Whereof, of the plague 917.			

The time when it began in the City of Weſtminſter, and theſe places following.

Buried in VVeſtminſter, from the 14 of Iuly to the 20. of October, in the whole number, 832. whereof of the plague 723.

Buried in the Sauoy, from the firſt of Iune to the 20.of October, in the whole number, 185. whereof of the plague, 172.

Buried in the pariſh of Stepney, from the 15.of March, to the 20.of October, in all 2598. whereof of the plague 1877.

Buried at Newington-but from the 14.of Iune to the 20.of October, in all 626. whereof of the plague 562.

Buried in Iſlington, 201. whereof of the plague, 170.
Buried in Lambeth, 373. whereof of the plague, 361.
Buried in Hackney, 101. whereof of the plague, 169.

The whole number that hath beene buried in all, both within London, and the Liberties, and the 7.other ſeuerall places laſt before mentioned is, 3979. whereof, of the number of the plague, 3207.

Printed by Iohn Windet, Printer to the Honourable City of London.

business to his Council. But the plague was still in
attendance, and two of the Queen's household were
stricken and died.[1] Many of the poorer sort were lodged
in tents near the Manor gate, particularly the kitchen
and stable servants appointed to receive provisions from
the country people. One or other died in these tents
every week.[2] All who had not urgent business were
refused admittance, and no one was allowed to enter the
Palace without a certificate that he had come from an
uninfected district.[3] Woodstock was considered very
unwholesome, as the house stood upon springs and the
place smelt of nothing but of cows and pigs. After a few
weeks' stay the King went first to Southampton and then
to Winchester. Winchester was infected by 3 October,[4]
and the Court removed to Wilton near Salisbury. The
big drop in the mortality at London was hailed with
delight, for these frequent removals caused great misery
and discomfort to all, and no matter where the Court went
the country was so impoverished as to be quite unable
to supply its wants.[5]

The fifteen years immediately preceding 1603 had been
years of great depression. The increased taxation resulting from the wars with Spain had reacted on trade, and
a succession of bad harvests from 1594 to 1598, and again
in 1600, had caused widespread poverty. Corn which in
1594 and 1595 was quoted at 53s. 4d. to 56s. a quarter
rose in 1596 to 80s. and later to 120s.[6] The distress in the

[1] *Cal. S. P. Ven.*, 1603–1607, 87, 90, and 92.

[2] J. Nichols, *The Progresses of James I*, i. 268 and 272.

[3] *Cal. S. P. Ven.*, 1603–1607, 98.

[4] E. Lodge, *Illustrations of British History*, iii. 183 ; *Cal. S. P.
Dom.*, 1603–1610, 40 ; *Cal. S. P. Ven.*, 1603–1607, 103.

[5] J. Nichols, *The Progresses of James I*, iv. 1,059.

[6] W. R. Scott, *Joint Stock Companies*, i. 100.

parish of St. Bartholomew Exchange was so great in 1596 that special prayers were offered, and the parish entered into a resolution binding each family to avoid eating suppers on Wednesdays and Fridays and to give the amount saved by this abstention to the poor.[1] Trade revived after the accession of James, but the revival was only momentary, for the infection brought commerce to a standstill. Foreigners were loth to receive any goods from England, and particularly from London. The Governor of Dieppe, for example, evidently suspecting that Rye was infected, had refused to allow travellers and goods from that town to land. On 10 August the Mayor and Justices of Rye protested that the town and the country for twenty miles around were free from infection, and that no goods, wares, or merchandise from London or other infected places were allowed to be brought into the town.[2] There was a general agreement in France not to receive broadcloth from England. Broadcloth and especially kerseys were made all over the kingdom, in hamlets and villages as well as in large towns, and the French attitude was much disliked by the English merchants who were endeavouring to secure discrimination between goods from infected and uninfected districts.[3]

But if the plague had put an end to export trade, it had been equally destructive to domestic trade. Distress

[1] *The Vestry Minute Books* (ed. E. Freshfield), 37. Cf. also *Sundrie new and Artificiall remedies against Famine. Written by H[ugh]. P[latt]. Esq. uppon thoccasion of this present Dearth* (1596).

[2] *Hist. MSS. Comm.*, 13th Report, Appendix, pt. iv, 130. The people of Rye were accused of bringing the infection to Dieppe in October 1536. Cf. *Letters and Papers Foreign and Domestic, Henry VIII*, vol. xi, No. 631.

[3] *Cal. S. P. Ven.*, 1603–1607, 104. See also *ibid.* 87.

amongst the clothiers was acute. He who formerly
employed many hundreds could not now help twenty
poor, for there was no sale of cloth at London or abroad.
' And in this case what should the Clothier doo ; some
come to him on their knees, some with wringing hands,
some crying with Infants in their armes, but all of them
with such pittifull lamentation, that it pitties the amazed
Clothier in such sort, that he is weary of life.' [1] All
orders on London merchants were recalled, and every uninfected town or village kept watch with bills and staves,
refusing admittance to those who came from infected
parts.[2]   The fleet of the London East India Company had
set sail on its first voyage in February 1601, and returned
to England when the plague was at its height. So completely was trade disorganized that the Company found it
impossible to realize the cargoes, and, in order to start the
second voyage, was forced to apply all its resources to
the equipment of the fleet.[3]

In London the flight of the wealthiest citizens had put
a stop to the merely local trade. The difficulty of collecting money also hindered the transaction of business, for
no one would pay his debts when the chances were that
his creditor would die.[4] Goods were bought gingerly
and sparingly. In Middleton's *Your five Gallants* (I. i)
a London broker conducts his business with a bill of
mortality by his side. A customer from St. Clement's is

[1] H. Petowe, *Londoners Their Entertainment in the Countrie*
(1604), sig. C 4 and C 4ᵛ.
[2] Garnet thought that a Londoner, when asked at a town's
gates whether he came from London, might in certain circum-
stances give an ' equivocating' answer. Cf. S. R. Gardiner,
History of England 1603–1642, i. 281.
[3] W. R. Scott, *Joint Stock Companies*, ii. 97.
[4] *Cal. S. P. Ven.*, 1603–1607, 106.

rejected : ' 3. at *Clements*, away with your pawne sir, your parish is infected ' ; a customer from St. Martin's-in-the-Fields is accepted : ' Saint *Martins* none, her 's an honest fellow . . . Welcome : good Saint *Martins* in the field, welcome, welcome, I know no other name.'

The theatres were closed for nearly a year. On 19 March 1603 the Privy Council sent letters to the Lord Mayor and to the Justices of Middlesex ordering ' the restraint of Stage plays till other direction be given '.[1] The infection can hardly have been the cause of this prohibition, since the reported plague-mortality in London and the liberties during the week ending 17 March was only three. The prohibition was perhaps due to the season of Lent (which had begun on 9 March) or to the serious illness of the Queen. Easter Sunday fell on 24 April, and the theatres probably opened the next day. On 5 May the Admiral's Company ceased playing at the Fortune Theatre ' now at the King's coming '. The King arrived in London on 7 May, and Worcester's Company and possibly the other two Companies began to act two days later.[2] But the players had little time to enjoy the blessings of a crowded London, for the theatres were closed before 17 May.[3] The plague-deaths in London and the liberties for the week ending 12 May were only 18, but the mortality in the out-parishes was doubtless more serious. Anyhow the Privy Council and the City would be more than ordinarily cautious because of their earnest desire that the plague should not interfere with the ceremonies of the coronation.

The players were busy in the provinces during the

[1] B.M. Addit. MS. 11402, fo. 86.
[2] *Henslowe's Diary* (ed. W. W. Greg), i. 174 and 190.
[3] J. O. Halliwell-Phillipps, *Outlines of the Life of Shakespeare* (1887), ii. 82.

summer. The King's players visited Richmond, Bath, Coventry, Shrewsbury, Mortlake, and Wilton House ; Worcester's men (afterwards Queen Anne's men) appeared at Leicester, Coventry, and Barnstaple, while the Admiral's men (afterwards the Prince's men) acted at Coventry, Leicester, York, and Bath.[1] That the players were back in London by 21 October appears from Joan Alleyn's letter to her husband : ' about us the sickness doth cease, . . . All the companies be come home and well for aught we know.' [2] The decrease in the sickness was too slow to permit of any acting in London until the following April, but James showed his appreciation of English plays and players by giving plentiful employment to the London Companies at the Court's Christmas festivities. The King's Company (to which Shakespeare belonged) acted before the King or Prince at Wilton House on 2 December ; at Hampton Court on 26, 27, 28, 30 December, 1 January (twice), and 2 February ; and at Whitehall on 19 February. The Prince's Company (to which Alleyn belonged) acted before the King or Prince on 4, 15, 21, 22 January and 20 February, the Queen's Company (to which Thomas Heywood belonged) played before the Prince on 2 and 13 January, and the Queen's Revels Children (whose plays were under the ' approbation and allowance ' of Samuel Daniel) played before the King on 21 February. The same day, Shrove Tuesday, Philip Henslowe presented before the King ' the game of Bearbaiting '. The King's men received £103 for their services at Court, and on 8 February James gave Richard Burbage £30 ' by way of his Majesty's free gift ' for the relief and maintenance

---

[1] J. T. Murray, op. cit., i. 58, 147, and 206.
[2] Henslowe Papers (ed. W. W. Greg), 59.

of him and his Company seeing that they were prevented from playing publicly in or near London owing to the plague.[1]   The theatres reopened on Easter Monday, 9 April.[2]

The playwrights also had a lean year. New plays were no longer in demand, for the travelling companies would act old pieces which had stood out all appeals, rather than pay money for new ones and risk failures. Dramatists then were even harder hit than players, and were forced to seek out other means of earning a livelihood. Dekker and Middleton turned pamphleteers, and made capital out of the very plague which had threatened them with poverty. Michael Drayton retired to the country, where he wrote *Moyses In A Map Of his Miracles*,[3] a poem in which the affliction of London served him for ' a booke, Whereby to modell *Egipts* miserie '.   Samuel Daniel's *The Vision Of The Twelve Goddesses* was the first of a long line of famous masques to be produced at James's court. It was ' Presented at Hampton Court, upon Sunday night, being the eight of January. 1604. And Personated by the Queenes most Excellent Majestie, attended by Eleven Ladies of Honour.' Jonson had left his wife and family in London, and was staying with old Camden at Sir Robert Cotton's house at Connington in Huntingdon. There he saw in a vision, says Drummond, his eldest son ' with the mark of a bloody cross on his forehead, as if it had been cutted with a sword '. Soon afterwards letters came from his wife with information of the boy's death from the infection.

---

[1] P. Cunningham, *Extracts from the Accounts of the Revels at Court*, xxxiv–xxxvii.   [2] See above, p. 54.
[3] Entered on the Stationers' Register on 25 June 1604 and published in the same year. Drayton refers to the plague of 1603 on p. 57.

This bereavement was the occasion of the fine poem beginning ' Farewell, thou child of my right hand, and joy '.
We do not know whether Shakespeare accompanied the
King's men in their travels. The Globe Theatre was closed
for eleven months.

IV

THE PLAGUE FROM 1603 TO 1624

SOME account has already been given of the disorganiza-tion of both public and private affairs during the plague of 1603. Taxes, duties, and customs brought in nothing, the Treasury was penniless and in confusion, and the King and his Council were at their wits' end what to do. Early in November James's request to the City for a loan of £40,000 was refused. Thereupon he asked for £30,000, then £20,000, and finally £10,000, but always met with a refusal. The excuse pleaded was the complete stoppage of trade, but ill-will was also suspected as the cause.[1]

London recovered with astonishing rapidity from the confusion and poverty which had overwhelmed it. During the whole year (from 23 December 1602 to 22 December 1603) no less than 38,244 people had died, and 30,578 of the plague.[2] Adding the deaths in Westminster, Lambeth, Newington Butts, the Savoy, Stepney, Hackney, and Islington, we get a grand total of 43,154 deaths, of which 35,104 were of the plague.[3] The population of London at the time could hardly have exceeded 250,000,[4]

[1] *Cal. S. P. Ven.*, 1603–1607, 106 and 112.

[2] Stow, *Annales* (1605), 1425, and a bill for 1603 (see the illus-tration) printed by Stansby in 1625. The general bill for 1625 for Westminster, Lambeth, &c., in MS. Rawl. D. 859 gives 4,910 deaths for 1603 and 4,526 of the plague. It gives a grand total of 43,411 in all, and 37,054 of the plague. See Note K, p. 185, for the number of deaths in the most heavily afflicted parishes.

[3] The figures for the eight out-parishes and the seven outlying districts are not given for the whole year (see p. 195 and Note H, p. 184), so that the true total is somewhat greater.

[4] See the Appendix, pp. 213–15.

1602. 1603.

A TRVE REPORT OF ALL THE BVRIALS AND CHRISTNINGS

within the City of LONDON and the Liberties thereof, from the 23. of December, 1602 to the
22. of December, 1603. Whereunto is adeed the number of euery seuerall Parish, from the 14. of Iuly, to the
22. of December, aswell within the Citie of LONDON and the Liberties thereof, as in other
Parishes in the skirtes of the Citie, and out of the Freedome, adioyning to the
Citie: According to the report made to the Kings most excellent Maiestie,
by the Company of Parish Clearks of the same
CITIE.

		Buried in all.	Of the plague.	Christnings.
December	23	83	3	96
Ianuary	6	78	0	97
Ianuary	13	81	1	114
Ianuary	20	80	0	103
Ianuary	27	80	4	128
February	3	104	4	102
February	10	76	0	108
February	17	96	3	109
February	24	85	3	108
March	3	82	3	110
March	10	101	2	110
March	17	108	3	106
March	24	65	2	106
March	31	78	6	59
Aprill	7	66	4	143
Aprill	14	79	4	86
Aprill	21	98	8	84
Aprill	28	109	10	85
May	5	90	11	78
May	12	112	18	103
May	19	122	22	81
May	26	122	32	98
Iune	2	114	30	82
Iune	9	131	43	110
Iune	16	144	59	90
Iune	23	182	72	95
Iune	30	267	158	82
Iuly	7	445	263	89
Iuly	14	612	424	88

This weeke was the Out-parishes
brought in to be ioyned
with the City and
Liberties.

		Buried in all	Of the plague	Christnings.
Iuly	21	1186	917	50
Iuly	28	1728	1396	138
August	4	2256	1922	115
August	11	2077	1745	110
August	18	3054	2713	95
August	25	2853	2539	127
September	1	3385	3035	97
September	8	3078	2724	105
September	15	3129	2818	89
September	22	2456	2195	90
September	29	1961	1732	81
October	6	1831	1641	71
October	13	1312	1146	73
October	20	766	642	67
October	27	625	508	75
November	3	737	594	70
November	10	585	442	65
November	17	384	251	64
November	24	198	105	58
December	1	223	102	64
December	8	163	55	72
December	15	200	96	71
December	22	168	74	70

The totall of all that hath beene buried
this yeare——————38244
Whereof of the Plague——30578
Christnings——————4789

	Buried in all	Of the Plague	
Albones in Woodstreet	183	164	London within the Walles.
Alhallowes Lumberstreet	159	98	
Alhallowes the great	286	250	
Athalowes the lesse	227	182	
Alhallowes Bredstreet	33		
Alhallowes stayings	123	103	
Aloallowes the Wall	216	174	
Alhallowes Hony-lane	12	5	
Alhallowes Barking	390	339	
Alphage at Cripplegate	174	182	
Androwes in the Wardrope	29	256	
Androwes Eastcheape	114	108	
Androwes vndershaft	165	142	
Annes at Aldersgate	146	125	
Annes Blacke Fryers	235	226	
Auntlins Parish	32	27	
Auslins Parish	92	78	
Barthelmew at the Exch.	93	83	
Bennets at Pauls Wharf	199	136	
Bennets Grace-Church	47		
Bennets Finck	95		
Bennets Sherhogg	26		
Buttols Billingsgate	91	73	
Christ Church Parish	334	271	
Christophers Parish	41	35	
Clementes Eastcheape	48	40	
Dennis Backe Church	112	88	
Dunstones in the East	227	197	
Edmundes in Lumbard-st.	78	67	
Ethelburow within Bishopsg.	163	124	
S. Faithes	115	96	
S. Fosters in Foster-lane	94	81	
Gabriel Fan-Church	56		
George Botolph lane	36		
Gregories by Paules	272	217	
Hellens within Bishopsg.	98	83	
Iames by Garlicke hithe	141	110	
Iohn Euangelist	9		
Iohn Zacharie	111		
Iohns in the Walbrooke	136	118	
Katherines Cree-Church	400		
Katherine Colemans	190	167	
Laurence in the Iury	88		
Laurence Pountney	161	114	
Leonards Foster-lane	230	212	
Leonards Eastcheape	54	39	
Magnus parish by the Bridge	109	76	
Margrets New fishstreete	83	61	
Margrets Pattons	54	44	
Margrets Moyses	70	63	
Margrets Lothbery	106	83	
Martins in the Vintry	238	190	
Martins Orgars	90	77	
Martins Iremonger lane	27	19	
Martins at Ludgate	199	161	
Martins Outwich	39	32	
Mary le Bote	26	24	
Mary Bothaw	35	31	
Mary at the hill	131	126	
Mary Abchurch	123	11	
Mary Woolchurch		17	
Mary Colchurch		8	
Mary Woolnoth			
Mary Aldermary		68	
Mary Aldermanbury			
Mary Staynings			
Mary Mount-haw	97	43	
Mary Sommerset	97	177	
Mary Fanchurch	16		
Martin Milke-street	32		
Maudlins in Oldfishstreet	126	109	
Mighels Bassieshawe	141		
Mighels Corne hill		91	
Mighels in Woodstreet	156	137	
Mighels in the Ryall	110	79	
Mighels in the Querne	61	46	
Mighels Quene-hithe	138	105	
Mighels Crooked lane	110	97	
Mildreds Poultry	81	62	
Mildreds Bredstreet	41	32	
Nicholas Acons	41	32	
Nicholas Cole-abbay	147	12	
Nicholas Olaues	83	69	
Olaues in the Iury	41	33	
Olaues in Hartstreet	171		
Olaues in Siluer street	113	92	
Pancras by Sopar lane	20	16	
Peters in Cornehill	141	80	
Peters in the cheape	58	37	
Peters the poore in broad st.	44	39	
Peters at Pauls wharf	97	88	
Stephens in Colman street	363	315	
Stephens in the Walbrook	24	20	
Swithines at London-stone	120	95	
Thomas Apostles	86	64	
Trinity parish	116	108	
Androwes in Holborn	1191	1125	Dunstones in the West	510	412	London without the Walls, and within the Liberties.
Barthelmew the lesse Smith	86	74	Georges in Southwarke	913	804	
Barthelmew the great Smith	195	165	Giles without Cripplegate	2408	1745	
Brides parish	933	805	Olanes in Southwarke	2541	2383	
Buttols Algate	1413	1280	Sauiours in Southwarke	1914	1773	
Bridewell Precinct	108	105	Sepulchers parish	2223	1861	
Buttols Bishopsg.	1228	1094	Thomas in Southwarke	249	221	
Buttols without Aldersg.	576	548	Trinity in the Minories	49	33	
Clements without Templeb.	662	502	Martins in the Fields	505	425	Out Parishes adioyning to the City.
Giles in the fields	456	402	Mary Whitechappell	1539	1352	
Iames at Clarkenwel	725	619	Magdalens in Barmondsey			
Katherines by the Tower	653	585	streete	597	562	
Leonards in Sboreditch	871	740	At the Pest-house	135	135	

Buried in all, within these 33 weekes————33681.
Whereof, of the Plague————29033.

Printed by Iohn Windet, Printer to the Honourable City of London.

The Yearly Bill for 1603

so that almost a sixth of the inhabitants perished in one
year. And yet in spite of this appalling mortality the
christenings, reduced in 1604, had regained their customary
number in 1605. London's vitality is also clearly shown
in the speed with which it returned to its normal activities.
A spell of cold weather set in towards the end of November and the infection rapidly diminished. By the first
week of December the rich runaways were returning,[1] and
emigrants from the country began to fill the gaps left by the
plague's victims. The usual revels held from St. Stephen's
Day to Twelfth Night were pursued as energetically as ever,
and, in spite of the poverty of the Court and of the City,
money was spent lavishly upon plays and fêtes, banquets
and jousts.[2]

With the decrease of the infection the authorities once
more resumed their hold upon the City and enforced the
plague-orders with the utmost rigour. Repeated searches
were made for idle persons and vagabonds, and at the
approach of the dark winter evenings lantern and candle-
light were ordered to be set out at every man's door
' according to ancient order and usage '.[3] Towards the
end of January 1604 the deaths from the plague had
fallen to 15. A fortnight later there were 27 in the City
alone, seventeen parishes being infected. The increase
may be attributed to the careless use of the bedding and
clothes of infected persons.[4] The long-deferred ceremony
of the King's triumphal entry into the City took place on
15 March, the three poets commissioned to write the

[1] *The First Letter Book of the East India Company* (ed. Sir G.
Birdwood), 39.
[2] *Cal. S. P. Ven.*, 1603–1607, 126 and 129. See also above,
p. 111.   [3] *J.* xxvi. 141 b.
[4] *Cal. S. P. Ven.*, 1603–1607, 130, 132, 133.

pageants being Dekker, Jonson, and Middleton. Dekker tells us that

' The Streets seemde to bee paved with men : Stalles in stead of rich wares were set out with children, open Casements fild up with women . . . hee that should have compared the emptie and untroden walkes of *London*, which were to be seen in that late mortally-destroying Deluge, with the thronged streetes now, might have believed, that upon this day, began a new *Creation*, and that the Citie was the onely Workhouse wherein sundry Nations were made '.[1]

The weekly deaths from the plague in March were 15, 10, 17, and 16.[2] The longer days and warmer weather were approaching and the plague had not yet been shaken off. On 29 March the Lord Mayor had again to complain of the negligence with which all orders were observed, particularly by constables, beadles, and parish clerks.[3] James's first Parliament, after waiting for some time for the sickness to cease, met at Westminster on 19 March, and two months later was read the Bill ' for the charitable Relief and ordering of persons infected with the Plague '. The fear that any increase in the mortality would lead to the adjournment of Parliament elsewhere caused the Lord Mayor and his colleagues to redouble their activities. The deaths from the plague in April were 17, 20, 10, 19, and in May 20, 20, 24, 34. A further rise was expected, and all who could began to look out for a house in the country. But to everybody's joy and surprise the infection greatly diminished, and the weekly plague-deaths in June were only 14, 11, 16, and 9.[4] The weather was

---

[1] *The Magnificent Entertainment* (1604), sig. B 3ᵛ (Dekker's *Dramatic Works*, 1873, i. 277).

[2] See *Cal. S. P. Ven.* for these figures.

[3] *J.* xxvi. 188.

[4] The figures are from *Cal. S. P. Ven.*

extraordinarily cold for the time of the year, furs being worn even so late as 20 June,[1] and this, it was thought, had much to do with the decrease.

In the country, however, the plague was raging fiercely, so that London was now the healthiest place in the kingdom. The tables were turned with a vengeance, and citizens, with bitter memories of the treatment they had received in 1603, took pleasure in discouraging the approach of the ' country Hobbinols '. The King abandoned all thought of making a progress into the country, and spent most of his time at Greenwich, Oatlands, Windsor, Theobalds, and other residences near London. The City took alarm in August when the infection increased in ' extraordinary sort ', but more attention was paid to the segregation of the sick and to the cleanliness of the streets, and the mortality rapidly decreased. Several orders relating to the condition of the poor in parishes like St. Sepulchre's and St. Giles's, Cripplegate, show that though the plague had diminished it had left an aftermath of misery.[2]   In December Parliament, which had been prorogued on 7 July 1604 and was to have met on 7 February 1605, was put off until October for fear of bringing the infection to London. The plague frequently served James as a convenient pretext for the prorogation of a parliament which had already incurred his displeasure.

It is unnecessary to examine in detail the history of the plague during the next few years. In none of these years was the City entirely clear, and in none was the plague serious enough to cause a recurrence of the scenes

---

[1] *Cal. S. P. Ven.*, 1603–1607, 164.
[2] *J.* xxvi. 240, 241 b, and 292.

witnessed in 1603. The annual mortality and number of christenings were as follows : [1]

				Total deaths.	*Of the plague.*	*Christened.*
1604	.	.	.	5,219	896	5,458
1605	.	.	.	6,392	444	6,504
1606	.	.	.	7,920	2,124	6,614
1607	.	.	.	8,022	2,352	6,582
1608	.	.	.	9,020	2,262	6,845
1609	.	.	.	11,785	4,240	6,388
1610	.	.	.	9,087 [2]	1,803	6,785
1611	.	.	.	7,343	627	7,014

Throughout this period the plague was most deadly in the hot weather, and in several years its activities were confined almost entirely to the autumn. In 1605 it did not become serious until September. It is true that on 28 July Parliament was prorogued from 3 October to 5 November, but this was partly because of the greater convenience of the later date and partly because of the fear that the arrival of people from all quarters of the realm, ' in many parts whereof there may yet remain some part of the dregs of the late contagion ', might revive the infection. By 13 September the plague had invaded all parts of the City and suburbs, including Southwark and Middlesex.[3] Early in October, however, the weekly plague-deaths had fallen to 22, the smallpox being more serious than the plague.[4] But precautions and restrictions do not seem to have been relaxed until Christmas.

In 1606 the infection became noticeable in March, and

---

[1] John Graunt, *Natural and Political Observations* (1676) and John Bell, *Londons Remembrancer* (1665/6). The figures for 1605 and 1611 are only given by Graunt. For the weekly totals from July to December 1606–1610 see Note L, p. 186.

[2] Graunt gives 9,289.   [3] *J.* xxvi. 366 and 372.

[4] *Cal. S. P. Ven.*, 1603–1607, 281.

the authorities quickly and vigorously enforced the plague-orders.[1] In the last week of July the deaths from the plague were 66 and steadily increasing. The wrestling usually performed before the Lord Mayor and aldermen on St. Bartholomew's Day was prohibited, though the usual games of shooting were permitted. In September, Michaelmas Term was adjourned, and all trials by juries in the City forborne.[2] The plague decreased somewhat in November, but was still in Newgate on 9 December, when the keeper was allowed £2 a week towards the relief of the poor prisoners there for so long as the infection should continue.[3]

The plague survived the winter of 1606–1607 and was spreading in the suburbs in March. The increase was attributed to the weather, which was unseasonably hot, to the continuance of plays, and to the lack of good order in Middlesex, particularly in Whitechapel, Shoreditch, Clerkenwell, and other ' remote ' parts.[4] At the request of the Lord Mayor the Privy Council commanded the Justices of Middlesex to see that better order was preserved. By the end of the year the plague was almost overcome. The credit for the victory must be given to the weather rather than to the magistrates. On 15 December the City streets were pestered with snow and frost,[5] and by Twelfth Day the Thames above Westminster was quite frozen over, the Archbishop coming from Lambeth to Court over the ice.[6]

[1] Cf. *R.* xxvii. 191 and *J.* xxvii. 35 b, 72, and 74 b.
[2] *R.* xxvii. 256 b and 278.
[3] *R.* xxvii. 312 b. In July 1607 the warden of the Fleet prison was allowed to remove such prisoners as he thought fit to a convenient house in the country. Cf. B.M. Addit. MS. 11402, fo. 128 b.   [4] *Remembrancia*, ii. 90.   [5] *J.* xxvii. 205.
[6] *The Court and Times of James the First*, i. 71.

The dearth of corn and all kinds of food caused in the spring of 1608 by this severe weather was so serious that compulsory fast-days were appointed. In July the plague, assisted by the scarcity of food, again alarmed the magistrates. A new set of orders devised by the Lord Mayor and aldermen, in collaboration with the Privy Council and neighbouring Justices of the Peace, was read out in each parish church every Sunday,[1] and on 20 September Carleton was able to testify that ' there be very good order taken more than usual '.[2] But the sickness clung to the City throughout the winter.

In January 1609 the plague was more widely spread than it had ever been at that time of the year, and energetic measures were taken for the dispersal of rogues and vagabonds and the shutting up of infected houses.[3] In spite of these measures and the coldness of the season, by the end of January the plague was killing off about sixty a week and was spreading rapidly. People began to think of withdrawing into the country, as a great scourge was expected with the arrival of the hot season. In the week ending 23 February as many as twenty-six parishes were infected.[4] Carleton on 20 February wrote of the increase of the sickness in the past week, proceeding, he hoped, from the extreme sharp weather, ' which made a quick riddance of the sick and diseased whereby the whole will be better assured '.[5] The plague-deaths had decreased one-half by the beginning of March, but in April the infection again became active, and was rivalled

---

[1] *J.* xxvii. 238 b and 271 b.
[2] *S. P. Dom., Jas. I*, vol. 36, Doc. 23.
[3] *J.* xxvii. 319.   [4] See the plague-bill on p. 198.
[5] *S. P. Dom., Jas. I*, vol. 43, Doc. 81.

in deadliness by an epidemic of smallpox. By 8 June the town was very empty and solitary, ' there being nothing thought on, by reason of the sickness, but fugae et for- midines '.[1] The infection in the summer was not so deadly as was feared, though by the end of August, owing, it was said, to the unripe fruit which the poor ate, it was more serious than it had been for some years. The weather was so bad that the crops could not be gathered, and the harvest lay rotting in the fields. This was the more deplorable in that drought had ruined the hay-crop.[2] In spite of these calamities St. Bartholomew's Fair was held on 25 August to everybody's surprise, and the usual money prizes were bestowed by the City in a game of shooting held in the afternoon of that day in Finsbury Fields. [3] These reckless tactics, coupled with a continu- ance of the bad weather, spread the infection about the country, and the Court fled from one place to another harassed by fear of the sickness. In London the number of plague-deaths passed the second hundred in Septem- ber, when the infection had spread to the best and most open streets. By the end of October, however, the fall in the death-rate tempted the nobility back to town. Early in December the weather was cold and dry and the plague had almost disappeared. Its virulence in this year was far more severe than in any other year between 1603 and 1625, and the total mortality was greater by 2,000 than in any year from 1604 to 1623.

The year 1610 began auspiciously. The fourth session of James's first Parliament opened on 9 February when

[1] *The Court and Times of James the First*, i. 96 and 100 (Carleton to Edmondes).
[2] *Cal. S. P. Ven.*, 1607–1610, 326.   [3] *J.* xxvii. 399 b.

the City was freer from the infection than it had been for many months. The news that a Spanish proclamation had forbidden all trade with London at Seville and other places was the more surprising and caused the more offence. It was rumoured that this action was prompted by the desire of some other nation to stop English rivalry in trade.[1] The plague was fairly quiet until August when it greatly increased, though not to the extent of previous years. Yet the mortality was great enough to make the bills a common subject of conversation.[2] In September the infection was decreasing, and by 15 November the weekly deaths from the plague were only 22. A month later they were only 12, and for fourteen years the plague ceased to be a thorn in the side of the London populace.

In 1611 the deaths from the plague were 627, and in the following year 64, but from 1613 to 1624 the City was extraordinarily free. The plague-deaths in these years were 16, 22, 37, 9, 6, 18, 9, 21, 11, 16, 17, and 11.[3] This total of 193 in twelve years was easily surpassed in 1603 and 1625 by the weekly mortality of a single parish. A history of the disease during these years is a history of false alarms causing a renewed attention to precautionary measures for a few weeks but creating little disquietude outside the small circle of statesmen and magistrates whose business it was to safeguard the health of the City. In September 1617, for example, the plague was very prevalent and deadly in the United Provinces and had

[1] *Cal. S. P. Ven.*, 1607–1610, 427. See also *Cal. S. P. Dom.*, 1603–1610, 596.

[2] *J.* xxviii. 86. In Donne's fourteenth Elegy, written almost certainly in 1610, a gallant strikes up an acquaintance with a citizen and his wife by asking ' the number of the Plaguy Bill ' (*Poems*, ed. Grierson, i. 106).

[3] John Graunt, *Natural and Political Observations* (1676).

spread into the Archduke's dominions. The constant
traffic and commerce with the Low Countries made the
position of London very dangerous : in John Chamberlain's words, ' we cannot but apprehend that *nostra res
agitur*, when so near a neighbour's house is on fire '.[1] No
bedding, feathers, and other household stuff from
Amsterdam or any infected places in the Low Countries
were allowed to be landed at the Port of London or at any
other place on the Thames, until the sickness had ceased
in Holland.[2] In October 1619, when the plague was very
severe at Rouen, two ships from that town were forced to
remain at Tilbury for twenty-five days before they were
permitted to dispose of their cargo.[3] Again in July 1623
William Gore was fined by the Eastland merchants for
introducing hemp from Elbing, where the plague was then
raging,[4] and in the following month, when Paris and
several other French towns were infected, great care was
taken to prevent the infection from being introduced into
this country by the various commodities with which France
furnished Bartholomew Fair.[5]

But though the plague held off, the health of the City
was troubled by other diseases. The autumn of 1612 and
the summer and autumn of 1616 were noteworthy for two
severe agues which raged through the country and carried
off many people including several of good note. After
a hard winter and a cool summer, an epidemic of smallpox

---

[1] *The Court and Times of James the First*, ii. 30.

[2] *P. C. R.* xxix. 135, 138, and 147.

[3] *P. C. R.* xxx. 307. The Italian regulations as to quarantine
were much more drastic. At Venice in October 1614 restrictions
were still placed on goods coming from England, though that
country had been uninfected for at least two years. Cf. *Cal. S. P.
Ven.*, 1613–1615, 216.

[4] *Cal. S. P. Dom.*, 1623–1625, 18.   [5] *P. C. R.* xxxii. 93.

was rife in the December of 1621.[1] In the main, however, the health of the City from 1611 to 1622 was good, the average mortality for these twelve years being 8,158. But in the two years which heralded the plague of 1625, the total mortality was, in 1623, 11,112, and in 1624, 12,210. In 1623 ' a contagious, spotted or purple fever ' and the smallpox killed off men and women of all classes. In August 1624 many were sick of the ' spotted ague '. The weekly mortality in the middle of the month was 318, a greater number than had been reached since 1609.[2] By the end of the month the weekly mortality was 407, including 150 children.

But before describing the insidious approach of the epidemic of 1625 let us examine the effect which the plague had upon the theatre and the drama during the interval between the plagues of 1603 and 1625. It is a great stroke of good fortune that in those formative years of the Elizabethan drama, from 1584 to 1602, the theatres (except for the plague-years of 1592 and 1593) suffered little or no interruption from the plague. If the City had been as unhealthy in these years as it was from 1603 to 1610, the result might have been disastrous. It has been seen that from 1604 the theatres were usually closed when the plague-deaths reached 30 (and afterwards 40) a week. If we assume for the moment that the system of automatic restraint was carried out with absolute precision, then the theatres were closed during the following weeks and months from 1606 to 1610 : 10 July 1606 to 8 January 1607 (except the fortnight from 20 November to 4 December and the week from the 18th to the 25th December) ;

---

[1] *The Court and Times of James the First*, i. 203, 422, and ii. 278.
[2] J. Chamberlain, *Letters*, ed. McClure, ii. 531, 576, 579.

5–12 February 1607 ; 12–26 March ; 30 April–7 May ;
9 July–26 November ; 28 July 1608 to 7 December 1609 ; [1]
12 July 1610 to 15 November and during the week 22–9
November. From 1611 to 1625 the plague had little if
any effect upon the theatres, whatever may have been
the effect of diseases like the ague and smallpox.

It remains to mention the evidence from contemporary
documents which bears upon the closing of the theatres.
After the opening of the theatres on 9 April 1604 the
players seem to have been left alone for eighteen months :
then on 5 October 1605 the Lord Mayor and the Justices
of the Peace for Middlesex and Surrey were ordered to
forbid stage-plays on account of the infection. On
15 December the restraint was withdrawn and the King's,
Queen's, and Prince's players were permitted ' to play
and recite their interludes at their accustomed places '.[2]
On 12 April 1607 the Lord Mayor asked the Lord Chamberlain to put down all stage-plays on account of the increase
of infection in the skirts and confines of the City.[3] The
letter is characteristic of the City's hostility, for the
deaths from the plague in the preceding week were only 23.
From Dekker's *Jests to make you Merie* (entered in the Stationers' Register on 6 October 1607) it appears that during
the summer the players, much to the disgust and poverty

---

[1] By 1609 the number of plague-deaths sufficient to close the
theatres had changed from 30 to 40 (see above, p. 54). In this
year the plague-deaths were less than 40 but more than 30 in the
weeks ending 2 March, 16 March, and 15 June. I have only taken
into consideration those weeks in 1610 in which the plague-deaths
were 40 or more. Weekly statistics for 1604, 1605, and 1611 are
not extant : the total yearly deaths from the plague were 896,
444, and 627.

[2] B.M. Addit. MS. 11402, fos. 107 and 109.

[3] *Remembrancia*, ii. 90. Cf. P. Gawdy, *Letters*, ed. Jeayes, 160.

of the poets, were strolling in the country ' making fooles
of the poore countrey people, in driving them like flocks of
Geese to sit cackling in an old barne : and to swallow
downe those playes, for new, which here every punck and
her squire (like the Interpreter and his poppet) can rand
out by heart, they are so stale and therefore so stincking '.[1]
A proclamation forbidding plays was issued in the autumn
of 1608, and William Pollard and Rice Gwynn were
both committed to Newgate on 17 November by the
London Court of Aldermen ' for that they yesterday last
suffered a stage play to be publicly acted in the White-
friars during the time of the present infection contrary to
his Majesty's late proclamation '.[2]   The King's players
were granted a reward of £40 on 26 April 1609 ' for their
private practice in the time of infection that thereby they
might be enabled to perform their service before his
Majesty in Christmas holiday '.   In 1609, as we learn
from Dekker, the doors of the playhouses were all locked
and the flags taken down.   The poets' muses were as
sullen as old monkeys, for their patrons were gone.   The
bears of Paris Garden, however, still performed, and ' the
pide *Bul* heere keepes a tossing and a roaring, when the *Red
Bull* dares not stir '.[3]   On 10 March 1610 the King's
men received £30, ' being restrained from public playing
within the city of London in the time of infection during
the space of six weeks in which time they practised

[1] Sig. H 4ᵛ (*G.* ii. 352).   For records of the travels of London
companies in the country from 1604 to 1610 see J. T. Murray,
op. cit., i. 148–55 and 209.
[2] *R.* xxviii. 301.   Both men seem to be unknown to historians
of the theatre.   The proclamation is not known to be extant.
[3] *Worke for Armorours*, sig. B 1 (*G.* iv. 97).   Creighton (i. 494)
is in error in stating that the passage occurs in *The Seven deadly
Sinnes* (1606).

privately for his Majesty's service '.[1]   On 20 April 1610 Simon Forman saw *Macbeth* acted at the Globe Theatre, and ten days later *Othello* was played there before Lewis Frederick, Prince of Württemberg.

During these plague-stricken years from 1603 to 1611 Shakespeare wrote the tragedies which plumb the depths of human suffering, and the romantic comedies which unite so strangely scenes of an almost feverish excitement and of the deepest and loveliest serenity.   The London plagues may have caused him to spend the more time in Stratford, and may, indeed, have hastened his retirement : but when we remember that to these years belong his greatest masterpieces we cannot suppose that his plays suffered because they were not written ' under the same direct influence of playhouse atmosphere which inspired his earlier comedies and historical plays '.[2]   According to a contemporary playgoer, the work of other dramatists became worse instead of better after the cessation of the plague and the reopening of the theatres.   Writing on 5 January 1615, when Shakespeare had withdrawn to Stratford and was spending the remainder of his days ' in ease, retirement and the conversation of his friends ', John Chamberlain informed Sir Dudley Carleton that

' they have plays at Court every night both Holidays and working-days, wherein they shew great patience, being for

---

[1] P. Cunningham, *Extracts from the Accounts of the Revels at Court*, xxxix–xl.   The ' six weeks ' I take to be from the end of October, when the players would be waiting in London for the plague to cease, till the Christmas season of 1609–10, during which thirteen plays were acted before the Court by the King's players, and eleven by other companies.   Cf. the extracts from the Pipe Rolls printed by Sir Edmund Chambers in *The Modern Language Review*, iv. 154.   The private practice would be perhaps at the private theatre in the Blackfriars, which the King's players had acquired in 1608.   [2] Creighton, *op. cit.*, i. 496.

the most part such poor stuff that instead of delight they send the auditory away with discontent : indeed our poets' brains and invention are grown very dry insomuch that of five new plays there is not one pleases, and therefore are driven to furbish over their old, which stand them in best stead, and bring them most profit '.[1]

[1] *S. P. Dom., Jas. I*, vol. 80, Doc. 1.   Printed in *The Court and Times of James the First*, i. 290.

MEMENTO MORI

It is appointed for all men once to die, Heb: 9.2 ſ.

And as i am, ſo muſt you be,
Therefore prepare to follow me

ſOVLD BY THOMAS WRIGHT

A Memento Mori.

V

THE PLAGUE OF 1625

THE mortality during the latter half of 1624 was exceptionally high. Though the plague held aloof, the spotted fever then prevalent was thought to be cousin-german and made almost as quick riddance of its victims.[1] After an unusually hot and dry summer the fruit-crop was abundant, but the poverty of the other crops, following on the two bad harvests of 1622 and 1623, caused a famine in the northern shires, and many were forced to live on boiled nettles or to eat swine, sheep, and horses that had died by chance.[2] In September there was an extraordinary number of cucumbers, and the general ill-health was ingeniously ascribed to the gardeners' practice of watering them from ditches which owing to the drought were ' low, noisome and stinking '.[3] On 1 October Parliament was prorogued from 2 November to 16 February on account of ' a general sickness and disease which proves mortal to many and infectious to more ', which had dispersed itself in London and Westminster.[4] When the year 1625 opened, the weather was unseasonably warm and mild, and the bills continued high. On 26 February occurred the highest tide ' known in the memory of man '. Much damage was done in Thames Street and all along the river side. Westminster Hall was flooded with three feet of water. More serious still was ' the drowning of the

---

[1] *The Court and Times of James the First*, ii. 471, and *D. P. P.* 179.   [2] Wither, *Britain's Remembrancer* (1628), 124.
[3] *The Court and Times of James the First*, ii. 473.
[4] *J*. xxxii. 320 b.

marshes, and overthrowing the walls in Kent, Essex, Lincolnshire, Yorkshire, and other places near the sea, to an exceeding hindrance and desolation'.[1] March ushered in the spring with 'windy and obstreperous rage', and the month went out with snow, rain, hail, and winds.[2]

The returns for the first three months of 1625 were as follows : [3]

Week ending.		Buried in all.	Of the plague.	Parishes infected.
December	23	183	0	0
,,	30	211	0	0
January	6	220	1	1
,,	13	196	1	1
,,	20	240	0	0
,,	27	226	0	0
February	3	174	3	1
,,	10	204	5	2
,,	17	211	3	1
,,	24	252	1	1
March	3	207	0	0
,,	10	210	0	0
,,	17	262	4	3
,,	24	226	8	2
,,	31	243	11	4

The infection of 1625 like that of 1603 was perhaps introduced from Holland. In August 1624 the Hague and other towns in the Low Countries were infected ' with much contagious and pestilential sickness ', and precautions were taken by the Privy Council to prevent the importation of goods from these towns.[4] ' It is fresh in memory ', wrote the Lord Mayor of 1663, ' that the Contagion which proved so fatal in 1625 was conveyed hither from Holland.' [5]   But some were not content

[1] J. Chamberlain, Letters, ed. McClure, ii. 604.
[2] Thomas Heywood, A Funeral Elegie (1625), sig. B 4.
[3] The statistics of infected parishes are taken from John Bell's Londons Remembrancer (1665/6).
[4] P. C. R. xxxii. 420.   [5] Remembrancia, ix. 70.

with this simple explanation. One writer laid the
blame on some rotten mutton, another made guilty of
these disasters the sun, the moon, and the stars,[1] while
a zealous divine preached publicly that it was sent at
Easter time, ' when a multitude of miscreant people came
unprepared, and unworthily, hand over head, to receive
the Sacrament '.[2]

Of the eight plague-deaths in the week ending 24 March
no less than seven occurred in one parish.[3] This parish
was almost certainly St. Botolph's-without-Bishopsgate.
Its inhabitants were granted £10 by the Court of Aldermen
for ' their extraordinary charge and expenses ' in the
relief of infected poor as early as 31 March.[4] Wither
writes of the plague stealing into London and lurking in

> The well-fill'd Suburbs ; spreading there (no doubt)
> Infection unperceiv'd, in many a place
> Before the bleare-ey'd *Searchers*, knew her face ; . . .
> But at the length, she was discover'd at
> A *Frenchmans* house without the *Bishopsgate*.

The Privy Council noted the increase of the plague in
London on 25 March, and rebuked the Lord Mayor and
aldermen for neglecting to enforce the customary orders—
' which if you shall farther neglect, you may be assured

[1] See above, pp. 6 and 86.
[2] *Lachrymae Londinenses* (1626), 14.   [3] *P. C. R.* xxxii. 708.
[4] *R.* xxxix. 158. H. L'Estrange in *The Reign of King Charles*
(1656), p. 8, states that the plague broke out in Whitechapel on
the same day and under the same roof as that of 1603, and
the neighbourhood with its crowded dwellings and insanitary
slaughter-houses certainly offered a fruitful ground for the spread
of the infection. Cf. also *The City Remembrancer* (1769), i. 267,
and *Hist. MSS. Comm.*, 11th Report, Appendix I, 26. Richard
Kephale in *Medela Pestilentiae* (1665), p. 2, asserts that the plague
began in Stepney : but the first plague-death recorded in that
parish was in the week ending 21 April. See a bill of mortality
for outlying districts in *S. P. Dom., Chas. I*, vol. 12, Doc. 39.

that an Accompt will be demanded at your hands '. The
infection, the Council pointed out, had been on the increase for several weeks, and had preventive measures
been adopted at the outset, it might have been ' stayed '.[1]
But despite the care of privy councillors and magistrates
the plague steadily increased :

Week ending.	Buried in all.	Of the plague.	Parishes infected.
April 7	239	10	4
,, 14	256	24	10
,, 21	230	25	11
,, 28	305	26	9
May 5	292	30	10
,, 12	332	45	13
,, 19	379	71	17
,, 26	401	78	16
June 2	395	69	20
,, 9	434 [2]	91	25
,, 16	510	165	31
,, 23	640	239	32
,, 30	942	390	50

The weather during these months was not without its
influence on the infection. April was ' healthful ' and
there was a fine show of blossom,[3] but frosts spoilt the
promise of the spring, Chamberlain asserting on 12 June
that the country had experienced for a month together
' the extremest cold weather ever I knew in this season '.[4]
June was diseased, and a ' ceaseless ' rain fell for a month
to the great detriment of all kinds of crops.[5] ' And wee

[1] P. C. R. xxxii. 708–9. Another letter was sent four days later.
[2] So Bell. The bill reads in error ' 401 '. Salvetti, writing on
10 June 1625, gives 445. Cf. Hist. MSS. Comm., 11th Report,
Appendix I, 21.
[3] Taylor, The Fearefull Sommer (1625—the later and enlarged
edition), sig. A 5ᵛ, and Wither, op. cit., 124 b.
[4] The Court and Times of Charles the First, i. 28.
[5] See below, p. 138. On 1 July the Venetian ambassador wrote
of ' the bad weather which threatens scarcity ' (Cal. S. P. Ven.,
1625–1626, 107).

cannot forget ', wrote a London physician about Midsum-
mer, ' what a hot and dry parching Summer we had this
last yeare ; . . . which now being seconded with such
abundance of moyst weather all this Spring and Summer
hitherto ; we may well doubt that a deluge of destruction
is comming upon us '.[1]

The ' great ' plague of 1625 was heralded like that of
1603 by the death of the sovereign.   King James died on
27 March in the fifty-seventh year of his age and the
twenty-third of his reign.   He had outstayed his welcome,
and his decease was accompanied by none of the marks of
genuine sorrow with which the nation had shown its regard
for Elizabeth.   Charles quickly showed signs of his anxiety
for the welfare of his subjects by his efforts, directed
through the Privy Council, to check the growth of the
infection in London.[2]   On 5 April the Council pointed out
to the Justices of the Peace for Middlesex, Surrey, and
Westminster, the great danger which might ensue from the
infection ' unless the farther spreading thereof be carefully
prevented now at the beginning, especially considering
how great a confluence of people there will be in regard of
the funeral of our late Sovereign Lord, the Coronation of
his Majesty that now is, and the Parliament '.   The Lord
Mayor, it appears, had complained to the Council of the
multitude of poor and vagabond people who flocked into
the City from the outlying parts, and the Justices for these
districts were sternly charged to take better order for the
suppression of vagrants, for the removal of inmates, and
for the greater cleanliness of the streets.[3]

[1] Stephen Bradwell, *A Watch-Man for the Pest* (1625), 5.
[2] Cf. *The Court and Times of Charles the First*, i. 11 : ' Our king
is very careful for the whole city against the plague ' (13 April).
[3] *P. C. R.* xxxiii. 12.

The mortality from the plague in April was certainly greater than that returned in the bills. Pneumonic plague was more prevalent in 1625 than in 1603, and the absence of buboes upon so many corpses led physicians and searchers alike to mistake the cause of death. The bill for the week ending 28 April points clearly to wrong diagnosis. The total deaths were 75 more than in the preceding week, yet the plague-deaths showed an increase only of one. No doubt many of these 75 deaths were caused by pneumonic plague.[1]

By the end of April the infection had invaded the City itself, 3 of the 26 plague-deaths occurring within the walls, and 2 of the 9 infected parishes being in the City.[2] The Court of the East India Company were so alarmed that they paid £20 for a second-hand coach to avoid the danger of hiring 'mercenary coaches which are common to all kind of people whole or sick '.[3] At the beginning of May great preparations were made for shows and pageants to celebrate the public entrance of Charles and his Queen into the City, but this ceremony together with the coronation was postponed until October on account of the continued increase of the infection. King James's funeral took place on 7 May with much pomp, though with an abridged ceremonial.

The richer citizens who were not tied to London by official business had begun to leave for the country before the end of April.[4] By 9 June the infection had increased so rapidly and was scattered so dangerously that it was ' somewhat sensibly apprehended now by the Lords and

---

[1] See also below, pp. 207–8.
[2] *The Court and Times of Charles the First*, i. 17.
[3] *London Topographical Record*, viii. 123 (23 April).
[4] *Cal. S. P. Ven.*, 1625–1626, 30.

other strangers that by the occasion of the Parliament are
now about the City '.[1] But the arrival of the Queen and
the opening of Parliament kept many in town whom the
plague would otherwise have frightened away. ' Though
sickness incréase shrewdly upon us,' Chamberlain wrote on
25 June, 'yet we cannot find in our hearts to leave this
town, so long as here is such doings, by reason of the
queen's arrival, and the sitting of the parliament.'[2] Charles
was married to Henrietta Maria by proxy at Notre-
Dame on May Day, and met his bride at Dover on 13 June.
Three days later they entered London by water, and were
welcomed by the ordnance of the fleet at Blackwall and
by the Tower guns. The City bells rang continuously
for seven hours, bonfires were lit in the streets, and the
citizens were ordered to indulge in suitable rejoicings
and triumphs.[3] Parliament, which had been prorogued
on account of disease from 2 November 1624 to 16
February, was further prorogued to 15 March, and again
to 20 April. But owing to the death of James and the
increase of the infection it did not actually assemble till
18 June, to the great displeasure of the knights and burgesses, who had been kept in town for many weeks at
no small danger and expense.[4] Charles in his opening
speech begged the Houses to expedite their business on
account of the plague. A motion in the House of Commons
to adjourn till Michaelmas was rejected, but the members
were in no hurry to vote the subsidies so anxiously
desired by the King for the war against Spain.[5] In the

[1] S. P. Dom., Chas. I, vol. 3, Doc. 44.
[2] J. Chamberlain, Letters, ed. McClure, ii. 624.
[3] J. xxxiii. 129.   [4] Cal. S. P. Ven., 1625–1626, 62, 96.
[5] Cf. S. R. Gardiner, History of England, 1603–1642, vol. v,
chap. lii.

week following the opening of Parliament the plague increased by 74, and, more ominous still, obtained a footing in Westminster itself. In the last week of June eighteen more parishes were infected, making a total of fifty in all. The Houses actually sat for three weeks, and were adjourned on 11 July to meet at Oxford on 1 August. But most members had gone home a week or so before the adjournment,[1] preferring to risk the King's displeasure rather than run the gauntlet of the plague. Parliament was the last of the public assemblies to be put off. A proclamation issued on 17 May prohibited disorderly and unnecessary resort to the Court and postponed any touching for the king's evil until after the coronation. On 18 June Trinity Term was adjourned, and six days later all trials by juries were abandoned.

The plague-deaths for the week ending 30 June were many more than those for the corresponding week in 1603, and this in spite of the cold weather. The prophecy that the infection would increase when the heat should come and the fruit ripen was terribly fulfilled. The returns for July, August, and September show that London was in the clutches of a plague more deadly than any experienced since the days of the Black Death.

Week ending.		Buried in all.	Of the plague.	Parishes. infected.
July	7	1,222	593	57
,,	14	1,741	1,004	82
,,	21	2,850	1,819	96
,,	28	3,583	2,471	103
August	4	4,517	3,659	114
,,	11	4,855	4,115	112
,,	18	5,205	4,463	114
,,	25	4,841	4,218	114

[1] *S. P. Dom., Chas. I*, vol. iv, Doc. 29.

Week ending.	Buried in all.	Of the plague.	Parishes infected.
September 1	3,897	3,344	117
,, 8	3,157	2,550	116
,, 15	2,148	1,672 [1]	107
,, 22	1,994	1,561 [1]	111
,, 29	1,236	852	103

In the outlying districts the infection was slower in spreading, but its effects were not less deadly. The yearly bills of mortality give the following figures.[2] We realize more clearly the devastation wrought by the plague in these districts when we bear in mind that the average weekly mortality from January to April was—in Westminster 11, in Lambeth 3, in Newington 6, in Stepney 20, in Hackney 1, and in Islington 2.

Week ending.	West-minster.	Lam-beth.	Newing-ton.	Step-ney.	Hack-ney.	Isling-ton.
July 7	43·16	7·1	34·18	92·60	1·0	3·1
,, 14	65·27	9·7	37·23	136·104	1·1	10·7
,, 21	89·55	16·6	66·49	171·140	5·4	3·2
,, 28	114·80	16·9	74·55	228·207	15·13	6·6
Aug. 4	125·97	25·16	84·68	274·255	14·12	20·19
,, 11	138·116	32·28	86·65	263·240	27·25	21·16
,, 18	181·150	39·38	66·64	341·328	23·20	31·31
,, 25	137·121	56·52	47·22	299·284	27·25	29·25
Sept. 1	193·164	44·38	32·9	291·278	20·15	33·28
,, 8	175·150	47·36	26·2	271·257	19·13	22·17
,, 15	189·167	47·31	22·0	190·184	10·5	19·14
,, 22	167·150	52·37	22·5	164·144	14·8	24·20
,, 29	116·91	22·17	15·2	121·97	20·12	15·11

Before the adjournment of Parliament the members obtained permission to hold a general fast : ' 1. to give God thanks for the happy succession of his majesty after his father. 2. That his Divine Majesty be pleased to cease

[1] So the contemporary bill. Bell gives 1,652 instead of 1,672 and 1,551 instead of 1,561.

[2] See below, p. 200. The first figure gives the total mortality for the week, the second the mortality from the plague.

the plague. 3rd and lastly, to give good success to the
fleet.' [1] This fast was solemnly held in London on
Saturday, 2 July. The King himself, with the Lords of
the Upper House and the Judges, heard two sermons in
the Abbey. An earl, a bishop, and a baron took the
names of absentees.[2] The House of Commons heard three
sermons at St. Margaret's, Westminster. The first sermon
lasted three hours and each of the other sermons two hours,
yet not a man fainted.[3] On the same day two sermons
were delivered in each parish church in London. Salvetti,
the Tuscan resident at Court, comments with surprise and
some irony on this fast, ' which is performed in all the
parishes, and consists in staying in church all day, singing
psalms, hearing sermons, the one shortly after the other,
and making I know not how many prayers, imploring
God for the stoppage of the plague and of the ceaseless
rain which for a month past has fallen to the detriment
of all kinds of crops, and finally that He may be graciously
pleased to bless the people, to prosper their undertakings,
to give them the victory over all their enemies, and above
all to preserve the purity of their religion '.[4] In addition
to this special ceremony fasts were held on 20 July and
on following Wednesdays, trading being forborne and the

---

[1] *The Court and Times of Charles the First*, i. 34. The fleet
intended against Spain and the Mexican treasure-ships did not
actually sail till 8 October, and then to fail completely in the
accomplishment of its mission.

[2] *Ibid.* 38. See also *The Autobiography and Correspondence of
Sir Simonds D'Ewes* (ed. J. O. Halliwell, 1845), i. 272. A collection
was taken at the service, and those members of the House of Lords
who were absent on 2 July and then paid nothing to the poor,
were ordered to pay double on 10 August. See *Journals of the
House of Lords*, 1625, 1 *Car.* I. 486.

[3] *Diary of Walter Yonge* (Camden Soc., 1848), pp. 85, 86.

[4] *Hist. MSS. Comm.*, 11th Report, Appendix I, 26.

days observed as much as any festival day.[1] On the last
day of July, however, the Privy Council requested the
Archbishops of Canterbury and York to forbid infected
parishes to meet publicly for the celebration of the fast ;
they were to observe their devotions privately in their own
houses.   At the same time churchwardens in ' clear '
parishes were to be careful not to admit people from
infected parishes.[2] The Council's action was condemned
by many, Wither denying that any died in church :

> For, ev'n thither
> Resorted I, where thronged were together
> The greatest multitudes : And day by day
> I sate, where all the croud I could survay.
> Yet, I nor man, nor childe, nor woman saw,
> To sinke, looke pale, or from their place withdraw.

The rain which had fallen during most of the month of
June continued for the first few weeks of July, and it was
feared that the plague would be accompanied by a famine :
' the hands of God stretched out daily more and more
against us by the increase of His plague in this City, and
the spreading thereof in the country, doth cause such
a distraction and consternation in men's minds that the
like was never seen in our age. . . . Now men make hay
standing up to the ankles in water.' [3] The London bills

---

[1] Locke (*S. P. Dom.*, *Chas. I*, vol. iv, Doc. 29) writes that the
first Wednesday fast was held on 6 July, but in the proclamation
dated 3 July they were ordered to begin on 20 July. Copies of
the form of prayer observed at these services are in the British
Museum and the Bodleian.

[2] *P. C. R.* xxxiii. 86 b.   Yet five days later Sir Allen Apsley
informed Sir John Coke that without order, fear, or restraint the
infected and the sound went to church together as if they had
no plague among them. Cf. *Hist. MSS. Comm.*, 12th Report,
Appendix I, 209.

[3] *S. P. Dom.*, *Chas. I.*, vol. iv, Doc. 61 (16 July).

topped the third thousand in July. The air seemed infected, and many succumbed suddenly when walking in the streets.[1] Sir John Gore was unfortunate enough to be Lord Mayor in this year : his house was infected early in June, and he was forced to shut up his doors and forsake the town, leaving Sir Thomas Bennet as his deputy.[2] But even Wither, who had no love for those in power, admitted that Gore steered his Court with good diligence, and stayed at the helm till his place was filled. He had returned to his post by July. Most of the aldermen and minor officials fled into the country. On 6 August the Lord Mayor complained that many constables, church-wardens, and collectors for the poor had carelessly left the City ' void of all government ' and had run away without appointing deputies.[3]   The beadles took the names of all defaulters, but it was more difficult to fill their places.

The disorder in the City and especially in the suburbs became evident in July. On the 20th the Privy Council, reminding the Lord Mayor and aldermen of the enforced absence of the King and Council, implored them not to abandon the City, but to continue and increase all the usual means for repressing the contagion, and in particular to be very vigilant in all other emergencies concerning the Government.[4] Ten days later Gore replied with modest dignity that the plague had not then raged so fiercely within the walls and liberties of the City as in the outskirts, ' where the parishes stretch into other Counties, and where the

---

[1] *Cal. S. P. Ven.*, 1625–1626, 130.

[2] *The Court and Times of Charles the First*, i. 29.   Bennet had been Lord Mayor in 1603–1604, and the experience he gained in that year would be of great service to the City in 1625.

[3] *J.* xxxiii. 130.   [4] *Remembrancia*, vi. 62.

multitudes of Inmates are without measure. . . . I have
not hitherto been wanting in the personal execution of my
Charge without respect of the present danger.' [1]

Runaways from London were now carrying the infection
into the country. On 19 July the Privy Council called the
attention of the Justices of Middlesex to the multitudes
of inmates sheltered by the inhabitants of Tottenham.
Newcomers were ordered to be removed and no more were
to be received. The inhabitants of Godalming were so
frightened of London tradesmen and London wares that
on 14 June they petitioned the Privy Council to prohibit
their fair.[2] In June also the Mayor and aldermen of
Bristol, bearing in mind the great danger of pestilence and
remembering their ' lamentable success ' on the like
occasion in 1603, desired the Council to forbid the resort
of all Londoners and all London goods and merchandise
to St. James's Fair.[3] This request was granted, the
Londoners vainly submitting a counter-petition that the
restraint might not apply to those who obtained certificates of health from the Lord Mayor.[4]

An elaborate order issued at the Essex Assizes on
25 July enacted that all Londoners repairing into Essex,
either to their own houses or to those of others, were to
remain indoors for fourteen days, together with the whole
household. Higglers and carriers who resorted to London
were to be kept in their houses for fourteen days, and then
bound to good behaviour and to appear at the next assizes
to answer their misdemeanour and contempt. This order
was to be openly read every Sunday in the parish churches

[1] S. P. Dom., Chas. I, vol. iv, Doc. 146. Also in Remembrancia,
vi. 63.   [2] Cal. S. P. Dom., 1625–1626, 45 and 66.
[3] P. C. R. xxxiii. 74.
[4] Cal. S. P. Dom., 1625–1626, 51, and R. xxxix. 268.

of Essex.[1] The latter part of the order was a cooling card for the fancy of Londoners, and many scathing remarks were made upon the selfish and short-sighted policy of the Justices of Essex :

'There are a Generation of Justices of Peace, who devised an unjust and unpeaceable way to punish us that remained ; For, first, they hindred our *London* butchers to come into their adjacent Townes and Hamlets to fetch Cattell, for our food : Secondly, they made Decrees, Orders, and Inhibitions, which they caused to be read publikely in Churches, . . . that our Market-folke of the same Townes and Hamlets be restreyned, upon penalties, to bring us into *London* fresh Victuals, (as Mutton, Veale, Butter, Egges and the like,) for our Moneyes ; whiles they themselves drinke their Wine and strong Beere in Bowles, . . . follow their sports ; as Hawking, Gaming, Bowling, and the like.' [2]

But the Justices were not allowed their own way for long. On 1 August the Lord Mayor told the Privy Council that if the City should be deprived of food, it was to be feared that it would not be in the power of himself and the few remaining magistrates ' to restrain the violence that hunger may enforce '.[3] Four days later the Council informed the Essex Justices that owing to the restraint of higglers and other persons provisions and food of all kinds had risen to excessive rates : ' it may well be feared that in case of hunger and want those few magis-

---

[1] *S. P. Dom., Chas. I*, vol. v, Doc. 2, 1. The intercourse of carriers into the City was forbidden before 9 July (cf. *ibid.*, vol. iv, Doc. 29), and Hobson, the Cambridge carrier, was forced to abandon his weekly journey to London (*The Court and Times of Charles the First*, i. 41) ; but it was another matter to forbid the intercourse of higglers who supplied the City with food.

[2] *Lachrymae Londinenses*, 4. See also Benjamin Spenser, *Vox Civitatis* (1625), 2 and 26.

[3] *S. P. Dom., Chas. I*, vol. v, Doc. 2. Also in *Remembrancia*, vi. 64.

trates remaining in and about the City, will be the less able to restrain from resorting into the country for their better relief such persons as shall be pinched and suffer in this kind '. The restraint was to be withdrawn,[1] but the markets and rendezvous were to be held outside the City : for those carrying provisions from Essex and some parts of Middlesex in Mile End Green or in Woods Close, for those coming from Middlesex to Westminster in Tothill Fields and St. James's Fields, and for those from Kent and Surrey in St. George's Fields.[2]

The distress amongst the poor had become acute, and doles from the City Chamber could do little to alleviate it. The vote of £10 to St. Botolph's, Bishopsgate, on 31 March has already been mentioned. The inhabitants of St. Leonard's, Shoreditch, were forced to petition for relief by the end of May, as they were unable to relieve the infected or to maintain an adequate number of officials. Two Justices of the county of Middlesex were empowered to tax all inhabitants of the county within a radius of five miles and to levy the tax, if necessary, by sale of goods or in default by imprisonment.[3] On 10 June the Lord Mayor condemned the ' vain and riotous Custom of late taken up ' of the meeting of countrymen from various counties in the halls and taverns of London, a ' vain expense ' especially to be forborne ' in these times of God's visitation '.[4] On the last day of the month an allowance was made to St. James's, Duke's Place.[5] A week later the Lord Mayor pointed out to the clergymen and church-

---

[1] *P. C. R.* xxxiii. 88 b. The like letters were sent to the Justices of Middlesex, Surrey (who were about to order the same restraint), Kent, and Hertford.   [2] *Ibid.* 89.
[3] *Middlesex County Records* (ed. J. C. Jeaffreson), iii. 3
[4] *J.* xxxiii. 129.   [5] *R.* xxxix. 264 b.

wardens of each parish that tradesmen and many poor
householders ' do suffer great wants, and are like to perish
and starve in respect that timely relief and supply is not
ministered unto them '.   A collection for poor afflicted
people was to be made every Wednesday, and the rich were
to be visited and urged to give liberally. The sum collected
was to be entered in one of the parish books, and information
of its amount conveyed to the Lord Mayor every week.[1]
On the same day the master and wardens of each City
company were requested to forbear their usual feasts and
to pay the money saved, with any additional sums, to the
Chamber of London.[2] Westminster did not share in the
sums collected in and for the City of London, but on 25 July
the overseers of St. Margaret's, Westminster, received £100
from the King's bounty for the relief of their infected
poor.[3] Other sums were contributed by generous citizens.
In the accounts of the examiners of St. Martin's-in-the-
Fields the receipt of £20, ' the most liberal gift ' of the
Earl of Rutland, is acknowledged in letters of gold.
Parliament met at Oxford on 1 August, much to the
disgust of the members, who obtained lodgings with
difficulty and found that the plague was still with them.
On 6 August the House of Lords ordered the poor-rate in
London and Westminster to be doubled, and the houses
charged whose inhabitants had fled.[4]   Five days later
letters patent authorized the issue of briefs for a general
collection to be made throughout the whole kingdom for

[1] *J.* xxxiii. 129 b.
[2] *R.* xxxix. 268 b.   The Stationers' Company was among those
who abandoned their feasts. Cf. *A Transcript of the Registers
of the Company of Stationers of London* (ed. Arber), iii. 691
(29 October).   [3] *Cal. S. P. Dom.*, 1625–1626, 73.
[4] *Journals of the House of Lords,* 475 a.

the relief of the poor in London and Westminster. The amount collected was written on the back of the brief and published by the churchwardens in open congregation. The minister then carried the money to the dean appointed in each deanery, the dean to his ordinary, and so at length it reached the Bishop of London who apportioned its distribution by the advice of another bishop and two lords of Parliament.[1] The Chamber of London advanced £1,000 until the money could be collected.

The distress of the poor and the absence of the magistrates led many to fear outbreaks of violence. London was swarming with vagrants, ' ministering suspicion that their stay there is for no good intent, but as may be well feared to make prey by pilfering and breaking up of houses of such citizens and other persons which are left empty of any servant to look to them—a thing practised as we hear by dissolute and desperate persons in times of former contagion and plague '. An enemy swooping down upon the coast in these summer months would have made an easy conquest. The mustering of the train-bands in every county had been forbidden on 14 August.[2] By the 31st the plague was amongst the seafaring men in the river, the pressing of sailors was discontinued, and the coast and the Thames were left unguarded.[3]

The pen of a Defoe alone could adequately describe the condition of London in the grip of this plague. All the horrors of 1603 were to be witnessed in the City in 1625 but in a heightened degree. ' August is called the month of corruption, which is not yet come ; Lord, what will

[1] *Cal. S. P. Dom.*, 1625–1626, 83. See also *The Court and Times of Charles the First*, i. 46.
[2] *P. C. R.* xxxiii. 88 and 92.
[3] *Hist. MSS. Comm.*, 12th Report, Appendix I, 211.

become of the distressed city then ? Remember, O Lord, thy wonted mercies, and take pity upon their affliction.' [1] The apprehensions of the Reverend Joseph Mead were fully realized. In August and September the infection was so great that the magistrates in desperation abandoned every care. The empty houses of merchants were broken into and robbed.[2] The sick and the sound went without restraint to church, and were suffered to converse together in all parts of the City.[3] Segregation was impossible, for the healthy households would not half have served to keep the sick or bury the dead.[4] So uncertain was the tenure of life that the parting salutation of ' Good night ' became ' God send us a joyful Resurrection '.[5] The terror of some men was so great as almost to become ludicrous. Salvetti, who had retired to Richmond in July, wished profoundly that he was elsewhere : ' I sit with my boots upon my legs ready for flight from this great peril, which, besides the cost, is a source of great perturbation of mind.' [6]

The plight of prisoners was as pitiable in this year as it had been in 1603. Dekker, who had suffered for seven years in the King's Bench prison, was one of the few writers to plead for ' the distressed in *Ludgate*, the

---

[1] *The Court and Times of Charles the First*, i. 44 (30 July).

[2] *Hist. MSS. Comm.*, 11th Report, Appendix I, 28. See also below, p. 154.

[3] *Ibid.*, 12th Report, Appendix I, 209. See also *P. C. R.* xxxiii. 98 b.

[4] Wither, *op. cit.*, 50. A common saying. Cf. Dekker's *Foure Birdes of Noahs Arke* (1609), sig. F 10ᵛ (*G.* v. 58), and see also *D. P. P.*, p. 96, ll. 11, 12, and p. 203, ll. 4–6.

[5] Abraham Holland, *Hollandi Post-huma* (1626), sig. F 4ᵛ. The poem is reprinted as *London Look-Backe* at the end of the 1630 edition of J. D.'s *Salomons Pest-House*.

[6] *Hist. MSS. Comm.*, 11th Report, Appendix I, 28.

miserable soules in the Holes of the two *Counters*, the
afflicted in the *Marshallseas*, the Cryers-out for Bread in
the *Kings Bench*, and *White Lyon* '.[1] The City bestowed
some small charity upon them. On 30 June the Court of
Aldermen ' in compassion towards them ' gave £10 to the
poor in the Holes of the Poultry and Wood Street Compters, and five days later ordered the appointment of
a minister for the poor prisoners in the Hole of the Poultry
Compter.[2] On 6 July a petition was presented to the
House of Lords by the prisoners in the Fleet to have
the benefit of Habeas Corpus. After conferment with the
Commons the Lords decided that it was illegal to grant a
prisoner liberty upon Habeas Corpus without the assent of
all his creditors, and that this privilege had been much
abused by many prisoners.[3] But on 31 July the prisoners
in the King's Bench were granted permission to go abroad
with their keepers and employ themselves to labour.[4]
From an account of the charges incurred by the City
Chamber between 6 August 1625 and March 1626 it
appears that payments were made for poor prisoners
in the Poultry (£8) and Wood Street (£12) Compters, in
Ludgate (£14), in Newgate (£13 6s. 1d.), in the Marshal-
sea (£1 10s.), in the King's Bench (£1 10s.), and in the
White Lion (£1 10s.).[5] But these small sums, even if
they reached the right hands, were not bountiful. ' Bread
and meat for the poor prisoners, for Christ Jesus sake,
bread and meat ' : this pitiful cry, the like of which was
heard from London's prisons till the time of Dickens, was

[1] *D. P. P.* 149.
[2] *R.* xxxix. 265 and 268 b.
[3] *Journals of the House of Lords*, 458 b, 459 b, 462 a, and 463 a.
[4] *Cal. S. P. Dom.*, 1625–1626, 77.
[5] House of Lords MS., 5 April 1626, annex 3.

now fruitless. For the charitable who were wont to fill
the alms-baskets with broken meat had left the poorest
prisoners to languish and to die.[1]

The scenes in the streets were like those witnessed in
1603. Wither, who remained in town in the heat of the
infection, gives us some notion of the horrors of the
plague :

> Here, one man stagger'd by, with visage pale :
> There, lean'd another, grunting on a stall.
> A third, halfe dead, lay gasping for his grave ;
> A fourth did out at window call, and rave ;
> Yonn came the *Bearers*, sweating from the *Pit*,
> To fetch more bodies to replenish it.

Taylor paints the scene in the same lurid colours :

Thus it was June, July, August and September.
> Some frantick raving, some with anguish crying,
> Some singing, praying, groaning, and some dying,
> The healthfull grieving, and the sickly groaning,
> All in a mournefull diapason moaning.

Abraham Holland, who lived ' in Chelsey aire ', writes a
little less crudely than Taylor and Wither of the miserable estate of London :

> Where the pale Visages of men expresse
> Farre above Poetrie the Heavinesse
> Of Gods sharp Scourge, where the Red wand affrights
> The Starting Passenger and troubled Nights
> Are spent in Burials, when what e're we see
> Is but an Argument of Miserie ;
> The Wormewood-Nosegayes, and the trembling Pace
> Of them that passe, though they have Herbe of Grace
> And curious Boxes to repell the ayre
> Which might assault them, seeming to out-dare
> The will of Destinie.[2]

[1] *D. P. P.* 148, 149 ; *Pickwick Papers*, chap. xlii.
[2] *Op. cit.*, sig. E 1ᵛ.

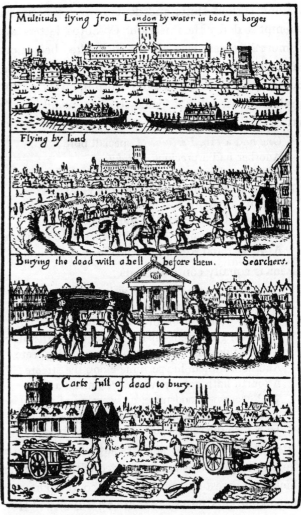

Scenes during the Great Plague.
From a contemporary print in the Pepysian Collection.

Many curious shifts and devices were practised in the attempt to dodge the infection. Corantos, letters, and bills of mortality were well aired and smoked before perusal,[1] and coins were washed in water before they were handled.[2] Both Wither and Taylor pour scorn upon the absurd pro- phylactics used by a panic-stricken populace. Wither writes :

> One had a rare *Perfume* of speciall note ;
> Another had a precious *Antidote*,
> Which at *Constantinople* had been tride
> When there two thousand on a day have di'de.
> A third, preferr'd a *Mixture* in a bag,
> Of whose large vertues he did largely brag,
> And said, the same they doe in Plague time, weare
> At *Rome*, (and so I think when he was there).

Taylor is equally contemptuous :

> One with a peece of tasseld well *tarr'd Rope*
> Doth with that nose-gay keepe himselfe in hope ;
> Another doth a wispe of worme-wood pull
> And with great Judgement crams his nostrils full ;
> A third takes off his socks from 's sweating feete,
> And makes them his perfume along the streete :
> A fourth hath got a pownc'd Pommander box,
> With woorme-wood juice, or sweating of a Fox,
> Rue steep'd in vineger, they hold it good
> To cheere the sences, and preserve the blood.

It was the quietness and desolation of this great City, whose streets were usually thronged with bustling crowds, which most arrested the attention of contemporary writers. They likened her misery to that of Jerusalem: ' How doth the city sit solitary that was full of people ? How is she

---

[1] *The Court and Times of Charles the First*, i. 44.

[2] Taylor, *op. cit.*, sig. A 5, and *A Looking-glasse for City and Countrey* (1630). See also *D. P. P.* 157 (in 1625) and 59 (in 1603).

become as a widow ? She that was great among the
nations, and princess among the provinces ... She weep-
eth sore in the night, and her tears are on her cheeks '
(*Lamentations* i. 1, 2). Streets and lanes were but thinly
manned with unhappy wretches who had no power to flee
and no means to stay.[1] William Lilly, the astrologer,
walking from his house over against Strand Bridge to St.
Antholin's Church about half-past six on a July morning,
met only three persons in the way, ' so few People were
then alive, and the Streets so unfrequented '.[2] A traveller
passing through the City at 1 p.m. at the end of August
' resembled the face thereof, at that time, to the appearance it useth to have at three of the clock in the morning,
in the month of June ; no more people stirring, no more
shops open '.[3] Most doors were shut up and padlocked,
and the notice ' Chambers ready furnished to be let ' was
supplanted by a cross and ' Lord Have Mercy Upon Us '.[4]
The cheerful sounds of the goings-on of a great City were
silenced : in their stead were heard the howling of dogs,
the raving of the sick, and the mourning of the bereaved.
The rich had all run away, so that people stared at any one
dressed in the habit of a courtier or gentleman ' as if they
had beheld the wandring Jew '.[5] Westminster, Whitehall,
the Strand, the Inns of Court, the Post, the Royal Exchange were all deserted. The woollen and linen drapers
had departed, and Watling Street was like an empty

[1] Taylor, *op. cit.*, sig. A 6.
[2] *Mr. William Lilly's True History of King James the First, and
King Charles the First* (1715), 19.
[3] *The Court and Times of Charles the First*, i. 48.
[4] Holland, *op. cit.*, sig. F 1ᵛ.
[5] Wither, *op. cit.*, 109 b. See also *Mr. William Lilly's History
of his Life and Times* (1715), 18, and *D. P. P.* 139.

cloister. In Cheapside it was almost impossible to change
a piece of gold, and if spice were needed to make ' com-
fortable Broth ', it was not to be had : for all the grocers
had fled.[1]   In some streets one or two shops stood open
' for small takings, and lesse gaine ', but for every shop open
sixteen were shut.[2]   Those trades alone flourished which
made capital out of sickness and death. Apothecaries,
sextons, herb-wives, physicians, quacks, nurses, and coffin-
makers did a roaring business and grew rich on their profits.
Butchers and cooks exacted exorbitant prices for meat and
food, while coachmen charged as much as forty shillings for
a six-mile ' jolting ' from London.[3]

Sad stories are told of the poverty to which so many
were reduced. It was feared that some died ' of the
stomacke sicknesse, as well as the *spotted sicknesse*, if there
were a Bill could be gotten of *All diseases* '. Many would
have been glad had their houses been infected, for their
parish would then have been forced to relieve them.[4]
A letter written on 1 September tells us that ' the want
and misery is the greatest here that ever any man living
knew : no trading at all ; the rich all gone ; housekeepers
and apprentices of manual trades begging in the streets,
and that in such a lamentable manner as will make the
strongest heart to yearn '.[5]

[1] Spenser, *op. cit.*, 24.
[2] Taylor, *op. cit.*, sig. A 6, and *D. P. P.* 138.
[3] Wither, *op. cit.*, 112 b ; Taylor, *op. cit.*, sig. A 8ᵛ; *D. P. P.* 139.
Lilly is the only writer to state that food was cheap in London at
the height of the infection. His food with that of his companion
came weekly to 6s. 6d. or 7s. ' so cheap Diet was at that Time '
(*History of His Life and Times*, 18). But most people in London
would have been unable to pay a half or a quarter of this price
for food.
[4] B. Spenser, *op. cit.*, 13.
[5] *The Court and Times of Charles the First*, i. 48.

The fear of sudden death throws a searching light upon
the hidden sources of character, and in great calamity
the extremes of conduct are revealed. Men are stripped
of their robes of pretence and convention. ' The mask is
torn off and the reality remains.' [1]

> Some streets had Churches full of people, weeping :
> Some others, *Tavernes* had, rude-revell keeping :
> Within some houses *Psalmes* and *Hymnes* were sung :
> With raylings, and loud scouldings, others rung.[2]

In the plague of Athens so poignantly described by the
genius of Thucydides, himself an eyewitness and a sufferer,
the calamity was so overwhelming that men, not knowing
what was to become of them, became careless of all law,
human and divine. Reflecting that life and riches were
alike transitory, they resolved to enjoy themselves while
they could and to think only of pleasure. ' Those who saw
all perishing alike, thought that the worship or neglect
of the Gods made no difference. For offences against
human law no punishment was to be feared ; no one
would live long enough to be called to account. Already
a far heavier sentence had been passed and was hanging
over a man's head ; before that fell, why should he
not take a little pleasure ? ' [3] So in seventeenth-century London many refused to observe the fasts, and
made merry in fields, streets, and taverns ; in the fields
' walking, talking, laughing, toying, and sporting together';
in the streets ' blaspheming, selling, buying, swearing ' ;
and in taverns and alehouses ' drinking, roaring, and
surfeiting '. Thieves wolfishly preyed upon the sick or

---

[1] Lucretius, *De Rerum Natura*, iii. 58, reading ' eripitur persona,
manet res '.

[2] Wither, *op. cit.*, 113 b.

[3] ii. 47–54. The quotation is from Jowett's translation (1881).

robbed the dead, and drunkards and whoremongers followed
their lusts with the sword of the pestilence hanging over
them.[1] The attitude of men who acted in the spirit of the
old song—

> Is 't not fine to dance and sing
> When the bells of death do ring ?

is nowhere more eloquently condemned than in a sermon
by John Donne. They cried out

' *Omnes Moriemur*, We can but die, and we must die : And,
Edamus, et bibamus, cras moriemur, . . . and so were cut off
by the hand of God, some even in their robberies, in half-
empty houses ; and in their lusts and wantonness in licentious
houses ; and so took an infection and death, like *Judas's* sop,
death dipt and soaked in sin. Men whose lust carried them
into the jaws of infection in lewd houses, and seeking one sore
perished with another ; men whose rapine and covetousness
broke into houses, and seeking the wardrobes of others, found
their own winding-sheet, in the infection of that house where
they stole their own death ; men who sought no other way to
divert sadness, but strong drink in riotous houses, and there
drank up *Davids* cup of Malediction, the cup of Condemned
men of death in the infection of that place.' [2]

On the other hand, the plague ' taught some religion,
that never knew what the word meant '.[3] The churches
were crowded with worshippers interceding for the health
of the country, and funeral sermons were attended in great
numbers by the sick as well as by the sound. Lilly gives
a vivid account of a service held on the 14 August :

' The *Sunday* before the great Bill came forth, which was

---

[1] *D. P. P.* 151 ; Wither, *op. cit.*, 113.

[2] *XXVI. Sermons* (*Never before Publish'd*) (1661), sig. Qqq 1ᵛ.

[3] Bodleian MS. Rawl. poet. 61, fo. 75ᵛ—a poem called 'London's
Lamentable Estate, in any great Visitation' by 'Ph.M.', i.e. Philip
Massinger. It has been printed by H. W. Garrod, *Genius Loci* (1950),
105–11.

of 5000 and odd Hundreds, there was appointed a Sacrament at *Clement Danes* ; during the distributing whereof I do well remember we sang thirteen Parts of the One hundred and nineteenth Psalm. One *Jacob* our Minister (for we had three that Day, the Communion was so great) fell sick as he was giving the Sacrament, went home, and was buryed of the Plague the *Thursday* following. Mr. *James* another of the Ministers fell sick, ere he had quite finished, had the Plague, and was thirteen Weeks ere he recovered. Mr. *Whitacre*, the last of the three, escaped not only then, but all the Contagion following without any Sickness at all ; though he Officiated at every Funeral, and buryed all manner of People, whether they died of the Plague or not. He was given to drink, seldom could preach more than one quarter of an Hour at a Time.' [1]

The flight of clergymen from the City was resented as bitterly in 1625 as in 1603. Those who had two benefices, and whose usual practice in the summer was to discharge their office to their ' Countrey sheep ' were excused, but for the runaways whose only cure and whose only care was a London parish there was neither excuse nor sympathy.[2] John Donne, Vicar of St. Dunstan's-in-the-West and Dean of St. Paul's, scattered his family and retired to Chelsea, where ' the infection multiplied so fast, as that it was no good Manners to go to any other place, and so I have been in a secular Monastery '. During these months of ' close imprisonment ', spent in the congenial company of George Herbert and his mother, he revised and wrote out his sermons.[3] We hear of the bravery of a few ministers who remained at their posts : of Dr. Meddus, rector of St. Gabriel's, Fenchurch, who was left alone with one man and a maid : of the ' learned ' Makernesse and the

[1] *History of His Life and Times* (1715), 18.
[2] Spenser, *op. cit.*, 18.
[3] *S. P. Dom., Chas. I*, vol. 10, Doc. 28.

' zealous ' Eton, whose courage cost them their lives.[1]
William Crashawe, rector of Whitechapel, was also among
the faithful. In his *Londons Lamentation for her Sinnes*
(1625) he tells how he walked ' hourely through the valley
of the shadow of Death, burying forty, fifty, sometime
sixty a day '. But most of these gallant gentlemen have
left no memorial behind them except the record of a burial
in the registers of their parish.

Little can be gleaned of the part played by doctors in
this calamity. Many, as in 1603, fled into the country
carrying with them their ' Electuaries, Pomanders, and
what not, whole Apothecaries shoppes full of conceits
and receipts, to keepe all the Cinque-Ports of mans
body inviolable '.[2] Stephen Bradwell, grandson to the
renowned Elizabethan surgeon, John Banister, stayed
in the City, issuing a tract to advertise his Antidotes,
Electuaries, Lozenges, Trochisks, and Pomanders, all of
his grandfather's invention and all ' imperious counters '
to repel the plague. He had two powders and one electuary which were of sovereign power : one cost a shilling
a dram, one threepence a grain, and the third half a crown
an ounce—' I confesse they are costly : but slight meanes
and cheape Medicines (how ever they promise) prove as
deare as death '.[3] Bradwell was in the field again in 1636
with the same remedies, but Raphael Thorius, also a
member of the Royal College of Physicians, died of the
infection in July or August. ' He acted more for the
publick (by exposing his person too much) then his most
dear concern.' [4] On a lower plane stood the quacksalvers,

[1] *The Court and Times of Charles the First*, i. 5 (note 3) and 43 ;
Wither, *op. cit.*, 130 b.   [2] Spenser, *op. cit.*, 17.
[3] *A Watch-Man For The Pest* (1625), sig. H 3^v.
[4] A. Wood, *Athenae Oxonienses* (1691), i. 423.

whose bills were plastered on many posts bragging in high
astounding terms of wonderful and impossible achieve-
ments. One of these ' impudent liars ' dwelt in Distaff
Lane, and annoyed Bradwell by protesting that he had
a medicine which had belonged to Banister. These impostors found a gullible public, and reaped a rich harvest
until death put an end to their roguery.

Clergymen and physicians were but a few among the
host of runaways. Most men who were financially or
physically able obeyed the sound advice of Hippocrates,
wonderfully garbled by the Earl of Melrose and Haddington
into ' flit sun and far of and be long a cuming bak agane '.[1]
Those who for business or other reasons were forced to
stay sent away their wives and children. ' For every
thousand dead here, five times as many ' fled away, and
gentry and poor swarmed ' from their City hive, like
Bees in May '.[2] Donne describes this flight in a letter
to Sir Thomas Roe, the English ambassador at Con-
stantinople : ' The Citizens fled away, as out of a house
on fire, and stuffed their pockets with their best ware,
and threw themselves into the highways, and were not
received, so much as into barns, and perished so, some
of them with more money about them than would have
bought the village where they died. A Justice of peace—
into his Examination it fell—told me of one that died so,
with 1400 l. about him.' [3] Locke writes of a Londoner
who died in the fields outside Southampton with much
money about him which was taken before he was cold.[4]

[1] Hist. MSS. Comm., 14th Report, Appendix III, 108.
[2] D. P. P. 147 and Wither, op. cit., 79.
[3] S. P. Dom., Chas. I, vol. 10, Doc. 28 (25 November). Cf. also
D. P. P. 162–4 and 170–1.
[4] Cal. S. P. Dom., 1625–1626, 90.

Dr. Meddus records a story of a woman dwelling near
Old Swan, who was removing into Surrey for fear of the
plague. Coming to the hill near Streatham, on the way
to Croydon, she turned round, looked on the City, and said,
' Farewell, London, and farewell, plague '. Soon afterwards she was taken sick and died. On her breast were
the tokens and these words distinctly to be read—' It is
in vain to fly from God, for He is everywhere '. The story
was passed on with the comment—' You may judge of
this, or suspend, as you shall see cause '.[1]

Any kind of shelter was gladly occupied by poor runaways. For miles round London it was difficult to find an
uninhabited shed or hovel, and stalls and barns were as
welcome as halls. Many found in flight the infection from
which they sought to escape. A man in Leadenhall Street
fled into the country with his seven children, buried them
all there, and returned to London.[2] Some died on the
road, others crept into ditches and there breathed their
last, while many perished in the fields :

> glad was he, they say,
> Who for his *Death-bed*, gain'd a Cock of Hay.[3]

Country villages and towns took great pains to ward
off the infection. At many towns no man was allowed to
enter without a ticket certifying that he had come from
an uninfected district.[4] At other places country yokels,
keeping their distance from suspicious strangers and get-
ting to windward of them, barred the way with halberds,
brown bills, pitchforks, staves, hooks, ' and such like
rustick weapons '.[5]   John Evelyn, the Diarist, travelled

---

[1] *The Court and Times of Charles the First*, i. 43.   [2] *Ibid.*
[3] Wither, *op. cit.*, 119 b.   [4] *Cal. S. P. Dom.*, 1625–1626, 90.
[5] Wither. *op. cit.*, 73 b, and H. Petowe, *The Countrie Ague* (1626),
sig. B 3ᵛ.

RUNAWAYS FLEEING FROM THE PLAGUE

in this year from his father's house at Wotton in Surrey
to his grandfather's at Lewes in Sussex, and, though but
a child of four or five years at the time, he never forgot
the strict watches and examinations to which his party
had to submit.[1] Constables in Norfolk were given instructions that no persons known or suspected to come
from infected places ' be suffered to abide or lodge in
your Town if by any fair means they may be kept
out '. A watch was to be kept both day and night,
and offenders brought before Justices of the Peace to be
committed to gaol.[2] Yet criminals often escaped scot-
free on pleading that they hailed from London, for few
Justices were courageous enough to examine them and few
constables to arrest them. Many country inns and alehouses took down their signs so that they might be under
no obligation to harbour travellers, whether sick or sound,
a trick which aroused the resentment of Londoners who
at other seasons had been welcomed with open arms.[3]
' That name (of Londoner) ', wrote the authors of *The Run-
awayes Answer*, ' which had wont to draw out a whole
Towne to stare upon him, and a *Church-yeard* full of
People (after Service) to gape upon his fine Cloathes,
spruce silke-Stockins, and neate steeletto-fied Beard : . . .
That *Name* is now so ill, that he is halfe hanged in the
Countrey that has it.' ' A murren on their manners when
they have any ', cried these gentlemen, and ' Grunting
Girgashites ' and ' Hog-making Gadarens ' may serve as
examples of the epithets hurled at the country people by
the indignant John Taylor. The Water-Poet, however,

[1] *Diary* (ed. Bray and Wheatley), i. 4.
[2] Bodleian Tanner MS. 177, fo. 46.
[3] Taylor, *op. cit.*, sig. A 5, B 3ᵛ, and B 5.

singled out the town of Hendon for commendation, in that it not only relieved the sick and buried the dead, allowing good weekly wages to two men to attend to these matters, but also sent £8 to relieve the poor of St. Andrew's, Holborn.

The Court during the summer also strove to run away from the infection, but owing to the rabble which followed its every movement it could not shake off the disease. Whitehall (3 July), Hampton Court, Oatlands, and Windsor (16 July) were in turn infected.[1] Charles then moved by way of Woking, Bisham, and Ricott[2] to Woodstock, where elaborate precautions were taken to ward off the plague. Elizabeth's custom was revived of setting up a gibbet at the Court gate in token of the punishment to be meted out to transgressors.[3] Parliament opened at Oxford on 1 August, but came to an end on the 12th. His Majesty then left Woodstock for Beaulieu in the New Forest where he employed himself in hunting.[4] In September he was at Southampton, Plymouth, and Wilton. The number of courtiers in attendance was greatly reduced so as to minimize the danger of infection and facilitate movement. Privy seals were sent out to supply the King's most pressing needs,[5] £10,000 was borrowed in August, and £98,000 was brought into the Exchequer in August and September on account of the Queen's portion. All this money went apparently to the equip-

---

[1] S. P. Dom., Chas. I, vol. iv, Docs. 29 and 61 ; The Court and Times of Charles the First, i. 41 and 44 ; Cal. S. P. Ven., 1625–1626, 115 ; J. xxxiii. 130 b.

[2] Cal. S. P. Dom., Addenda, 1625–1649, 37.

[3] Ibid., 1625–1626, 84.

[4] Hist. MSS. Comm., 11th Report, Appendix I, 31 ; Cal. S. P. Ven., 1625–1626, 154.

[5] Cal. S. P. Ven., 1625–1626, 165 ; Letters and Memorials of State (ed. Arthur Collins, 1746), ii. 360.

The cool reception of a Londoner visiting the country

ment of the fleet which was to attack Spain and to meet the many other expenses of the King and Council. No wages were paid at Court in October and it was even difficult to find money for the diet of the King and his officers. The poverty which was to prove so serious a hindrance to Charles was thus apparent in the first few months of his reign. The plague which interrupted trade and impoverished the whole country shut various ways of raising money which would otherwise have remained open to him.[1]

At London the infection had been so deadly in August that few thought to survive it. But the bill of mortality for the week ending 25 August showed a welcome decrease, and by the last week in September the plague-deaths were less than a thousand. The decrease was attributed by some to the proclamation of 14 August ordering the banishment of Jesuits. Mead, on the other hand, pointed out that the sickness decreased after the seventh general fast, just as the walls of Jericho fell down after the seventh blast of the trumpet.[2]

Week ending.		Buried in all.	Of the plague.	Parishes. infected.
October	6	838	538	99
,,	13	815	511	91
,,	20	651	331	76
,,	27	375	134	47
November	3	357	89	41
,,	10	319	92	35
,,	17	274	48	22
,,	24	231	27	16
December	1	190	15	12
,,	8	181	15	7
,,	15	168	6	5
,,	22	157	1	1

[1] *Letters and Memorials of State*, ii. 363 ; *Cal. S. P. Ven.*, 1625–1626, 148 and lv ; S. R. Gardiner, *History of England, 1603–1642*, vi. 3.   [2] *The Court and Times of Charles the First*, i. 46.

In the outlying districts the plague decreased as rapidly :

	West-minster.	Lam-beth.	Newing-ton.	Step-ney.	Hack-ney.	Isling-ton.
Oct.	294·216	77·48	34·2	329·231	25·14	45·34
Nov.	114·55	40·18	24·0	185·86	9·0	22·8
Dec.	54·1	11·3	19·0	124·7	11·0	13·3

With the decrease of the infection and the return of many magistrates, better measures were taken to enforce the regulations. In October the Privy Council reproved the Lord Mayor, the Lord Mayor reproved the aldermen, and the aldermen reproved the plague-officials. The Justices in the outlying districts were also reproved.[1] On the 21st the Council complained to the Lord Keeper of ' the indiscreet and unruly carriage ' of the inhabitants of Westminster, many of whom with running sores on them were mixing freely with the sound. The frequency of funeral sermons was deprecated—' which as in themselves they are of most excellent use, being applied with zeal and judgement, so in these times of contagion, they augment the danger by reason of the greater concourse of people '. A word of praise was given to ' Mr. Hayward ' who had behaved discreetly and warily in a most trying time.[2] On the 28th the City magistrates issued a precept to clear the streets of vagrants, who were present in unusually large numbers, and a few days later they enforced the ancient custom of hanging out lantern and candlelight.[3]

The authorities were now faced with the problem of securing the orderly return of the runaways. At the beginning of September the shops were shut and London was almost deserted. A month later the streets were full of people and the highways thronged with passengers on

---

[1] P. C. R. xxxiii. 127 b and 131 ; J. xxxiii. 140.
[2] P. C. R. xxxiii. 140.   [3] J. xxxiii. 140 b.

horse and foot.[1] Not all runaways were so timid as
Lovewit in *The Alchemist* who would not return while
there died one a week within the walls. In the week
ending 6 October the deaths from the plague decreased
by 314 and in the following week by only 27. This is
entirely attributable to the return of crowds of runaways.

London welcomes home her runaways.

Many expressed surprise that the decrease had not been
turned into an increase.

But the fury of the infection was spent, and poverty
rather than plague was now to be feared. The dislocation
of commerce in 1625 was even greater than in 1603.
Intercourse with foreign countries had practically ceased.
The loss on the farm of general customs in 1625, by
reason of the plague and the troubles with Spain, was
£5,041.[2] In this country, too, trade was almost at a

[1] *The Court and Times of Charles the First*, i. 54. People
driving into the City were greeted by the populace with jeers of
' Runaways '. Cf. Petowe, *The Countrie Ague* (1626), sig. C 1.

[2] *Cal. S. P. Dom.*, 1625–1626, 203.

standstill. The cloth trade had been very bad for some years, partly owing to the activity of the Dutch and partly to James's hazardous treatment of it in granting privileges to the New Merchant Adventurers.[1] The depression was aggravated by the plague. The delivery of cloths to be dyed and dressed was stopped,[2] and clothiers complained bitterly of ' a want of vent ' for their wares.[3] In September many clothiers in Gloucestershire, Berkshire, Wiltshire, and Somersetshire had quantities of cloths on their hands in Blackwell Hall (the London market-place for woollen cloths), and more still in their own houses which they dared not bring to London even if merchants would have ventured there to buy them.[4] Distress was also evident amongst the farmers. Money was so scarce with them that none was paid except for 'white-meats and such like victuals ' to relieve their urgent needs. The whole year's stocks of corn, cattle, and other winter provisions still lay on their hands, so that they could pay no rent. It was generally feared that many would abandon their land, and turn the farms into the hands of their landlords.[5] Graziers and marketmen were unable to sell their commodities because of the infection, hopmasters could not sell their hops either at Stourbridge Fair (which had been prohibited on 4 August together with Bartholomew Fair) or at London. To make matters worse, unusually heavy demands were being made upon the nation's resources. Rents were falling due with the approach of Michaelmas, subsidies were being raised

[1] W. R. Scott, *Joint Stock Companies*, i. 145 and 166.
[2] *London Topographical Record*, viii. 123.
[3] *S. P. Dom., Chas. I*, vol. 6, Doc. 77.
[4] *P. C. R.* xxxiii. 110 (3 September).
[5] *S. P. Dom., Chas. I*, vol. vi, Doc. 77, and vol. viii, Doc. 34.

to meet the needs of the King.[1] The position of trades-
people in London was deplorable. Nobody would buy
their merchandise : carts sent into the country laden with
goods returned as full as when they started.[2] The scarcity
of money was so great ' as the like hath not been seen '.[3]
Tradesmen and artificers, who were wont to pay subsidies,
relieve the poor, and discharge their country's duties by
watching and warding, were fain to crave relief themselves.
Prices rose all round. Coals which were selling before the
plague at 12s. a chaldron were fetching 33s. in March 1626.[4]
The outlook would not have been so black for the poor
if the harvests had been good. But the nation was
threatened with dearth and famine ; [5] in Essex few farmers
had even half their ordinary crop of corn ; [6] in Huntingdon
the grain was very coarse and only about a third of the
normal yield. Owing to the floods of an abnormally wet
spring the best meadows had been spoilt for feeding
cattle, and bad pasture had caused sheep-rot to spread.[7]
Dire distress was evident in London far into the next
year.[8] A note from the Privy Council on 27 November
called the attention of the Justices of Middlesex and
Surrey to the multitudes of poor and vagrant people

[1] The cost of the fleet fitted out this year for an attack on Spain
proved a heavy burden to the country : for the counties had to
pay for the press, clothe the soldiers, send them to Plymouth, and
feed them until they were taken over by the King's officers.
Cf. *Cal. S. P. Ven.*, 1625–1626, xi.   [2] *D. P. P.* 157.

[3] *S. P. Dom., Chas. I*, vol. 4, Doc. 29 (9 July).

[4] *Cal. S. P. Dom.*, 1625–1626, 295.

[5] *D. P. P.* 142. See also *Cal. S. P. Ven.*, 1625–1626, 158.

[6] *Cal. S. P. Dom.*, 1625–1626, 107.

[7] *S. P. Dom., Chas. I.*, vol. viii, Doc. 44.

[8] One of the reasons given by the City in 1626 for refusing
a loan to the King was the complete stoppage of trade caused by
the plague of 1625 to the great loss of the City merchants. Cf.
Hist. MSS. Comm., 11th Report, Appendix I, 77.

pestering the City and especially the suburbs. The Justices were charged to relieve the poor and set them to work, for their presence threatened another pestilence and gave foreigners a very poor opinion of the City. Many of the unemployed sought to obtain a living by acts of violence. Insolent robberies on the highways near London became frequent, and men went about ' in such Companies, and so armed (as we are informed) as if it were to the public affront of Justice and all authority '. On 13 December the Council required all inns, alehouses, and other hostelries on the highways or in suspicious places to be examined. Suspected persons with horses or pistols in their possession were to be searched, and unclaimed horses to be impounded until their owners appeared.[1]

The measures taken for the relief of the infected poor in London and Westminster have already been described. The City of London had advanced £1,000, to be returned when the money collected by briefs throughout the kingdom had been brought in. On 27 November the Privy Council instructed the Bishop of London, into whose hands such monies were sent, to repay this sum or as much of it as he had received, seeing that the City had heavy burdens and were likely to have heavier : for ' the poor are increased in many parts of the City by reason of the stand of trade, and the death and decay of many tradesmen who were wont heretofore to set them on work '.[2] Accounts of the money collected by briefs show that the total amount realized by the end of February 1626 was £1,128 2s. 11¾d. Eleven bishoprics had failed to send in any contributions by 25 April, and the money which

---

[1] *P. C. R.* xxxiii. 170 b and 183 b.
[2] *Ibid.* 170. Cf. also House of Lords MS., 24 March 1625/6.

came in after 26 June went to the redemption of English captives. The four dioceses contributing more than £100 were Bath and Wells (£251 13s.), Coventry and Lichfield (£169 13s. o½d.), Peterborough (£129 19s. 3d.), and Chester (£109 3s. 5¼d.).[1]

The joint account presented on 5 April 1626 by Allen Cotton, Lord Mayor, Sir John Gore, late Lord Mayor, and Cornelius Fish, Chamberlain, states that they had received for the relief of the poor sums amounting to £1,120, including £1,000 collected by briefs, £80 given by the House of Lords, and £40 given by the Bishop of London. £861 16s. 1d. had been spent for the relief of the poor in and near London since 6 August 1625. A detailed list is shown of the money given to each parish. The ten parishes which received more than £20 were those of St. Sepulchre, New-gate (£130 10s.) ; St. Olave, Southwark (£70) ; St. Giles, Cripplegate (£65) ; St. Botolph, Aldgate (£51) ; St. Andrew, Holborn (£37) ; St. Botolph, Bishopsgate (£32) ; St. Martin, Vintry (£28) ; St. Mary, Whitechapel (£27) ; St. Botolph, Aldersgate (£23) ; and St. Andrew, Wardrobe (£21).[2] All these parishes with the exception of St. Martin's, Vintry, St. Botolph's, Aldersgate, and St. Andrew's, Wardrobe, returned more than 600 deaths from all causes in 1625.[3]

In addition to this sum the City spent £1,671 14s. 6d. in the following ways :

	£	s.	d.
For the relief of poor visited people in and near London before 6 August 1625 . . .	171	0	0

[1] House of Lords MS., 25 April 1626, annexes 1 and 2 ; *Hist. MSS. Comm.*, 4th Report, Appendix, 19.

[2] House of Lords MS., 5 April 1626, annex 3.

[3] See Note M, p. 187.

	£	s.	d.
For doctors, physicians, surgeons, apothecaries and house-rent for them being wholly employed for the use of the infected poor . . .	290	6	8
For necessaries for the Pesthouse and for physic and diet of poor people sent thither . .	314	19	0
For the relief of the poor in hospitals then visited and not having other relief as in time of health	333	6	8
For the relief of the poor in Bridewell wanting relief	400	0	0
To an extraordinary Marshal and his men employed all the sickness time, day and night, to see to the good government of the sick, and to look into the safety of the City, and to attend upon the Lord Mayor besides the other Marshal and his men newly employed . . .	111	3	0
For many large printed orders and books concerning sickness to be delivered to the parishes of London	50	19	2

In 1603 the whole charge which the Chamber of London was at for the pesthouse and for all expenses was only £153 16s. 8d., so that in 1625 it spent £1,517 17s. 10d. beyond all precedents, excluding the sum of £861 16s. 1d. paid out of the money handed in by the Bishop of London.

In Westminster money had been advanced by the churchwardens and vestrymen of St. Margaret's for the relief of the poor, and had not been returned by 14 March 1626. A committee of the House of Lords, appointed on 25 April to consider how much of the money remaining from the general collections (£539 16s. 10¾d.) should be distributed amongst Westminster and the out-parishes, decided on 16 May to give Westminster £300 and to divide £220 16s. amongst Southwark, Stepney, St. Giles's, Cripplegate, and six of the out-parishes.[1]

[1] *Hist. MSS. Comm.*, 4th Report, Appendix, 6; *Journals of the House of Lords*, 526 b, 539 b, 572 b, and 628 b. The out-

Through the importunity of the Queen Charles left
Wilton for Salisbury early in October. He did not venture
to Hampton Court until 3 November.[1] Both the King and
his Council were eager to return to Whitehall, and on
4 December and again on the 13th urged the Lord Mayor
and aldermen thoroughly to disinfect all plague-stricken
houses, and especially household stuffs and bedding, by
frequent fires and by exposing them to the ' frosty and
kindly ' weather.[2] The City magistrates replied that they
were acting warily and circumspectly in airing and cleansing all houses, as also in the ' clean and sweet keeping '
of streets and lanes and in the ejection of inmates and
' undersitters '.[3] Charles, however, spent Christmas at
Hampton Court and did not remove to Whitehall till
7 January.[4] By that time the epidemic had almost run
its course. In London the deaths for the week ending
22 December were 157, the smallest return of the year :
in Westminster only four died of all diseases in the week
ending 29 December, a weekly total less than any known
for thirty years. In consequence the restraint upon the
citizens of London in attending fairs was removed on
30 December. John Donne's eloquent sermon on the
plague was delivered at St. Dunstan's on 15 January 1626
on the text ' For there was not a house where there was not

parish of St. James's, Clerkenwell, where Dekker lived and died,
received only £19 from the City of London in 1625, though it
suffered very heavily. On 16 May 1626 it was assigned £25, but
by a petition presented by the inhabitants on 7 May 1628 (when
all the available money had been spent) it appears that the parish
never received this sum. Cf. *Hist. MSS. Comm.*, 4th Report,
Appendix, 15.

[1] *Letters and Memorials of State*, ii. 361 and 365.
[2] *P. C. R.* xxxiii, 177 and 183 b. See also *Remembrancia*, viii. 65.
[3] B.M. Egerton MS. 2623, fo. 30.
[4] *Letters and Memorials of State*, ii. 367.

one dead '. A fortnight later a public thanksgiving for the
assuagement of the infection was held in London and
Westminster, when the Bishop of London preached at
St. Paul's Cross for two and a half hours.[1] On 2 February
Charles was crowned at Westminster, and his second Parliament met on the 6th. The decay and desolation of the
town was still very evident and very grievous.[2] A wet
spring raised fears of a famine. Happily the sky grew
clear, the floods sank,

> And *Harvest* came, which fild our Granards more
> Then in the fruitfull'st, of sev'n yeares before.[3]

At London and Westminster on 5 July and in the rest of
England on 2 August a general fast was observed : to
give thankful acknowledgement to God of the deliverance
from the plague, of the remembrance of the scarcity and
famine lately threatened throughout the kingdom, and of
the blessing of God upon the fruits of the earth in the time
of the country's greatest distress.

Players and dramatists were hard hit by the infection. The plague-deaths exceeded forty a week from
12 May till 24 November. Few of the companies travelled
in the country during the summer, for few towns or
villages would have admitted them. The King's Company
was much impoverished by its enforced inactivity, and in
December Charles made them a grant of £66 13s. 8d. ' for

[1] In the country the thanksgiving was held on 19 February
(*The Court and Times of Charles the First*, i. 74 and 81). A special
form of prayer was compiled by the bishops and printed with the
title ' A short Forme of Thankesgiving to God For staying the
contagious sickenesse of the Plague : To be used in Common
Prayer, on Sundayes Wednesdayes and Frydayes '. The verses
sung from the Psalms are the same as those in the Thanksgiving
Service of January 1564, a copy of which is in *S. P. Dom., Eliz.*,
vol. 33, Doc. 9.

[2] *Cal. S. P. Dom.*, 1625–1626, 225.   [3] Wither, *op. cit.*, 124 b.

the better furnishing them with apparel' for court performances.[1] On 18 December we hear that Christmas would be spent in plays and that the common players had leave to go to Court now that the plague-deaths had fallen to six.[2] The players at the Cockpit near Whitehall had opened their theatre by 6 December, but by order of

A Sermon at St. Paul's Cross in plague-time.

the Privy Council they were bidden by the Session of Peace held at Hicks Hall to cease their performances ' until his Majesty's pleasure be further signified '.[3] The London theatres were open by 21 December, when the Lord Mayor and aldermen of the City informed the Council that ' there is one thing of late begun which in our opinions will be as great a means as any . . . both to renew and increase the sickness, namely common stage plays about the City out of our jurisdictions '. They expressed the fear that if these theatres remained open,

[1] J. T. Murray, *English Dramatic Companies*, i. 163.
[2] *S. P. Dom., Chas. I*, vol. 12, Doc. 4.
[3] *Middlesex County Records* (ed. J. C. Jeaffreson), iii. 6.

they would draw together a great concourse of people ' of the meaner and lewder sort, who there make matches and appoint their meeting places ', and so would renew and spread the sickness which had so happily abated.[1] But as there was only one plague-death in the week ending 22 December and as it was most important that the companies should be able to rehearse plays both old and new before performing them at Court, it is likely that the City's unreasonable request to close the theatres was refused.

The plague is a poor man's disease, and flourishes in insanitary alleys and in swarming, rat-ridden tenements, amongst the ill-fed, ill-clothed, and ill-housed. It is exceptional to find a victim of mark and memory in a London plague.[2] With Gavin Douglas and (perhaps) William Lily in 1522, and Hans Holbein in 1543, the tale is almost taken. Among the thousands of men and women who died of the plague in 1625 three have left a name behind them, that their praises might be reported. Thomas Lodge probably became plague-doctor and died of the infection. John Florio, Italian tutor to Prince Henry and to Queen Anne, translator of Montaigne, a man much devoted to the English nation and to the English language, is said by Wood and Aubrey to have died of the plague at Fulham in August or September. Evidence points as strongly to the death in this epidemic of John Fletcher. He was buried at St. Saviour's, Southwark, on 29 August 1625. Aubrey notes that a knight of Norfolk or Suffolk invited the dramatist into the country. Fletcher stayed to have a suit of clothes made for him, but before the suit was ready he fell sick of the plague and died : ' This I

---

[1] B.M. Egerton MS. 2623, fo. 30.
[2] Cf. *D. P. P.*, p. 109, l. 20.

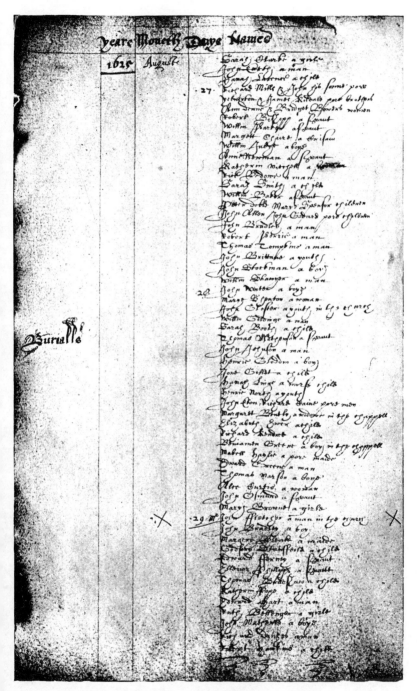

A page from the Register of St. Saviour's, Southwark

Recording the burial of John Fletcher, poet and dramatist

had from his Tailor, who is now a very old man, and clark
of St. Mary Overy's.' [1]

For the next ten years London was free from any
serious visitation of the plague. In 1626, 1627, 1628, and
1629 the plague-deaths were 134, 4, 3, and 0. In 1630 the
City experienced a minor plague which was the occasion
of two pamphlets by Thomas Dekker.[2] The infection was
noticed by the Court of Common Council on 18 March,
rose to its highest point in the week ending 29 July, when
77 died of the plague, fluctuated from 34 to 73 in August,
September, and October, and by the end of the year had
almost disappeared. The total number of deaths from the
plague throughout the year was but 1,317, and more than
a quarter of these died in the two parishes of St. Botolph,
Aldgate, and St. Mary, Whitechapel. But the memory of
1625 was so fresh that the terror of citizens was out of all
proportion to the danger threatened. The theatres again
suffered heavily. The weekly plague-deaths were more
than 40 from 8 July to 21 October and from the 4th to the
11th November, but the Privy Council was so alarmed at
the first appearance of the infection that it prohibited all
stage-plays, bear-baitings, and other assemblies for sports
and pastimes as early as 14 April.[3] The theatres were not

[1] MS. Aubrey 8, fo. 54 (*Brief Lives*, ed. A. Clark, i. 254). See the
illustration of the page on which Fletcher's burial is registered.
J. Chamberlain (*Letters*, ii. 623) says that Orlando Gibbons, organist
of the Chapel, 'that had the best hand in England', died at Canterbury on 5 June 'not without suspicion of the sickness', but Barclay
Squire showed that Gibbons died of an apoplectic seizure. See
Athenaeum, 14 November 1885, 664. John Harvard's father died
of the plague in Southwark on 20 August. See *NQ*, 7th Series, ii.
197.
[2] *London Looke Backe* and *The Blacke Rod* (D. P. P. 173–217).
[3] *P. C. R.* xxxix. 752.

permitted to reopen until 18 November.[1] The grounds upon which the genial Sir Thomas Roe lamented the idleness of the players are worth noting. He wrote to the Queen of Bohemia on 29 October :

' Your Majesty will give me leave to tell you another general calamity, we have had no plays this six months, and that makes our statesmen see the good use of them, by the want : for if our heads had been filled with the loves of Pyramus and Thisbe, or the various fortunes of Don Quixote, we should never have cared who had made peace or war, but on the stage. But now every fool is enquiring what the French do in Italy, and what they treat in Germany.' [2]

The one London plague of any importance between 1625 and 1665 was that of 1636. In this year there were buried in all 23,359 and of the plague 10,400, so that the epidemic was far less fatal than that of 1625. Indeed the plague-deaths returned in 1636 were surpassed in 1625 by those of five parishes alone.[3] The mortality in London from the week ending 23 December 1624 to that ending 22 December 1625 and in the outlying districts from the week ending 30 December 1624 to that ending 22 December 1625 was as follows :

	Buried in all.	Of the plague.
In London, the liberties, and the out-parishes	54,265	35,417
In Westminster, Lambeth, Newington, Stepney, Hackney, and Islington. .	8,736	5,896
Total	63,001	41,313

The population of London in 1625 was not more than

---

[1] *The Court and Times of Charles the First*, ii. 80.
[2] *S. P. Dom., Chas. I*, vol. 174, Doc. 102.
[3] For a list of the nineteen most heavily afflicted parishes in 1625 see Note M, p. 187.

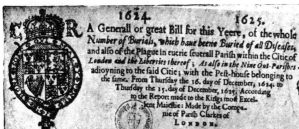

1624.   1625.

A Generall or great Bill for this Yeere, of the whole Number of Burials, which haue beene Buried of all Diseases, and also of the Plague in euerie seuerall Parish within the Citie of London and the Liberties thereof ; As also in the Nine Out-Parishes adioyning to the said Citie; with the Pest-house belonging to the same. From Thursday the 16. day of December, 1624. to Thursday the 15. day of December, 1625. According to the Report made to the Kings most Excellent Maiestie: Made by the Companie of Parish Clarkes of LONDON.

LONDON.	Bur.	Plag.	LONDON.	Bur.	Plag.	LONDON.	Bur.	Plag.
Albanes in Woodstreete	188	78	Gabriel Fen-church	71	54	Martins Iremonger-lane	25	18
Alhallowes Barking	357	263	George Botolph-lane	30	19	Martins at Ludgate	264	164
Alhallowes Breadstreet	38	14	Gregories by Pauls	296	196	Martins Orgars	88	47
Alhallowes the Great	442	302	Hellens within Bishopsgate	146	71	Martins Outwich	60	30
Alhallowes Hony-lane	18	8	Iames by Garlickhithe	186	109	Martins in the Vintrey	339	208
Alhallowes the Lesse	259	205	Iohn Baptist	122	79	Matthew Fridaystreete	34	11
Alhallowes in Lumberdstreet	86	44	Iohn Euangelist	7	0	Maudlins in Milkestreet	40	23
Alhallowes Stayninge	183	138	Iohn Zacharies	143	97	Maudlins by Oldfish-streete	225	141
Alhallowes the Wall	301	155	Iames Dukes place	310	253	Michael Basishaw	292	219
Alphage Cripple-gate	240	190	Katherine Coleman	263	175	Michael Corne-hill	144	79
Andrew Hubbard	146	101	Katherine Cree-church	48	373	Michael, Crooked-lane	144	91
Andrewes Vndershaft	219	149	Lawrence in the Iewrie	91	55	Michael Queenehithe	215	157
Andrewes by the Wardrobe	372	291	Lawrence Pountney	126	127	Michael in the Querne	53	30
Annes at Alders-gate	196	128	Leonards Eastcheape	51	26	Michael in the Ryall	111	62
Annes Black-Fryers	336	215	Leonards Fosterlane	29	209	Michael in Woodstreet	189	68
Antholins Parish	62	31	Magnus Parish by the Bridge	137	85	Mildreds Breadstreete	60	44
Austines Parish	72	40	Margarets Lothburie	114	64	Mildreds Poultrey	94	45
Bartholomew at the Exchange	52	24	Margarets Moses	37	25	Nicholas Acons	33	23
Bennets Fincke	108	57	Margarets new Fishstreete	143	82	Nicholas Cole-abby	87	67
Bennets Grace-church	48	14	Margarets Pattons	37	50	Nicholas Olaues	70	43
Bennets at Pauls Wharfe	226	131	Marie Ab-church	88	58	Olaues in Hartstreet	266	195
Bennets Sherhogge	24	8	Marie Aldermanbury	130	79	Olaues in the Iurie	42	21
Botolphs Billings-gate	99	66	Marie Aldermarie	89	54	Olaues in Siluerstreet	274	204
Christs-Church Parish	611	371	Marie le Bow	55	19	Pancras by Soperlane	37	8
Christophers Parish	48	28	Marie Bothaw	22	14	Peters in Cheape	68	44
Clements by Eastcheape	87	72	Marie Colechurch	26	11	Peters in Corne-hill	238	72
Dionis Back-church	99	59	Marie at the Hill	152	84	Peters at Pauls Wharfe	97	68
Dunstanes in the East	335	225	Marie Mounthaw	76	58	Peters the poore in Broadstr.	52	27
Edmonds in Lumberdstreet	78	49	Marie Summerset	270	192	Steuens in Colemanstreete	506	350
Ethelborow within Bishopsg.	205	101	Marie Stayninge	70	44	Steuens in Walbrooke	25	13
Faiths Parish	89	45	Marie Woolchurch	58	35	Swithins at London-stone	99	60
Fosters in Fosterlane	149	102	Marie Woolnoth	82	50	Thomas Apostles	141	107
						Trinitie Parish	148	87

Buried within the 97. Parishes within the Wals, of all Diseases. — 14340, *Whereof of the Plague* — 9197.

	Bur.	Plag.		Bur.	Plag.		Bur.	Plag.
Andrewes in Holborne	2190	1636	Botolph Bishopsgate	2334	714	Olaues in Southwarke	3689	2609
Bartholomew the Great	516	360	Botolph without Aldersgate	178	394	Sauiours in Southwark	2746	1671
Bartholomew the Lesse	113	65	Dunstanes in the West	860	642	Sepulchres Parish	3425	2420
Brides Parish	1481	1031	Georges in Southwarke	1608	912	Thomas in Southwarke	335	277
Botolph Aigate	2573	1653	Giles without Crippelgate	3988	2338	Trinitie in the Minories	131	87
Bridewell Precinct	213	152				At the Pest-house	194	189

Buried in the 16. Parishes without the Wals, standing part within the Liberties and part without : in Middlesex and Surrey, and at the Pest-house. — 26972, *Whereof of the Plague* — 17153.

Buried in the nine out Parishes.

	Bur.	Plag.		Bur.	Plag.		Bur.	Plag.
Clements Templebar	1284	755	Katherines by the Tower	998	744	Marie White-chappell	3505	2172
Giles in the Fields	1333	947	Leonards in Shoreditch	1995	1407	Magdalens in Bermondsey st.	1127	889
Iames at Clarkenwell	1191	903	Martins in the Fields	1470	974	Sauoy Parish	250	176

Buried in the nine Out-Parishes, in Middlesex and Surrey. — 12953, *Whereof of the Plague* — 9067.

The totall of all the Burials of all Diseases, within the Wals, without the Wals, in the Liberties, Middlesex and Surrey : with the nine Out-Parishes and the Pest-house — 54265, *Whereof buried of the Plague, this present yeere, is* — 35417.

Christnings this present yeere, is — 6983.
Parishes cleare this yeere, is — 0.
Parishes infected this yeere, is — 121.

London, Printed by William Stansby, 1625.

The Yearly Bill for 1625

320,000,[1] so that at least one-sixth of the population perished. The true proportion of the plague's victims was even greater, for perhaps a sixth of the City's inhabitants fled into the country. The horrors of this plague left a lasting impression upon the minds of Londoners. Their attitude towards it is well expressed by the author of *Lachrymae Londinenses* in words which were soon to be tragically falsified :

' to this present Plague of Pestilence, all former Plagues were but pettie ones. . . . This, to future Ages and Historiographers must needs be Kalendred the *Great Plague*.'

[1] See the Appendix, pp. 213–15.

NOTES

A (see p. 19)

THE unwillingness of the examiners to serve and their remissness in the performance of their duties suggested the need of still more authoritative control, and in December 1609 seven Commissioners of Health were appointed to hold office for six months—all of them aldermen and men of high position, and each one exercising supervision over a seventh part of the City. They kept a register book with the names and districts of the examiners, searchers, and watchmen in their division, and every Friday examiners and constables were required to attend at their homes and give an account of the number of deaths and infected houses, the details of which were entered in the register.[1] After the cessation of the plague in 1610 their services were no longer required. The office was not revived in the next epidemic of 1625.

B (see p. 47)

In 1548 one bell at least was ordered to be rung for three quarters of an hour at each burial.[2] Turner of Boulogne objected in 1563 that it ' did the party departing no good, neither afore their death nor after '.[3] The continual ' jangling ' of the bells gave great offence to the sick, and in September 1592 ' extraordinary ringing ' was forbidden. There were 114 churches in the 26 wards : London was a city of many towers and spires and of many bells. Bells were rung in July 1603 (see above, p. 96), but not when the plague was at its height. Dekker speaks of corpses being buried in this year ' without the dead mans musick (his *Bell*) '.[4] Ben Jonson refers to this nerve-racking noise in *The Silent Woman* (I. i). The ' perpetuitie of ringing ' in plague-time led Morose to ' devise a roome, with double walls, and treble seelings ; the

---

[1] *J.* xxviii. 24 b and 25.
[2] Stow, *Annales* (1605), 1,004.
[3] Cited by Creighton, *A History of Epidemics*, i. 336.
[4] *The Seven deadly Sinnes* (1606), sig. G 1ᵛ (*G.* ii. 76).

windores close shut, and calk'd ; and there he lives by candle-light '. More troublesome was the ' everlasting voyce ' of fine Madam Would-be (*Volpone*, III. v) :

> The bells, in time of pestilence, ne're made
> Like noise, or were in that perpetuall motion.

In 1625 Nehemiah Wallington, a strict Puritan with a tormented conscience, remained ' in this doleful City ' with his wife and children, ' hearing of bells tolling and ringing out continually '.[1] ' In the daytime ', wrote the author of *Lachrymae Londinenses*, ' what else heare we almost but the Bells ringing of Knells ? and in the night season (when we should take our rest,) we are interrupted by the continuall tolling of Passing-Bells, and anon the ringing out of the same ' ; and Holland, who could hear at Chelsea the murmuring of London's bells, remarked that no clocks were heard to strike, for nothing was rung

> but death-lamenting Knells.
> Strange, that the Houres should faile to tell the Day,
> When Time to thousands ran so fast away.[2]

By the orders of 1636 the ringing of bells at private funerals was strictly forbidden. In 1665 ' the Bells seemed hoarse with continual tolling, until at last they quite ceased '.[3]

The funeral charges at St. Botolph's, Aldgate, in 1588 were as follows : [4]

	s.	*d.*
ffor the menester	11	0
ffor the afternoones knell with the greate bell . .	6	8
ffor the ground in the Churche	6	8

---

[1] His diary is at the Guildhall Library (MS. 204).

[2] *Op. cit.*, sig. F 4ᵛ. Cf. also Wither, *op. cit.*, 104, and Taylor, *The Fearefull Sommer* (1625), sig. A 6ᵛ.

[3] N. Hodges, *Loimologia* (translated by John Quincy, 1720), 18. Pepys heard the bell of his parish toll five or six times on 30 July (*Diary*, ed. H. B. Wheatley, v. 31).

[4] A. G. B. Atkinson, *St. Botolph Aldgate* (1898), 113. For the charges for the ringing of bells at Stepney in 1602, at St. Christopher's in 1625, and at St. Saviour's, Southwark, in 1613, see *Memorials of Stepney Parish* (ed. G. W. Hill and W. H. Frere), 42 ; *Accomptes of the Church-wardens of St. Christopher's* (ed. E. Freshfield), 60 ; and a broadsheet (No. 136), *St. Saviour of Southwarke*, in the possession of the Society of Antiquaries.

	s.	d.
ffor the best cloth not used [1]		9
ffor takinge up the stones	11	0
ffor the peales which weare not runge . . .	2	0
ffor the pitt and knell the corse being coffined . .		18
ffor the Clarkes attendance		8
ffor the sextens attendance		4
ffor three passinge bells		12
ffor iiij bearers		16

C (see p. 56)

The wand or rod was usually two or three feet in length. A white rod was carried in the country. In London the colour was changed from white to red in May 1583.[2] It was a common trick to conceal the wand under the cloak or garment (see below, p. 180) : for this reason bearers were sometimes forbidden to carry cloaks. After the order of 1583 that all inhabitants of an infected house, whether themselves infected or not, were to keep at home, the wand became the distinctive mark of those who waited on the infected, as searchers, nurses, buriers, and plague-doctors. The mark was borrowed from the Continent. In 1480 infected persons at Lille were required to carry ' une blanque verghe ' three feet long.[3] At Moret in 1580 the Venetian ambassador met a man and a woman carrying wands and asking alms.[4] Many healthy beggars used them to frighten people into giving money.

D (see p. 58)

Providers of food, fuel, and other necessaries to infected houses were first appointed in 1564. They were usually women. About the year 1578 the Privy Council (who wished them to be styled ' purveyors ' or ' acaters ') suggested that they should deal only with certain specified poulterers, butchers, bakers, &c., and not attend the common markets ;

[1] By order of the vestry it had to be paid for, whether used or not.
[2] I know of only one instance of the use of a white wand in London after 1583 : purveyors of necessaries were ordered to carry white rods on 11 August 1592 (*J.* xxiii. 126), but red rods were carried on 7 September (*ibid.* 129 b).
[3] É. Caplet, *La Peste à Lille au XVIIe Siècle* (1898), 36.
[4] *Cal. S. P. Ven.*, 1558–1580, 649.

but the aldermen did not consider the suggestion feasible.[1]
In 1583, 1592, and 1603, when the plague was so heavy that it
became impossible to obtain providers for all the segregated,
one member from each infected household (and ' not sundry
at sundry times ') was appointed by the surveyor to act as
provider : he was required to walk by the channel, to shun
crowded thoroughfares, and to carry a red wand without
concealing any part of it under his cloak or garment.[2] In
the seventeenth century the duties of providers were usually
performed by watchmen.[3]

E (see p. 64)

The task of setting up crosses and ' papers ' was given sometimes to the beadles or constables of the ward, sometimes to
the clerk or sexton of the parish, and sometimes (as in 1583)[4] to
officials specially appointed for the purpose. Anthony Copley
tells the story of the constable who, hearing his neighbour's
wife ' sore lamming ' her husband, set up a red cross on their
door. The neighbour was highly offended, and complained to
the alderman of the ward of the great injury done to him. The
constable's defence was: ' And like your Worship, his wife sore
beate him yesterday, and I thinke there cannot be a greater
plague in a house then that, and therefore I did it.' [5]

The usual payment for setting up a single cross was twopence : [6] in 1592 a man earned £4 by setting up and watching
bills.[7] Defacement of these marks was a common offence. The
punishment in 1574 was a fine of 40s. or imprisonment for 18
days,[8] and in 1583 confinement for an additional 28 days.[9]
In 1592 a bricklayer who pulled down a bill was committed

---

[1] *S. P. Dom., Eliz.*, vol. 98, Doc. 38.

[2] *J.* xxi. 285 (1583) ; xxiii. 129 b (1592) ; xxvi. 127 (1603).

[3] *J.* xxvi. 372 (1605) ; xxvii. 275 (1608) and 365 b (1609). See also
the orders for 1665 and see above, p. 69.   [4] *R.* xx. 466.

[5] *Wits, Fits and Fancies* (1614), 87.

[6] J. M. S. Brooke and A. W. C. Hallen, *Transcripts of the Registers
of . . . S. Mary Woolnoth and S. Mary Woolchurch Haw*, xxv.

[7] *R.* xxii. 445 b.

[8] *J.* xx, pt. i, 263 b. This mayoral proclamation was printed by
John Day and is reprinted in Grose and Astle's *The Antiquarian
Repertory* (1807), i. 350. In 1578 the punishment was 40s. or 20 days
(*J.* xx, pt. ii, 429 b).   [9] *J.* xxi. 285 b.

to the nearest Cage, there to remain during the pleasure of the Court of Aldermen,[1] and in 1630 a watchman was stocked for wiping a cross off a door in Westminster.[2]

F (see p. 77)

The land chosen by a special committee appointed in 1583 to discover a site for the pesthouse is described as

' three Acres or thereaboutes belonginge to Saint Bartholo-mewes hospitall, Lyinge in a common feilde apperteyninge to the Prebende of wenlockes barne in the tenure of John Millyon, Abuttinge on the gardyns of John Cornwall on the west, And vppon the foote path ledinge from London to Canbery on the east, And alsoe vj Acres or thereaboutes lyinge towardes the northe of the said field, whereof two acres parcell thereof are of the demaynes of the Prebend of More, one Acre and a half of thinheritance of william Plighton, And the other three Acres beinge on the Northsyde belonginge to the said prebend in the tenure of the saide John Cornewall which peece of grounde this Courte Lyked well of.' [3]

G (see p. 84)

There is abundant evidence of the rates charged to inmates of the pesthouse. In July 1603 the Court of Aldermen decreed that persons carried there from any part of the City or liberties were to be maintained by the householder with whom they had resided, if he was of ability, and alter-natively by the parish whence they came. It was further ordered that ' every person who shall send any infected person to the pesthouse shall send with them xiij$s$. iiij$d$. towards the charge of surgery, women keepers, and other extraordinary charges '. By 13 September the Chamberlain had spent £115 for bedding, physic, and other necessaries for poor sick people sent to the pesthouse.[4]

In May 1604 Henry ' Chetham ' or ' Cheetam ' or ' Chittam ', Keeper of the Pesthouse, sent a petition to the Court of Alder-men, asking no doubt for certain reforms in the management of the house and for a revision of the rates of payment. A report on this petition, presented on 18 May, proposed the

[1] R. xxii. 425.   [2] S. P. Dom., Chas. I, vol. 175, Doc. 3.
[3] J. xxi. 283 b.   [4] R. xxvi, pt. i, 176 b, 189, and 191 b.

following resolutions which the Court afterwards adopted.[1] A register was to be kept recording the names of persons sent to the pesthouse, the date of their arrival, the parish and dwelling from which they were brought, and the time of their death and burial or delivery. No person was to be received there without a warrant from the Lord Mayor or the alderman of the ward or his deputy or the provost-marshal. The keeper had to ensure that the parent or governor of the sick person or the churchwardens of his parish would pay the patient's expenses. If the sick man were a vagrant without a permanent dwelling-place, this had to be recorded in the warrant. A list of the rates which the keeper might charge is sufficiently interesting to quote in full.

> The rates for duties to be receaved by the keeper of the Pestehowse which wee thinke meete he doe not in anie wise exceede

ffor the dyett of everie persone whose father mother Master Mistres or other parent or governor shalbe of abillitie by the daie . . . . . . viij^d

ffor the dyett of the poore by the daie . . . vj^d
Lodginge everie nighte . . . . . . ij^d

watchinge and attendance (if anie shall neede) for a daie and a nighte dureinge three daies and three nightes . vj^d

Phisick and surgerie by the daie . . . . iiij^d
If anie shall dye then for the shrowde . . . ij^s
ffor buriall . . . . xvj^d

for fyer in winter from Michaelmas to the feaste of the Anunciacon of the blessed virgyn Mary in case where fire shalbe needfull by the daie . . . . ij^d

And to the ende there maie be a register keepte and faire written that maie sett furthe the truthe in particulers as shalbe meete and as is hereby before mencioned and intended It is thoughtt meete that there be allowed for mayntenance thereof and for the paines and chardges of the Clarke whoe shall keepe the same booke to be paide for everie persone whoe shalbe receaved in to the saide howse at the tyme of the firste receivinge of suche persone in to the same howse . . . . viij^d

---

[1] *Letter Book*, BB, 271 b and 272. In July 1611 Chetham and William Upton petitioned for and obtained an increase of wages. Both men are

And to thende there maie be from tyme to tyme⎫
speedie supplie of provisions necessarie for ease and ⎪
reliefe of suche as shalbe receaved in to the saide howse ⎪
wee houlde it meete that there shalbe paide unto ⎪
Cheetam nowe keeper of the saide howse Tenn shillinges ⎪
aforehande towardes the defrayinge of the chardges of ⎪
everie suche persone dureinge suche tyme as suche ⎪
persone shall continue in the same howse And if anie ⎬ x^s
suche persone shall dye before that money be dulie ⎪
expended accordinge to the ordinarie rates and allow- ⎪
ances of the howse then the saide Cheetam shall repaie ⎪
the sorplusage thereof which after the buriall shall ⎪
remaine unexpended unto the father mother Master ⎪
Mistres Parent or other governor of suche persone ⎪
which shall soe dye or to anie other to whome the same ⎪
in righte oughte to be paide   .   .   .   .   .⎭

ffurther wee doe houlde it meete that he maie⎫
have vj[11] xiij[s] iiij[d] per Annum for his wages that ⎪
he maie be encouraged to keepe his place and ⎬vj[11] xiij[s] iiij[d]
office for the better goverment of the saide ⎪
howse soe longe as he shalbe officer there   .⎭

These rates were practically unaltered in 1625. An interesting instance from the parish books of St. Margaret's, Lothbury,
throws light on this point. On 1 May 1625 William Miller,
brazier, petitioned the parish for relief and maintenance on
the ground that his house was infected and shut up, and that
he was destitute of all means. The vestry agreed to lend him
£3. Eight days later, however, Miller petitioned for more
money to the great astonishment of the whole parish, who
marvelled that he had spent so much money in so short a time.
In the end it was decided, with Miller's consent, that he and
his household (eight persons in all) should be sent to the
pesthouse for a month, at the weekly charge per person
of seven shillings, a total monthly charge to the parish of
£11 4s.[1]

styled keepers of the pesthouse (*Letter Book*, DD, 303 b). The office was
not abolished until 1730 (*J*. lvii. 212).
   [1] *Archaeologia*, xlv. 71. See also above, pp. 73–4.

H (see p. 106)

In a general bill of mortality for Westminster, Lambeth, &c., in 1625 (MS. Rawl. D. 859), the following statistics are given for the outlying districts in 1603 :

	Total deaths.	Of the plague.
City of Westminster (14 July–15 December) .	1,019	879
Lambeth (no period specified)	410	387
Newington Butts (14 June–15 December) . .	657	577
Savoy (1 June–15 December)	211	196
Stepney (25 March–15 December) . . .	2,129	2,059
Hackney (no period specified)	210	187
Islington (no period specified)	274	239
Total	4,910	4,526 [1]

J (see p. 106)

The term was held at Hertford in the plague-year of 1592, when the inhabitants charged excessive prices for food and lodging.[2] In 1603 St. Albans, Hertford, Northampton, and Coventry all sued to have the term in their midst,[3] but Winchester was preferred. This town was as extortionate as Hertford. ' Six howres sleepe could not be bought under five shillings.' ' A bottle of hay was sold deerer then a bottle of wine at *London.*' Dekker's satirical account in *Newes from Graves-end* (D. P. P. 74–8) may be compared with the following ballad from All Souls MS. clv, fo. 91. I am indebted to Sir Charles Firth for calling my attention to it and to the Warden and Fellows of All Souls College for allowing me to print it. The scribe appears to be Christopher Yelverton, Speaker in the parliament of 1597 (cf. fo. 62) and author of the epilogue to the *Jocasta* (1566) of two other members of Gray's Inn, George Gascoigne and Francis Kinwelmersh.

On the term being kept at Winchester.

Which is the waye to Winchester
    here 's one woulde by a goose
Men saye the tearme shalbe kept there
    I thinke the Devills brocke loose

---

[1] The figures add up to 4,524.
[2] *Acts of the Privy Council,* 1592, 273–4.
[3] E. Lodge, *Illustrations of British History* (1791), iii. 172.

Neyther fyer nor forrage there's to be had
  howe hanges this geare together
They that maye chuse I hold them madd
  will make any arraunt thether.

ffrom Westminster to Winchester
  is threscore mile save three
And I doe dwell at Nottingham
  tearme that tearme list for me
They need neyther plague nor pestilence
  that make their travell thether
They shalbe plagud ere they come there
  with durtie waye and weather.

It might have ben at Saint Albans towne
  a thousande tymes more fitter
Then to goe toyling up and downe
  to seeke for haye and litter
I will tarry still at Nottingham
  the waye is farr to wander
Ile paye for none of their powdred sauce
  for eyther goose or gander.

Soe farewell tearme at Winchester
  with all thy fowerten dayes
The ende will shewe howe the worlde will goe
  full litle to thy praise.

K (see p. 114)

Fourteen parishes returned more than 600 deaths from 14 July to 22 December 1603 : St. Andrew, Holborn (1,191—1,125) ; St. Bride (933—805) ; St. Botolph, Aldgate (1,413—1,280) ; St. Botolph, Bishopsgate (1,228—1,094) ; St. George, Southwark (915–804) ; St. Giles, Cripplegate (2,408—1,745) ; St. Olave, Southwark (2,541—2,383) ; St. Saviour, Southwark (1,914—1,773) ; St. Sepulchre (2,223—1,861) ; St. Clement, Temple Bar (662—502) ; St. James, Clerkenwell (725—619) ; St. Katherine-by-the-Tower (653—585) ; St. Leonard, Shoreditch (871—740) ; St. Mary, Whitechapel (1,539—1,352). The last five parishes are out-parishes, the rest are parishes without the walls and within the liberties. The parish which suffered most in the City proper was St. Katherine Cree Church

(400—337). In the ninety-six parishes within the walls there died in these months 11,408, and of the plague 9,452 : in the sixteen parishes without the walls there died in all 16,530, and of the plague 14,388 : in the eight out-parishes and at the pesthouse there died in all 6,143, and of the plague 5,302. The total was 34,081, and of the plague 29,142. See the bill of mortality at p. 114, where the figures are wrongly added up.

L (see p. 118)

These statistics are taken from John Bell's *Londons Remembrancer* (1665-6), sigs. B_3–B_4.[1] The original weekly bills from which Bell derived them were burnt in the Fire of 1666.

1606

		Buried in all.	*Of the plague.*			*Buried in all.*	*Of the plague.*
July	3	110	25	October	2	256	141
	10	134	33	,,	9	218	106
,,	17	146	50	,,	16	227	117
,,	24	140	46	,,	23	224	109
,,	31	178	66	,,	30	226	101
August	7	181	67	November	6	183	68
,,	14	197	75	,,	13	162	41
,,	21	189	85	,,	20	145	28
,,	28	207	85	,,	27	123	22
September	4	241	116	December	4	160	45
,,	11	216	105	,,	11	137	38
,,	18	214	92	,,	18	132	28
,,	25	204	87	,,	25	135	38

1607

July	2	112	27	October	1	283	150
,,	9	117	33	,,	8	230	113
,,	16	154	37	,,	15	223	110
,,	23	152	51	,,	22	215	82
,,	30	156	43	,,	29	198	68
August	6	187	77	November	5	196	66
,,	13	172	69	,,	12	186	55
,,	20	189	76	,,	19	148	46
,,	27	175	71	,,	26	130	21
September	3	232	105	December	3	126	19
,,	10	243	121	,,	10	122	28
,,	17	264	124	,,	17	131	7
,,	24	302	177	,,	24	129	9

1608

July	7	134	16	August	4	184	45
,,	14	162	26	,,	11	191	70
,,	21	156	24	,,	18	203	79
,,	28	233	50	,,	25	197	73

[1] The weekly plague-deaths for 1606–1610, 1625, 1630, 1636, 1637, 1640–1642 are reprinted by J. T. Murray, *op. cit.*, ii. 186–9.

1608 (cont.)

		Buried in all.	Of the plague.			Buried in all.	Of the plague.
September	1	275	123	November	3	236	109
,,	8	250	136	,,	10	189	72
,,	15	248	107	,,	17	205	69
,,	22	273	143	,,	24	205	70
,,	29	296	147	December	1	240	90
October	6	239	103	,,	8	194	68
,,	13	258	131	,,	15	197	75
,,	20	247	124	,,	22	190	53
,,	27	241	102	,,	29	165	39

1609

		Buried	Plague			Buried	Plague
July	6	194	60	October	5	306	154
,,	13	198	57	,,	12	335	177
,,	20	189	58	,,	19	313	131
,,	27	229	91	,,	26	199	55
August	3	239	100	November	2	237	84
,,	10	280	126	,,	9	224	69
,,	17	264	101	,,	16	234	67
,,	24	296	150	,,	23	187	59
,,	31	364	177	,,	30	181	51
September	7	300	141	December	7	139	18
,,	14	335	158	,,	14	150	23
,,	21	386	210	,,	21	148	23
,,	28	311	144	,,	28	161	39

1610

		Buried	Plague			Buried	Plague
July	5	194	38	October	4	219	63
,,	12	187	45	,,	11	221	79
,,	19	171	45	,,	18	197	59
,,	26	187	40	,,	25	187	49
August	2	187	47	November	1	187	58
,,	9	234	50	,,	8	196	40
,,	16	250	73	,,	15	160	22
,,	23	208	60	,,	22	163	42
,,	30	294	99	,,	29	179	39
September	6	286	96	December	6	142	15
,,	13	272	89	,,	13	146	12
,,	20	256	86	,,	20	148	26
,,	27	254	72	,	23	183	0
				,,	30	211	0

M (see p. 174)

Nineteen parishes returned more than 600 deaths from 22 December 1624 to 23 December 1625 : Christchurch (611—371) ; St. Andrew, Holborn (2,190—1,636) ; St. Bride (1,481—1,031) ; St. Botolph, Aldgate (2,573—1,653) ; St. Botolph, Bishopsgate (2,334—714) ; St. Dunstan - in - the - West (860—642) ; St. George, Southwark (1,608—912) ;

St. Giles, Cripplegate (3,988—2,338) ; St. Olave, Southwark (3,689—2,609) ; St. Saviour, Southwark (2,746—1,671) ; St. Sepulchre (3,425—2,420) ; St. Clement, Temple Bar (1,284—755) ; St. Giles-in-the-Fields (1,333—947) ; St. James, Clerkenwell (1,191 [1]—903) ; St. Katherine - by - the - Tower (998—744) ; St. Leonard, Shoreditch (1,995—1,407) ; St. Martin-in-the-Fields (1,470—974) ; St. Mary, Whitechapel (3,305—2,272) ; St. Magdalen, Bermondsey Street (1,127—889). Of these parishes the first was within the walls, the next ten without the walls, and the remainder in the out-parishes. In the ninety-seven parishes within the walls there died in all 14,340, and of the plague 9,197 : in the sixteen parishes without the walls and at the pesthouse there died in all 26,972, and of the plague 17,153 : in the nine out-parishes in Middlesex and Surrey there died in all 12,953, and of the plague 9,067.

[1] A contemporary bill (MS. Rawl. D. 859) gives 1,121 as the total of deaths. Bell and contemporary bills in the Guildhall (see facsimile at p. 174) and in *S. P. Dom.*, *Chas. I*, vol. 11, Doc. 70, give 1,191, the correct figure.

THE BILLS OF MORTALITY

THE aim of this section of the Appendix is to give a summary account of the origin and contents of the London
weekly and yearly bills of mortality in the sixteenth and
early seventeenth centuries and of the machinery which
produced them ; a list of extant bills ; [1] and an estimate of
their trustworthiness. Some of the material upon which
this section is based has been used before by W. Ogle in
‘ An Inquiry into the Trustworthiness of the Old Bills of
Mortality ’ (*Journal of the Royal Statistical Society*, September 1892), by C. Creighton in *A History of Epidemics*
(vol. i, 1891), and in ‘ The Population of Old London ’
(*Blackwood's Magazine*, April 1891), by J. Christie in *Some
Account of Parish Clerks* (1893), and by C. H. Hull in *The
Economic Writings of Sir William Petty* (1899).

THE WEEKLY BILLS

England owed many of her plague-measures to France,
but in establishing bills of mortality she led the way by
150 years. Bills were first compiled in Paris in 1667, and
the idea was probably suggested to the counsellors of
Louis XIV by John Graunt’s *Natural and Political Observations* (1662), the book which first showed their statistical
value.[2] The earliest reference to a London bill of mortality
that has so far been discovered is dated 30 August 1519.
On that day the Court of Aldermen agreed that the

---

[1] It was intended at first to stop at 1630, but references have
been added to the most important collections of later bills.

[2] Hull, *op. cit.*, ii. 422.

Chamberlain should pay 22d. to ' John Ward one of the
yeomen of the Waterside for boat hire to my lord Cardinal's
and to Mr. Lark with the bill of the number of such
persons as be deceased of the common sickness sithence
the beginning of the search thereof'.[1] Lark was the brother
of Wolsey's mistress. The next reference is in a letter
written by Sir Thomas Audley, Lord Keeper, in October
1532 : ' The Council here have commanded the mayor to
certify to them to-morrow what number of persons have
died of the plague in London this last week.' [2] Bills were
also prepared in 1535, 1536, and 1537, all plague-years.[3] It
is probable that they were not compiled in healthy years
until the latter half of the century.

Statistics for the bills of 1519 seem to have been obtained by organized searches. The system of segregation
established in January 1518 would assist their compilation.
The parish-clerks of London had been incorporated as
the Guild of St. Nicholas in 1233,[4] but in the early part
of their existence their duties were mainly choral. The
return of bills is not mentioned in the Ordinances of 1529,[5]
but it had become a part of their duties by July 1536
when the wardens were instructed that every parish church
in London was to deliver to the Lord Mayor weekly and
in writing the names of the infected and of the dead.[6] In
September 1538 Thomas Cromwell issued injunctions for

[1] R. v. 142 b. The statement in October 1513 (Cal. S. P. Ven.,
1509–1519, 151) that the plague-deaths varied from three to four
hundred a day was probably a guess.

[2] State Papers, Henry VIII, § 71, fo. 139.

[3] R. ix. 187 ; Letters and Papers, Foreign and Domestic,
Henry VIII, vol. ix, Nos. 151, 209, 274, 279, 341, 451, and vol. xii,
pt. ii, No. 298.

[4] Stow is the only authority for this statement. See Christie,
op. cit., 24.   [5] Ibid. 65–75.   [6] R. ix. 187.

the provision of a book and a coffer with two locks in every parish in England and Wales. On Sundays the minister was required to enter in the book, in the presence of the churchwardens or one of them, all the christenings, marriages, and burials of the preceding week.[1] The parish registers were no doubt used by the clerks in making their returns, though many discrepancies exist between the numbers in the bills and in the registers. According to the Ordinances of 1553 the wardens had to ' write, or cause to be written weekly, the certificates of all such persons as shall die or depart within the City of London and the liberties thereof, in such manner and form as heretofore hath been accustomed, and thereupon make a certificate to the Lord Mayor of this City for the time being, as often and as long as commandment shall be given so to continue by the said Lord Mayor for the time being, and so from time to time '.[2] In 1555 the clerks were ordered to return ' the numbers of all the persons that do die and whereof they die ', but the only disease which was differentiated before 1607 was that of the plague. An interesting variant from the ordinary bill is recorded in January 1583 when the City compiled a list of infected inns, victualling houses, and lodging houses : it was printed on one side of a sheet of paper, and displayed in conspicuous places about the City so that citizens might know which houses to avoid.[3]

Only four weekly bills of the sixteenth century appear to have survived : a bill for a week ending 23 November,[4]

---

[1] Public Record Office, *Theological Tracts*, iii. 1.

[2] Christie, *op. cit.*, 133–4. See also *R.* xiii. 43 b–49.

[3] *Remembrancia* (ed. W. H. and H. C. Overall), 336.

[4] B.M. Egerton MS. 2603, fo. 4. It has been dated 1532 by Creighton and others, but it may very well be earlier. A facsimile

two bills covering the period 5–14 August 1535,[1] and a bill for the week ending 22 November 1582.[2] Seventeenth-century bills are extant for the weeks ending 20 October (see facsimile at p. 106) and 3 November 1603,[3] 12 November 1607 (a plague-bill: see below, pp. 198–9),[4] 23 February 1609 (a plague-bill : see facsimile on p. 198),[5] 17 August 1609,[6] 15 April 1613,[7] and in 1625 for the weeks ending 21 July,[8] 11 August,[9] 27 October, and 15 December (a plague-bill : see facsimile at p. 196).[10] There are series of weekly bills from 1636 to 1683 in the Bodleian,[11] from

of a part of this bill is given in Traill's *Social England* (illustrated edition), iii. 195.

[1] *State Papers, Henry VIII*, § 49, fos. 219–26. Cf. Creighton, *op. cit.*, i. 296–9.

[2] *Hist. MSS. Comm., Salisbury MSS.*, pt. xiii, p. 212. I have not seen this bill.

[3] Guildhall Library. These bills are printed by John Windet ' Printer to the Honourable City of London '. For Windet's licence, see below, p. 196. Another bill in the possession of Sir Charles Firth gives statistics up to 20 October 1603. It was (piratically) ' Printed by J. R. [? James Roberts] for John Trundle '. This bill is probably that described in J. E. Hodgkin's *Rariora* (1902), iii. 7, and sold by Messrs. Sotheby on 28 April 1914 (*Sale Catalogue*, No. 206).

[4] *S. P. Dom., Jas. I*, vol. 28, Doc. 88. Part of this plague-bill is reprinted in *The Home Counties Magazine*, vol. vi (1904), p. 75.

[5] Trinity College, Dublin (*Hist. MSS. Comm.*, 4th Report, 594).

[6] *S. P. Dom., Jas. I*, vol. 47, Docs. 85, 86. This bill is in MS. See p. 197, *n.* 3.

[7] B.M. Reg. 7. C. XVI, fos. 154–7 b. This bill is in MS.

[8] Bodleian MS. Rawl. D. 859.   [9] B.M. 1298. m. 11. (18).

[10] Bodleian MS. Rawl. D. 859.

[11] Gough Adds. Lond. 4⁰. 95. This important series appears to have escaped attention. There are many gaps. Creighton (*op. cit.*, i. 532), regretting that Graunt omitted to give statistics for 1637–1646, writes : ' The omitted years are not only those of great political revolution, which may have had an effect upon the public health, but they are of special interest for the beginning of that great period of fever and small-pox in London which continued all through the eighteenth century.'

1662 to 1680, from 1702 to 1829, and from 1832 to 1853 in the Guildhall, and from 1665 to 1773, and from 1831 to 1838 in the British Museum.

There are also statistics, abstracted from the weekly bills, which give the total weekly deaths and the total weekly plague-deaths, but not the weekly mortality in each parish. Summaries of this kind are extant for each week from 9 July 1563 to 26 July 1566,[1] for 21–28 October 1574,[2] from 26 December 1577 to 31 January 1583,[3] and from December 1596 to December 1600.[4] Many bills were burnt in the fire at the Parish Clerks' Hall in 1666, but not before some of them had been printed in John Bell's *Londons Remembrancer* (1665/6). From this work we learn the weekly totals of deaths and christenings from 26 December 1605–20 December 1610, 23 December 1624– 15 December 1625, 24 December 1629–16 December 1630, 24 December 1635–14 December 1637, 19 December 1639– 14 December 1647, and 27 December 1664–19 December 1665.[5]

---

[1] *Three Fifteenth Century Chronicles, with Historical Memoranda By John Stowe* (ed. J. Gairdner, Camden Society), 123–5 and 144–7: Stow evidently derived his information from the weekly bills, but only gave the numbers of those dying of the plague. Statistics of the deaths from all causes in each parish during 1563 are reprinted in *Notes and Queries*, 9th Series, vi. 384, from a collection of extracts made by William Lambarde, *c.* 1568.

[2] Holinshed, *Chronicles* (1577), ii. 1870.

[3] *Hist. MSS. Comm.*, 4th Report, Appendix, 222 (Salisbury MSS.). These are the bills delivered to Burghley. They are reprinted in Creighton, *op. cit.*, i. 341–4. There are gaps from 9 November to 28 December 1581, and for the week ending 20 December 1582.   [4] Bodleian MS. Ash. 824, fos. 195–216.

[5] Bell also gives the yearly totals for 1593 and 1604 : John Grant (*Natural and Political Observations*, 5th edn., 1676) gives them from 1604 to 1664. The yearly total for 1593 is also given in the bill for the week ending 20 October 1603. On the weekly

Several changes were made from time to time in the arrangement and contents of the bills. In the earliest bills the order in which the parishes are mentioned seems quite haphazard, but on 1 August 1570 the wardens of the parish clerks were ordered to divide the returns into three parts, showing : (1) the number of deaths within the City walls ; (2) the number in the parishes without the walls and within the liberties ; and (3) the number in the out-parishes.[1]

Changes were also made in the number of parishes included in the bills. The bill in Egerton MS. 2603 mentions 100 parishes within the walls, and without the walls but within the liberties.[2] One of the 1535 bills gives 102 parishes, the other 98. In 1563 108 parishes are mentioned.[3] Statistics for 1582 derived from the weekly reports[4] include 96 parishes within the walls, 11 without the walls and within the liberties, and the two hospitals of St. Thomas and St. Bartholomew. In 1605 the Court of Aldermen ordered the parish clerks to include the weekly number of christenings in the Dutch and French churches.[5] St. James's, Duke's Place, was added to the 96 parishes within the walls in 1622. In 1603 and 1625 the number of parishes without the walls and within the liberties was 16. The

figures for 1592–1593 given in some broadsheets and by Graunt, see Creighton, *op. cit.*, i. 354 ; C. H. Hull, *op. cit.*, ii. 426–7 ; and E. K. Chambers, *The Elizabethan Stage*, iv. 348, 349. I have not attempted to collect the statistics to be found here and there in contemporary notes and letters. Many letters contain the plague-deaths for the current week. Thus in a letter in my possession Burghley gives the plague-deaths in London and in Westminster for the week ending 27 September 1576.

[1] *Letter Book*, V, 307.

[2] Thirty-seven parishes are mentioned by name, 23 of them being infected : 63 parishes are reported ' clear ', i. e. as returning no deaths.   [3] Stow, *Annales* (1605), 1,112.

[4] See below, p. 200.   [5] *R.* xxvi, pt. ii, 494 b.

deaths in the out-parishes, as we have seen, were ordered to be shown in the bills in August 1570, but they were not regularly included until much later. In 1603 they were not given until the week ending 21 July.[1] The Court of Aldermen again ordered their inclusion on 14 January 1605.[2] There were eight out-parishes in 1603: St. Clement Danes; St. Giles-in-the-Fields; St. James, Clerkenwell; St. Katherine-by-the-Tower; St. Leonard, Shoreditch; St. Martin-in-the-Fields; St. Mary, Whitechapel; and St. Magdalen, Bermondsey Street. St. Mary, Savoy, was added in 1606. Burials in St. Paul's Cathedral, Westminster Abbey, the Temple Church, St. Peter's-in-the-Tower, the Rolls and Lincoln's Inn Chapels, the Charterhouse and several other chapels belonging to hospitals, were not included in the bills.[3]

The three Westminster parishes of St. Margaret, St. Martin-in-the-Fields, and St. Clement Danes were required to send their weekly bills to the Lord Mayor of London from 1593.[4] In 1626 Westminster was included in the weekly bills of London. The outlying districts of Islington, Hackney, Stepney, Rotherhithe (or Redriffe), Newington, and Lambeth were added during the plague of 1636. The inclusion of the thickly populated parish of Stepney greatly annoyed the citizens of London, who unsuccessfully petitioned against it on the ground that country people were led to suppose that the plague was more serious in London

[1] See the yearly bill for 1603 at p. 114.
[2] R. xxvi, pt. ii, 494 b.
[3] W. Maitland, *The History of London* (1775 edn.), ii. 472.
[4] *Acts of the Privy Council*, 1592–1593, 442. Westminster bills (in manuscript) for the weeks ending 4 October 1605 and 15 September 1608 are in *S. P. Dom., Jas. I*, vol. 15, Doc. 76, and vol. 36, Doc. 16. St. Martin-in-the-Fields and St. Clement Danes were also included in the out-parishes of the City of London.

than it really was and so were chary of visiting, or receiving goods from, the City.[1]

In 1607 (perhaps earlier) the clerks were required to specify the several diseases on the backs of the bills. The bill for the week ending 12 November 1607 is so drawn up. This practice, which seems to have fallen into disuse, was renewed in October 1624.[2] These lists of diseases and casualties were based upon the reports of the searchers. The diagnoses of these ancient and ignorant women were sometimes vague and sometimes precise : ' greefe ', ' Liver-growne ',' Rising of the Lights ', ' Starved at nurse ', ' Aged ', ' Murthered by his mother ', ' King's Evill ', ' Meagrome ', ' Suddenly ', ' Brused ', ' Plannet struck '. The obsolete phraseology of the searchers was still bringing the bills into disrepute when the office was abolished by the Registration Act of 1836.

The weekly bills were perhaps first printed in 1593. The bills of that year printed by John Wolfe were graced with an ' eloquent *post-script* ' from the pen of Gabriel Harvey.[3]   On 1 August 1603 John Windet obtained permission to print ' the bills of such as die and are buried this year of the plague and other sicknesses provided that he shall print London and the Liberties thereof by themselves in one sheet, and the places in Middlesex and Surrey by themselves in another sheet '.[4] The earliest printed weekly bill now extant appears to be

---

[1] *The Court and Times of Charles the First*, ii. 244.

[2] *R*. xxxviii. 267 b.   See also above, p. 190.

[3] G. Harvey, *Works* (ed. Grosart), i. 259; T. Nashe, *Works* (ed. McKerrow), iii. 89. On 14 July 1593 Wolfe then City Printer was licensed to print 'the bills, briefs, notes and larges given out for the sickness weekly or otherwise'. Arber's *Transcript*, ii. 634.

[4] Arber's *Transcript*, iii. 243.

A Plague-Bill for the week ending 15 December 1625

that printed by Windet for the week ending 21 July 1603. The bill for the week ending 20 October (p. 106) gives the weekly figures in the parishes within and without the walls and in the out-parishes, also the total figures for each week from 14–21 July to 11–20 October, in London and in Westminster, the Savoy, Stepney, Newington, 'and sundry other places, since the sicknesse began there'. In September 1611 the right to print the weekly bills passed to William Stansby.[1] From his press came the bills of 1625. In 1626 a press for printing the weekly bills was set up in the Parish Clerks' Hall. The printer had to be a person approved of by the Archbishop of Canterbury and the Bishop of London.[2] Before 1626 and possibly for some time afterwards the weekly bills were only printed in plague-years: the one extant copy of the bill for the week ending 15 April 1613, for example, is in manuscript.[3] In 1625 the bills were not printed until the week ending 21 July. The plague was then so serious that a bill must have sold as readily as a ballad.

On 1 August 1603 Windet was licensed to print not only the bills of mortality for the year, but also ' the briefs

---

[1] *A Transcript of the Registers of the Company of Stationers of London* (ed. Arber), iii. 467. We should have expected this right to pass to William Jaggard who had succeeded Windet as printer to the City on 17 December 1610 (*Letter Book*, DD, 225 b). Isaac Jaggard, who succeeded his father as City Printer in November 1623, printed the plague-orders in 1625. See the accounts of the examiners of St. Martin's-in-the-Fields (City Hall, Westminster, MS. 4512).

[2] Christie, *op. cit.*, 187.

[3] The bill for the week ending 17 August 1609 is also in manuscript ; the other extant bills of the seventeenth century (see p. 192 above) are printed. Threepence was paid for a bill of the plague in 1624 (*Archaeologia*, xv. 161), but this, if not in manuscript, was probably the yearly bill.

thereof within London which the Clerks deliver forth '
These briefs were blank printed forms which were filled in
every week in ink by the Clerk of the Hall.   They were

1608.

From the 16 februwary
to the , 23

Buried in London within
the wals this weeke.——} 64
Whereof the Plague——— 13

Buried without the walles and}
the Pesthouse. ——————} 90
beeing in the Liberties' ——
Whereof the Plague——— 22

The whole number in ——}
London and the Liberties.} 154
Whereof the plague ——— 35
Chriftned in thofe places 135

Buried in the 9.out parifhes — 23
Whereof the plague. ——— 4

The totall of al——}
the burials in the.——} 177
places aforefaid.——
Wherof the plague—— 46
Chriftned in the 121.parifhes 152
Parifhes cleare ——— 95
Parifhes infected —— 26

A Plague-Bill for the week ending 23 February, 1608/9.

plague-bills rather than bills of mortality : deaths from
the plague were recorded against each parish, the total
mortality from all causes being entered only in the
summary.   Four of them were printed on one sheet of
paper, so that they were half the size of the ordinary
printed bill.   Bills of this kind are extant for the weeks

ending 12 November 1607 and 15 December 1625 (see the illustration at p. 196). The parishes were grouped as in the bills of mortality, except that from July 1609 the deaths in the parishes without the walls and in the out-parishes were arranged in columns according as they were in London, Middlesex, or Surrey.[1] The plague-bill for the week ending 23 February 1609 (see the illustration on p. 198) is more summary : it does not give the figures for each parish but only the total christenings and the total deaths from the plague and from all causes.

The bills throw an interesting sidelight upon the religious dissensions of the seventeenth century. In the extant weekly bills of 1603 and 1625 only two parishes have the title of Saint : it does not appear why St. Faith's and St. Foster's (a corruption of St. Vedast's) should have been so preferred. Even these parishes are deprived of their title in the plague-bill for the week ending 15 December 1625. All parishes were sainted from the week ending 22 January 1634,[2] all of them were unsainted from the week ending 3 November 1642, and all were sainted again from the week ending 7 August 1660.

THE YEARLY BILLS

A yearly bill shows the total deaths in each parish for the preceding year. In the early seventeenth century they seem only to have been printed in years of extraordinary mortality. The earliest known copy of a printed

---

[1] Cf. *R.* xxix. 64 b, and compare the blank forms for 1610 in *S. P. Dom., Jas. I,* vol. 58, Doc. 102, with the bill for 5–12 November 1607.

[2] Stow's *Survey,* ed. J. Strype (1755), ii. 123. Cf. the accident which happened to Sir Roger de Coverley when asking a Roundhead for St. Anne's Lane and a Catholic for Anne's Lane (*Spectator,* No. 125).

yearly bill belongs to the year 1603 (p. 114). The Parish Clerks' Company, London, possesses a printed document which gives the following statistics for the year 28 December 1581 to 27 December 1582: (1) the plague-deaths in each parish in London and the liberties; (2) the total number of christenings and of deaths from all causes and from the plague in London and the liberties; (3) the total number of deaths from all causes and from the plague in the out-parishes. But this, which is printed in octavo form and not as a single sheet, is not strictly speaking a bill of mortality. It is probably the fifth sheet of a printed pamphlet, for the signature of the one leaf which is signed is E ij, and the author of the remarks which follow the statistics uses the first person singular, though no name whether of editor, printer, or publisher is given on the title-page.[1]

The yearly bills for 1603 and 1625 in Bodl. MS. Rawl. D. 859 were printed together on one sheet by William Stansby in 1625.[2] Slightly different copies from the same press are in the Guildhall. A copy of Stansby's bill of 1625 is also in *S. P. Dom., Chas. I*, vol. 11, Doc. 70. The Guildhall copy is reproduced at p. 174. The same Bodleian MS. contains a printed yearly bill for Westminster, Lambeth, Newington, Stepney, Hackney, and Islington in 1625: other copies, with slight differences, are in the Guildhall and in *S. P. Dom., Chas. I*, vol. 12, Doc. 39. London bills

---

[1] There are eight leaves : the first is the title-page, the last is blank. The pamphlet was bought at Jolley's Sale (*Sale Catalogue*, 92).

[2] In the bill for 1603 the weekly totals are given for the whole year (except for the week ending 30 December 1602), but the burials in each several parish are given only for the twenty-three weeks from 14 July to 22 December.

for 1629, 1630,[1] 1631, and 1632 are in the Forster and
Guildhall Libraries. The Guildhall Library also possesses
yearly bills for 1633, 1634, 1635, 1636, 1641, 1652, 1653,
1658, and 1660. The yearly bills from 1658 to 1849 are in
the British Museum.

In 1603 the right to print the yearly bills belonged to
John Windet. This right passed to William Stansby in
September 1611 and from his press came the general bills
for 1625. In December 1626 the Company of Parish
Clerks ' agreed with Mr. Stansby to print the yearly bills
at such prices as shall then be concluded on, under the
penalty of 100l. for divulging or allowing copies to be
dispersed before the 7th January next ensuing '.[2] The
yearly bill for 1629 was printed by Richard Hodgkinson :
the later bills are without imprint.

DELIVERY AND PAYMENT

By the Parish Clerks' Ordinance of 1553 the Lord Mayor
received a weekly bill from the wardens of the Company,
and each alderman from the clerk of his parish.[3] The
King also received a copy. In October 1543 Henry VIII,
then on progress, severely admonished the Lord Mayor
for not informing him of the weekly deaths. The ad-
monishment was undeserved, for the Lord Mayor had
informed the Lord Chancellor, thinking that he would
surely hand on the information to the King.[4] Again, in
November 1608, James ' somewhat passionately complained that he heard not from my Lord Chamberlain of

[1] Another copy of the 1630 bill is in B.M. Egerton MS. 2645,
fo. 234.
[2] Christie, op. cit., 187.   [3] Ibid. 134.
[4] J. xv. 55 and verso. When London was free from the plague
the sergeant or yeoman of the Channel rode to the Court every
week with the bill. Cf. R. xv. 340 b (May 1564) and xxvi. 435 b
(September 1604).

the bill of the sickness, and was the more moved because he had found himself offended with the same fault before and was promised it should be amended '.[1]

The normal yearly payment made by the City to the parish clerks for compiling and printing the bills was £3 6s. 8d.[2] In September 1607, when they were ordered to deliver bills to the Queen and the Lord Chancellor as well as to the King, their allowance was raised to £8 a year, but in February 1608 this was decreased to £5 on the ground that the clerks had been relieved of the charges which they had formerly defrayed of providing vestments and other things for St. Mary Magdalen's Chapel by the Guildhall.[3] In 1609 they again received the sum of £3 6s. 8d.,[4] but in February 1625, because they were specifying the several diseases on the backs of the bills, their allowance was raised to £4.[5] In June 1626, when the clerks possessed a printing press of their own, the payment fell once more to £3 6s. 8d. or five marks ; they were then required to present bills to every alderman and officer of the Court of Common Council every Thursday.[6]

COMPILATION

By orders issued in February 1570 [7] parish clerks and sextons were required to swear that ' if you at any time or times . . . shall know or be informed or have vehement

---

[1] S. P. Dom., Jas. I, vol. 37, Doc. 95.

[2] Cf. R. xxvii. 24 b (June 1605) and 221 b (June 1606), xxviii. 34 b (June 1607).

[3] R. xxviii. 93 and 160.

[4] R. xxix. 50 (June 1609), 235 b (June 1610), xxx. 3 o (June 1612).   [5] R. xxxix. 92.

[6] Letter Book, II, 253. The subscription for the weekly bills was four shillings per annum in 1662 (Graunt in Hull, op. cit., ii. 346).

[7] J. xix. 219.

suspicion that any person or persons in your parish is now or shall be either dead diseased or infected with the plague, that then you within the space of three hours next after such knowledge, information or véhement suspicion, or as soon after as ye conveniently may, shall in writing certify or cause the same to be certified to the Deputy or in his absence to the Alderman of the ward '. Any one breaking this oath was sent to Newgate and further punished. The same ordinance threatened with imprisonment those who falsely informed a minister, clerk, or sexton that a person did not die of the infection. In 1578 two honest and discreet matrons were sworn in every parish to search and view the body of every person dying in the parish, and to make true report to the clerk of all who died of the plague, so that the clerk might make like report to the wardens of the parish clerks.[1] In 1583 the searchers or viewers of dead bodies were required to report to the constable, the constable to the clerk, and the clerk to the chief of clerks.[2] This method of procedure remained practically unaltered for many years. ' When any one dies,' observes Graunt, ' then, either by tolling, or ringing of a Bell, or by bespeaking of a Grave of the *Sexton*, the same is known to the *Searchers*, corresponding with the said *Sexton*. The *Searchers* hereupon (who are ancient Matrons, sworn to their Office) repair to the place where the dead Corps lies, and by view of the same, and by other enquiries, they examine by what *Disease* or *Casualty* the Corps died. Hereupon they make their Report to the *Parish Clerk*.' [3]

Once a week the parish clerk took to the Clerk of the Hall

---

[1] See above, p. 65.   [2] *J*. xxi. 285 b.
[3] Graunt in Hull, *op. cit.*, ii. 346.

a list of all the burials and christenings during the preceding week. The returns for the out-parishes in Middlesex and Surrey were also sent to the Hall.[1] The general account was then made up. The bills were issued from Friday to Friday in 1563–1566, from Thursday to Thursday from 1574 to 1646, and afterwards from Tuesday to Tuesday.[2] In June 1609 the wardens were ordered to deliver bills to the Lord Mayor and the Court of Aldermen by 8 o'clock every Thursday morning and to deliver no bills to any other person before 10 o'clock.[3] This order seems to have been very necessary, for in the following year a minute of the Company complained that many false and untrue bills were issued by members, thus bringing the bills into disrepute both at home and abroad. In future it was ordered that any member who should ' by any cunning device, practice, or means, give away, disperse, utter, or declare, or by any sinister device, cast forth at any window, hole, or crevice of a wall of this house, any bills or notes, whereby the reports of these returns for that week may be known or uttered abroad, before the book is given to the Lord Mayor, shall pay 10s. fine, one-half to the Chamber of London and one-half to the poor of this Company, and shall suffer in addition such punishment as shall seem fit to the masters and wardens of this Company '.[4]

---

[1] B.M. Addit. MS. 29597, fos. 13 and verso.

[2] Some of the statistics given by Stow for July 1563 run from Saturday to Saturday. Bell (*op. cit.*, sig. D 1) says that the general and weekly bills were changed from Thursday to Tuesday in 1629. The change was made in December 1646, when bills were issued from 10 to 17 December (Thursday to Thursday) and also from 15 to 22 December (Tuesday to Tuesday). See the weekly bills in the Bodleian (Gough Adds. Lond. 4°. 95).

[3] *R*. xxix. 45 b.   [4] Christie, *op. cit.*, 136–7.

TRUSTWORTHINESS

In 1729 Maitland showed that at least 3,038 burials were omitted during the year from the London bills of mortality, an error chiefly caused by the omission of the burials in dissenters' burial-grounds.[1] But in the first quarter of the seventeenth century there were no such burial-grounds. Secret burials would be a more serious cause of error, but the little evidence that there is seems to show that, except in plague-time, this practice was rare in the sixteenth and early seventeenth centuries. About the year 1578 the Privy Council suggested that the names of persons of all sexes and ages in each house should be kept in registers, that a weekly view of them should be taken in times of infection, and that no one should leave his house or service without giving notice. The Lord Mayor and aldermen objected to this scheme partly because it was too elaborate and expensive, partly because the necessity for it arose only from a slander concerning secret burials, which they evidently discredited and which they craved might be examined.[2] If the number of unreported burials was small, we may suppose that the returns of total mortality are substantially accurate.

The bills are in general agreement with the parish registers. A rough comparison of the mortality of fourteen London parishes as shown in the yearly bill for 1625 and in the registers has given the following results. The two totals agree in only three instances. The greatest discrepancy is in the figures for St. James's, Clerkenwell, the bill giving 1,191 deaths, the register 1,164. The aggregate returns of the fourteen parishes are 2,517 in the bill and

[1] *The History of London* (1775 ed.), ii. 740–2.
[2] *S. P. Dom., Eliz.*, vol. 98, Doc. 38

2,495 in the registers. The discrepancy is, therefore, only 22 in 2,517 or 1 in 114.[1]

The returns of plague-deaths are not so trustworthy. Innumerable complaints were made about their inaccuracy.   In February 1570 the Lord Mayor complained of ' corrupt and colourable dealing by the clerk, sexton, beadle, and others ', and of their failure ' either for corruption or friendship ' to notify the aldermen of houses visited with the plague.   Eight years later the Privy Council rebuked the Lord Mayor because the bills ' are not done with that care that behoveth ', and again in 1590 it had great suspicion that the weekly certificates were not truly reported, the numbers of those dying of the plague being especially inaccurate.   The churchwardens of every parish were ordered to call the searchers before them and to charge them carefully to view every corpse in their parish and to make true certificate weekly in writing. If they were at all doubtful about the cause of death, they were to invoke the aid of the searchers of the next parish, or some others of skill, their fee to be paid by the parish to which they were called.   The Council complained again in April 1603 of the concealment and misreporting of plague-deaths.   The abuse was denied by the Lord Mayor, who championed the honesty of the searchers.[2]   The same charges against

---

[1] Out of 120 comparisons made by Ogle (op. cit., 443) between the annual return in the bills and the entries in the registers, there were only twenty occasions in which bill and register gave the same number.   On the other hand, ' as these errors occurring indifferently in contrary directions tended . . . to correct each other, the total amount of error was but slight when a sufficiently long series of years was taken into account '.

[2] J. xix. 213 b ; Acts of the Privy Council, 1577–1578, 387 , J. xxii. 401 ; Remembrancia, ii. 74. According to a letter dated

the inaccuracy of the returns of plague-deaths were made in 1625.[1]

We may safely acquit the magistrates of intentionally falsifying the certificates, except perhaps in the early stages of the infection. The falsification resulted in part from the incompetence of the parish-clerks and largely from the ignorance and corruptibility of the searchers. These were not above taking bribes to return a disease as consumption or spotted fever instead of the plague.[2] In many cases, particularly in deaths from pneumonic plague when no plague-sore was visible, ignorant women and many Elizabethan and even modern physicians would be unable to diagnose the disease correctly.[3] For this reason it seems certain that pneumonic plague was more prevalent in 1625 than in 1603.[4] For in 1603 the deaths

4 July 1603 (B.M. Stowe MS. 150, fo. 190), ' The certificate of the plague the last week was 158 within the freedom of the City and the king having information of more sent to my lord mayor for a true certificate who certified 800 and odd in the city and suburbs.' One hundred and fifty-eight deaths from the plague were returned for the week ending 30 June. It is not clear whether the figure 800 includes deaths from all causes or only from the plague. It should also be noted that the number 158 includes only deaths in London and the liberties whereas the number 800 includes the deaths in the suburbs where the mortality was very heavy.

[1] *Hist. MSS. Comm.*, 11th Report, Appendix I, 21, and *S. P. Dom., Chas. I*, vol. iv, Doc. 29.

[2] In 1630, 1,910 deaths were returned as from consumption, 1,091 from fever, and 1,317 from plague.

[3] Cf. W. J. Simpson, *Report on Plague in the Gold Coast in 1908*, p. 13 : there were some cases ' in which there was an absence of any special symptoms of illness until a few hours before death, and in these, unless suspicion had been aroused by the fact that they had been in association with patients suffering from pneumonic plague, even the most experienced might have been misled in the diagnosis of the disease '.

[4] Cf. *The Court and Times of Charles the First*, i. 15 (23 April 1625) : ' the physicians do in a manner agree that this sickness is not directly the plague, as not leaving any sore, or any such like

I *

from causes other than the plague were 7,566, in 1625 18,654. The average annual mortality in 1603 was between 4,500 and 5,500, and in 1625 between 8,000 and 9,000, [1] so that the excess of deaths other than plague-deaths over the average annual mortality was in 1603 at least 2,066 and in 1625 at least 9,654. Some of these deaths, no doubt, were caused by influenza or typhus, which often accompanied an epidemic of plague in this country, but many may be attributed to the infection.

accident, but only contagious in blood or kindred '. Cf. also John Woodall, *The Surgeons Mate* (1639), 321 : ' in *Anno 1625,* we had many signes contrarie to the *Plagues* in other times ; yea, and many did dye dayly, without any signes or markes on their bodies at all '. See also above, p. 134.

[1] The years 1623 and 1624—when the total mortality was 11,095 and 12,199—were exceptionally unhealthy.

II

THE POPULATION OF LONDON IN THE EARLY SEVENTEENTH CENTURY

ACCORDING to a report made in 1557 by Giovanni Michiel, a Venetian ambassador, the population of London and the liberties (including Westminster) was 185,000.[1] Giovanni Botero, an Italian writer, estimated the population of London and the liberties in 1590 at about 160,000.[2] In 1606 the estimate of the Venetian ambassador was 300,000.[3] All these figures are conjectural. In 1631 a census taken by the Lord Mayor at the request of the Privy Council found the number of persons in the City and liberties (omitting the out-parishes) to be 130,178,[4] but the method by which the search was conducted was no doubt defective. The deaths in the out-parishes being in this year about one-third of those in the City and liberties, the population within the bills may be calculated on this basis to be about 170,000, too low a figure for the London of 1631. In his *Londinopolis* (1657) James Howell, eager that London should outdo Paris, claimed that in 1636 a census found the population to be above 700,000. ' Mr. Howell did in that point mistake.' [5]

---

[1] *Cal. S. P. Ven.*, 1556–1557, p. 1045.

[2] *A Treatise, Concerning the Causes of the Magnificencie and greatnes of Cities, . . . now done into English by Robert Peterson* (1606).

[3] W. B. Rye, *English as seen by Foreigners*, 272.

[4] John Graunt, *Natural and Political Observations* (1676), reprinted in Hull, *op. cit.*, ii. 407, 408. Cf. also *Notes and Queries*, 11th Series, i. 426.

[5] Sir Peter Pett, *The Happy Future State of England* (cited by Hull, *op. cit.*, i. xliv).

As the contemporary estimates are not to be trusted, the bills of mortality are now our best clue to the population of early seventeenth-century London. It is claimed above that in the early years of the century the returns of total mortality, especially in years unaffected by the plague, are substantially accurate. The following figures are taken from the *Natural and Political Observations* of John Graunt, of which the first edition appeared in 1662, the fifth in 1676. Graunt took them from the bills of mortality preserved at the Parish Clerks' Hall until the Great Fire of 1666. His figures have been checked by the weekly statistics for 1606–1610 given from the same source in John Bell's *Londons Remembrancer* (1665/6) and by the original bills for 1625 and for 1629–1635.

The Table of Burials, and Christenings in London.

Anno Dom.	97 parishes.	16 parishes.	Out-parishes.	Buried in all.	Besides of the Plague.	Chris-tened.
1604 .	1,518	2,097	708	4,323	896	5,458
1605 .	2,014	2,974	960	5,948	444	6,504
1606 .	1,941	2,920	935	5,796	2,124	6,614
1607 .	1,879	2,772	1,019	5,670	2,352	6,582
1608 .	2,391	3,218	1,149	6,760 [1]	2,262	6,845
1609 .	2,494	3,610	1,441	7,545	4,240	6,388
1610 .	2,326	3,791	1,369	7,284 [1]	1,803	6,785
1611 .	2,152	3,398	1,166	6,716	627	7,014
	16,715	24,780	8,747	50,042	14,752 [2]	52,190

[1] For '6,760' Graunt reads '6,758' and for '7,284' he reads 7,486'. I follow Bell's figures, which agree with the summation of the weekly bills. Graunt's total of '50,242' is corrected to '50,042', but it is not possible to correct the detailed figures for the 97, 16, and out-parishes. Fortunately the error is negligible.

[2] The figures add up to '14,748'.

Anno Dom.	97 parishes.	16 parishes.	Out-parishes.	Buried in all.	Besides of the Plague.	Chris-tened.
1612 .	2,473	3,843	1,462	7,778	64	6,986
1613 .	2,406	3,679	1,418	7,503	16	6,846
1614 .	2,369	3,504	1,494	7,367	22	7,208
1615 .	2,446	3,791	1,613	7,850	37	7,682
1616 .	2,490	3,876	1,697	8,063	9	7,985
1617 .	2,397	4,109	1,774	8,280	6	7,747
1618 .	2,815	4,715	2,066	9,596	18	7,735
1619 .	2,339	3,857	1,804	7,999	9	8,127
	19,735	31,374	13,328	64,436	171 [1]	60,316
1620 .	2,726	4,819	2,146	9,691	21	7,845
1621 .	2,438	3,759	1,915	8,112	11	8,039
1622 .	2,811	4,217	2,392	8,943	16	7,894
1623 .	3,591	4,721	2,783	11,095	17	7,945
1624 .	3,385	5,919	2,895	12,199	11	8,299
1625 .	5,143	9,819	3,886	18,848	35,417	6,983
1626 .	2,150	3,286	1,965	7,401	134	6,701
1627 .	2,325	3,400	1,988	7,711	4	8,408
	24,569	39,940	19,970	84,000	35,631	62,114
1628 .	2,412	3,311	2,017	7,740	3	8,564
1629 .	2,536	3,992	2,243	8,771	—	9,901
1630 .	2,506	4,201	2,521	9,237	1,317	9,315
1631 .	2,459	3,697	2,132	8,288	274	8,524
1632 .	2,704	4,412	2,411	9,527	8	9,584
1633 .	2,378	3,936	2,078	8,392	—	9,997
1634 .	2,937	4,980	2,982	10,899	1	9,855
1635 .	2,742	4,966	2,943	10,651	—	10,034
	20,694 [2]	33,495	19,327	73,505	1,603	75,774

These statistics exhibit clearly the rapid growth of London in the early seventeenth century. The baptismal returns for 1628–1635 show an increase of 45 per cent. over those of 1604–1611, and this in spite of the set-back caused by the plague of 1625. In the tables of burials Graunt

[1] The figures add up to ' 181 '.
[2] The figures add up to ' 20,674 '.

does not distinguish between the plague-deaths within the walls, in the liberties, and in the out-parishes, but most of these took place outside the walls. In 1625 the division was 9,197, 17,153, and 9,067, and in 1630 it was 190, 603, and 524. If we suppose that as in 1625 about one-quarter of the plague-deaths occurred within the walls, one-half in the liberties, and one-quarter in the out-parishes, then the total burials in these three areas in 1604–1611 were 20,403, 32,156, and 12,435, and in 1628–1635 they were 21,095, 34,297, and 19,728. The increase in population in the parishes outside the walls becomes more apparent if we compare the figures for years unaffected by the plague, say, 1605 and 1627. The burials in the out-parishes have doubled. It is no wonder that the authorities found the housing problem too much for them. Within the walls there was little room for expansion after the sixteenth century. The slight increase is mainly due to the building-up of garden spaces and to the division of large houses into tenements.

The latter half of the seventeenth century saw the foundation of the Royal Society and the establishment in England of the modern science of statistics. Several attempts were then made to calculate the population of London. John Graunt, the first man to treat the bills of mortality as anything but ' as a Text to talk upon in the next Company ', estimated the population of London in 1665 at about 460,000, a figure which includes the out-parishes added to the bills in 1636 (see above, p. 195). His calculations are based in part upon the assumption that 3 persons out of 11 families died per annum (that is to say, allowing 8 persons in a family, 1 person died in every 30 per annum), and in part upon a rough estimate of

the number of houses.[1] Sir William Petty, to whom
(says Evelyn) ' there was nothing difficult ', reckoned the
population to be about 696,000 in 1686. His figures are
based on a death-rate of 1 in 30, on information from the
makers of a general map of London that in 1682 there
were 84,000 houses in London, and on the statement of the
Hearth Office that in 1686 the houses within the bills were
105,315.[2] He allows 6 persons in a family.[3] In 1690
Gregory King, basing his calculations on the books of the
Hearth Office, found the number of inhabited houses in
London to be 105,000. An allowance of 4·57 persons a
house (doubtless too low a figure) gives a total of 479,600
souls. With 10 per cent. for omissions and 2,440 for
transitory persons (e.g. seamen, soldiers, vagrants) he
settles on a total of about 530,000.[4]

These attempts are more ingenious than convincing.
Graunt's death-rate of 1 in 30 is quite arbitrary, and even
if we admit the accuracy of the returns of the Hearth
Office we can place little confidence in calculations based
on this source, seeing that the estimate of the number of
persons in each house fluctuates from 4·57 to 8. Estimates
of the population of eighteenth-century London are almost
as unsatisfactory. It is not until the first census of 1801
that the statistical ground becomes firm and sure. In this
census it was found that the population in the parishes

---

[1] Graunt in Hull, *op. cit.*, ii. 331, 332, 384, 385.

[2] Hearth money was imposed by 14 Charles II, c. 10 (1662).

[3] Hull, *op. cit.*, ii. 533–6. Elsewhere (p. 459) it suits Petty's
convenience to allow 8 persons in a family. The map of London
would be that entitled ' London &c:.actually surveyed by William
Morgan his Majesty's Cosmographer 168½ '. It is said to be the
first survey of London made on scientific lines. See above, p. ix.

[4] G. Chalmers, *An Estimate of the Comparative Strength of Great
Britain* (2nd ed., 1794), pp. 54–6.

then included in the bills of mortality amounted to about 745,000. The average number of burials, after the deficiencies of the bills had been duly corrected, was 25,000. The proportion of burials to population was, therefore, about 1 to 30.[1] Let us apply this ratio to the average yearly number of burials for 1612–1614, 1620–1622, and 1632–1634, all years of normal health, first adding a correction of 10 per cent. for omissions (see above, p. 195) and possible errors in the returns and for the excess of persons dying in London but buried in the country over persons dying in the country but buried in London.[2] Then the population in 1612–1614 would be 250,256, in 1620–1622 it would be 294,734, and in 1632–1634 it would be 317,097.[3]

There can be no doubt that the London death-rate was higher in the early seventeenth century than in 1801.[4] In calculating the population of early seventeenth-century

[1] W. Heberden, ' On the Mortality of London ' (1808) in *Medical Transactions Published by the College of Physicians*, iv. 111.

[2] C. H. Hull (*op. cit.*, i. xci) would add a correction of 15 per cent. for the early seventeenth century and of 10 per cent. for the late seventeenth century. But the differentiation does not seem to be necessary.

[3] If we apply Graunt's ratio of 1 in 28 to the average number of baptisms in these years, we arrive at a population in 1612–1614 of 196,364, in 1620–1622 of 221,928, and in 1632–1634 of 274,652. A large correction, however, would need to be added to these figures, for the baptismal returns do not represent the floating population, and they are naturally more imperfect than the burial returns. A man has to be buried, but he need not be baptized. A correction of 20 per cent. would give us totals of 235,637, 266,314, and 329,582. The error in baptismal returns becomes still more serious later in the century owing to religious scruples. In 1652 and 1653, when the bills also included some outlying districts (see above, p. 195), the baptisms were only 6,128 and 6,155.

[4] The census of 1631, which we cannot accept as accurate, gives a ratio of about 1 in 21.

London, therefore, on a ratio of 1 in 30, we tend to over-estimate the true figure. Hence the statements made above that in 1603 the population was not more than 250,000 and in 1625 not more than 320,000 appear to be sufficiently cautious. 'Although these numbers are not (as they cannot be) a demonstrated truth, yet they will serve for a good supposition, which is as much as we want at present.' [1] But the subject needs to be handled by a competent authority on vital statistics.

A population of 250,000 or 320,000 may now seem small to us, but it must be remembered that the population of the whole of England in 1600 was probably not more than 4,460,000.[2] London was many times larger than her nearest rivals. As late as 1841 Manchester (with Salford) was the second largest town in the British Isles with a population still under 300,000. Already in the mid-seventeenth century there were some who thought that ' London, the Metropolis of England, is perhaps a Head too big for the Body, and possibly too strong'. According to the astrologer William Lilly, Charles I was of this opinion, and not surprisingly. Dr. Johnson, a lover of London, while admitting that London was too large, denied that there was any similarity to a head connected with a body. 'It would be as much too big, though the body were ever so large ; that is to say, though the country were ever so extensive.' [3]

[1] Petty's words slightly altered (Hull, op. cit., ii. 460).

[2] So estimated by John Rickman, the statistician responsible for the Census Reports from 1801 to 1831. Cf. Parliamentary Papers, Reports from Commissioners, 1843, vol. xi, p. 37.

[3] Graunt, Natural and Political Observations (1662), sig. A2ᵛ. Lilly, Monarchy or no Monarchy in England, 1651, 78. Boswell's Life, ed. Hill, ii. 356.

INDEX

Abbot, Thomas, surgeon, 82.

ague, 123–4.

air : corruption of the, 5, 7, 44–5 ; correction of the, 8–10, 31.

aldermen, 15, 17, 19, 20–1, 52, 72, 76, 171, 177, 182, 202–3 ; court of, 15, 17, 22, 34–5, 52, 68, 78, 83, 89, 126, 131, 147, 162, 181, 189, 194, 204 ; runaways, 94–5, 102, 140.

Aldgate Bars, 60.

alehouses, 25, 28, 95, 153, 159, 166 ; see inns, taverns.

Alleyn, Edward, 9, 111.

Allhallows, Dowgate Ward, 41.

Amsterdam, 85–6, 123.

amulets, 10.

Andrewes, Lancelot, 70 n.

apothecaries, 12, 21, 152, 168 ; see the illustration at p. 20.

apprentices, 50, 73, 152.

assemblies, prohibition of, 49–51, 90–2, 96, 106, 139, 173 ; at funerals, 40–1, 94–6 ; see fairs, theatres.

astrology, 5–7 ; see Forman, Simon ; Gadbury, John ; Lilly, William.

Athens, the plague of, 153.

Aubrey, John : quoted, 12, 172–3.

Audley, Sir Thomas, 190.

Avicenna, 8, 10.

ballad on the term being kept at Winchester in 1603, 184–5 ; ballad-singing, 50.

Bamford, James, vicar of St. Olave's, 67, 70, 84, 100.

Banister, John, surgeon, 156–7.

barber-surgeons, see surgeons.

Barnstaple, 111.

Barry, Lording : quoted, 54 n.

Bath, 111 ; Bath and Wells, diocese of, 167.

beadles, 17, 18, 62, 100, 102, 116, 140, 180, 206.

bearbaiting, 50, 52, 111, 126, 173.

bearers of the dead, 45–7, 60, 148, 179 ; see the illustrations on pp. 47, 149.

Beaulieu, 160.

Beaumont, Francis, and Fletcher, John : plays quoted, 10, 40 n., 69 ; see Fletcher.

beggars, 18, 25, 51, 133, 165–6, 179 ; see rogues and vagabonds.

Bell, John, 186, 193, 210.

bells, tolling of, 96–7, 99, 177–9.

Bennet, Sir Thomas, Lord Mayor in 1603–4, 140.

Berkshire, 164.

Bethnal Green, 47.

Bhagavata Parana : quoted, 36.

Bible : quoted, 3–4, 36, 150–1, 169.

bills of mortality : 122, 150, 189–208 ; origin and contents of weekly bills, 189–99 ; list of extant weekly bills, 191–3 ; plague-bills, 192, 197–9 ; yearly bills, 199–201 ; delivery and payment, 201–2 ; compilation, 202–4 ; printing, 196–8, 200–202 ; estimate of trustworthiness, 205–8, 209–10 ; inaccuracy of plague-returns, 91, 134, 206–8 ; see the illustrations at pp. 106, 114, 174, 196, 198.

Bisham, 160.

Black Death, 6 n., 15, 50, 55 n., 56.

Blackwall, 47, 135.

Blackwell Hall, 164.

Bombay, plague in, 1.

Borough, Sir John, 78.

Botero, Giovanni, 209.

bowling, 25, 50.

Bradwell, Stephen, physician, 132–3, 156–7.

Bridewell, 35, 81, 89, 168.

INDEX

Paddington, 82.
Paddy, Sir William, 21.
Paracelsus, 8.
Paris, 123, 135 ; plague-orders of, 62, 189.
Paris Garden, 126.
parish-clerks : duties of, 17, 41–2, 62–3, 65, 179–80, 202–3 ; responsible for bills of mortality, 190–1, 194–8, 201–7 ; fraud and ignorance of, 41, 47–8, 116, 204, 206–7.
parliament, meetings of : 116–18, 121–2, 129, 134–8, 144, 147, 160, 170 ; act of, establishing plague-orders and officials, 19, 58–60, 116, and illustration on p. 59.
Paston, Margaret, 13.
Pepys, Samuel, 73, 98 n., 178 n.
pesthouse, London, 74–84, 94, 168, 181–3 ; makeshifts, 74–6 ; site, 77, 79–80, 181 ; progress of building, 76–9 ; cost, 77–8 ; rates, 168, 181–3 ; accommodation, 80–2 ; plan, 82 ; officials, 82–3, 181–3 ; unpopularity, 84 ; other pesthouses, 74 n., 81 n. ; see the illustrations at pp. 80 and 82.
Pesthouse Row (now Bath St.), 80.
Peterborough, diocese of, 167.
Petticoat Lane, 47.
Petty, Sir William, 213.
Phayre (or Thayre), Thomas : quoted, 6.
Phillips, Peter, 28.
physicians, 7, 13, 20–2, 102–3, 134, 152, 156, 168, 182 ; college of, 21, 23, 31, 48, 156 ; Bradwell, Stephen, 132–3, 156–7 ; Burnett, Dr., 73 ; Coghan, Thomas, 5 ; Forman, Simon, 102, 127 ; Hering, Francis, 10, 29, 104 ; Kellwaye, Simon, 11 ; Lodge, Thomas, 7, 10, 12, 22, 79, 84, 102–4, 172 ; Paddy, Sir William, 21 ; the ' Spanish Doctor ', 22 ; Thorius, Raphael, 156 ; see empirics ; see also the illustrations at pp. 20, 22, and 104.
Piers Plowman, 28.

pigeons, 13 n., 36.
plague, *see* medical.
plague-bills, *see* bills of mortality.
plague-orders : London orders in 1518, 15, 34–5, 56–7, 61–2, 190 ; in 1519, 188–90 ; in 1521, 62 ; in 1535, 28, 49 ; in 1543, 15, 35, 38, 45, 51 ; in 1547, 28 ; in 1548, 41, 177 ; in 1563, 15, 31, 35, 38–9, 50–1, 57, 63 ; in 1564, 24, 38, 52, 57, 179 ; in 1569, 20, 29, 40, 49, 51 ; in 1568, 63 ; in 1569, 20, 29, 40, 49, 51 ; in 1570, 15, 194, 202 ; in 1574, 15, 53, 180 ; in 1578, 39, 63, 65, 67 ; in 1581, 36, 49 ; in 1583, 15–16, 19, 21, 28, 38–40, 58, 65, 76–7, 179–80 ; in 1592, 42, 64, 68, 70, 177, 179–80 ; in 1593, 64, 78 ; in 1594, 53, 64, 68, 78–9 ; in 1603, 31–2, 35, 40, 42, 64, 89, 91, 180–1 ; in 1604, 19, 54, 58–60, 68, 115–17, 181 ; in 1605, 125, 195 ; in 1606, 38, 119 ; in 1607, 25, 49, 119, 196 ; in 1608, 36, 42, 120, 126 ; in 1609, 18, 20–1, 40, 48, 69, 120, 177, 204 ; in 1625, 21–2, 31, 45, 47, 74, 131–3, 139–45, 162, 166, 169 ; in 1630, 36, 42, 173–4 ; in 1636, 48, 55, 178, 195 ; in 1665, 16, 31, 42, 48, 57, 64 ; general orders, 8–9, 12, 14, 16, 42, 57 n., 68, 70 ; neglect of plague-orders, *see* sanitation, segregation.
plague-pits, 41, 43–5, and the illustration on p. 149.
plagues in London : from 1597 to 1603, 85–6 ; in 1603, 86–115, 177, 184–6 ; from 1603 to 1625, 114–28, 186–7, 210–11 ; in 1625, 129–76, 178, 187–8 ; in 1630, 173–4, 211 ; from 1625 to 1635, 211 ; in 1636, 174.
plays, players, *see* theatres.
Plighton, William, 181.
Plymouth, 160, 165 n.
pneumonic plague, *see* medical.
Pollard, William, 126.
pomanders, 8, 10, 150, 156.

OTHER TITLES IN THIS HARDBACK REPRINT PROGRAMME FROM
SANDPIPER BOOKS LTD (LONDON) AND POWELLS BOOKS (CHICAGO)

8111649	PHEIFER J.D.	Old English Glosses in the Epinal-Erfurt Glossary
8142277	PICKARD–CAMBRIDGE A.W.	Dithyramb Tragedy and Comedy
8269765	PLATER & WHITE	Grammar of the Vulgate
8213891	PLUMMER Charles	Lives of Irish Saints (2 vols)
820695X	POWICKE Michael	Military Obligation in Medieval England
8269684	POWICKE Sir Maurice	Stephen Langton
821460X	POWICKE Sir Maurice	The Christian Life in the Middle Ages
8225369	PRAWER Joshua	Crusader Institutions
8225571	PRAWER Joshua	The History of The Jews in the Latin Kingdom of Jerusalem
8143249	RABY F.J.E.	A History of Christian Latin Poetry
8143257	RABY F.J.E.	A History of Secular Latin Poetry in the Middle Ages (2 vols)
8214316	RASHDALL & POWICKE	The Universities of Europe in the Middle Ages (3 vols)
8154488	REYMOND E.A.E & BARNS J.W.B.	Four Martyrdoms from the Pierpont Morgan Coptic Codices
8148380	RICKMAN Geoffrey	The Corn Supply of Ancient Rome
8141076	ROSS Sir David	Aristotle: Metaphysics (2 vols)
8141092	ROSS Sir David	Aristotle: Physics
8142307	ROSTOVTZEFF M.	Social and Economic History of the Hellenistic World, 3 vols.
8142315	ROSTOVTZEFF M.	Social and Economic History of the Roman Empire, 2 vols.
8264178	RUNCIMAN Sir Steven	The Eastern Schism
814833X	SALMON J.B.	Wealthy Corinth
8171587	SALZMAN L.F.	Building in England Down to 1540
8218362	SAYERS Jane E.	Papal Judges Delegate in the Province of Canterbury 1198–1254
8221657	SCHEIN Sylvia	Fideles Crucis
8148135	SHERWIN WHITE A.N.	The Roman Citizenship
9240167	SINGER Charles	Galen: On Anatomical Procedures
8113927	SISAM, Kenneth	Studies in the History of Old English Literature
8642040	SOUTER Alexander	A Glossary of Later Latin to 600 AD
8270011	SOUTER Alexander	Earliest Latin Commentaries on the Epistles of St Paul
8222254	SOUTHERN R.W.	Eadmer: Life of St. Anselm
8251408	SQUIBB G.	The High Court of Chivalry
8212011	STEVENSON & WHITELOCK	Asser's Life of King Alfred
8212011	SWEET Henry	A Second Anglo-Saxon Reader—Archaic and Dialectical
8148259	SYME Sir Ronald	History in Ovid
8143273	SYME Sir Ronald	Tacitus (2 vols)
8200951	THOMPSON Sally	Women Religious
8201745	WALKER Simon	The Lancastrian Affinity 1361–1399
8161115	WELLESZ Egon	A History of Byzantine Music and Hymnography
8140185	WEST M.L.	Greek Metre
8141696	WEST M.L.	Hesiod: Theogony
8148542	WEST M.L.	The Orphic Poems
8140053	WEST M.L.	Hesiod: Works & Days
8152663	WEST M.L.	Iambi et Elegi Graeci
9240221	WHEELWRIGHT Philip	Heraclitus
822799X	WHITBY M. & M.	The History of Theophylact Simocatta
8206186	WILLIAMSON, E.W.	Letters of Osbert of Clare
8208103	WILSON F.P.	Plague in Shakespeare's London
8114877	WOOLF Rosemary	The English Religious Lyric in the Middle Ages
8119224	WRIGHT Joseph	Grammar of the Gothic Language